THE CULTURALLY SUST

SERIES EDITOR: Django Paris, *Univer...,*

ADVISORY BOARD: H. Samy Alim, Maggie Beneke, Jeremy Garcia, Gloria Ladson-Billings, Tiffany Lee, Danny Martinez, Teresa McCarty, Timothy San Pedro, Valerie Shirley

The overarching purpose of the Culturally Sustaining Pedagogies (CSP) Series is to offer preparing and practicing educators, graduate students, and scholars a comprehensive series of books dedicated to educational settings engaged in sustaining Indigenous, Black, Latinx, Asian, and Pacific Islander young people, families, and communities as these memberships necessarily intersect with gender and sexuality, disability, migration, language, land, class, and more. The CSP Series is defined by its coherent focus on the strengths and wisdom of young people, families, elders, communities, and educators who use education—in Pre-K through college classrooms, across content areas, in community organizations, and in peer and family settings—as a tool of positive social transformation and revitalization.

Native Presence and Sovereignty in College:
Sustaining Indigenous Weapons to Defeat Systemic Monsters
AMANDA R. TACHINE

Culturally Relevant Pedagogy:
Asking a Different Question
GLORIA LADSON-BILLINGS

Protecting the Promise:
Indigenous Education Between Mothers and Their Children
TIMOTHY SAN PEDRO

Native Presence and Sovereignty in College

Sustaining Indigenous Weapons to Defeat Systemic Monsters

Amanda R. Tachine

TEACHERS COLLEGE PRESS

TEACHERS COLLEGE | COLUMBIA UNIVERSITY
NEW YORK AND LONDON

Published by Teachers College Press,® 1234 Amsterdam Avenue, New York, NY 10027

Copyright © 2022 by Teachers College, Columbia University

Front cover illustration by Lynne Hardy.

An excerpt from the poem "American Arithmetic" from *Postcolonial Love Poem*, by Natalie Diaz, is reprinted with permission of The Permissions Company, LLC, on behalf of Graywolf Press (graywolfpress.org), and Faber and Faber Ltd. Copyright © 2020 by Natalie Diaz.

The poem "We Must Remember" from *A Radiant Curve*, by Luci Tapahonso, is reprinted with permission of the University of Arizona Press. Copyright © 2008 by Luci Tapahonso.

Library of Congress Cataloging-in-Publication Data is available at loc.gov

ISBN 978-0-8077-6613-2 (paper)
ISBN 978-0-8077-6614-9 (hardcover)
ISBN 978-0-8077-7996-5 (ebook)

Printed on acid-free paper
Manufactured in the United States of America

*We must remember the worlds our ancestors
traveled. Always wear the songs they gave us.
Remember we are made of prayers. Now we leave
wrapped in old blankets of love and wisdom.*
—Diné poet Luci Tapahonso[1]

*Dedicated to our beautiful relatives who dreamed
and sang for us*

Portions of the proceeds from the sale of the book will go to the
Office of Navajo Nation Scholarship and Financial Assistance.

Contents

Series Foreword

Greetings! I am so glad you have chosen to learn with this powerful book, *Native Presence and Sovereignty in College: Sustaining Indigenous Weapons to Defeat Systemic Monsters.* And learn deeply each of us must, as we join Amanda Tachine in community with 10 Navajo teenagers—Jessie, Lauryn, Joy, Chris, Mike, Cecilia, Sam, Sarah, Wesley, and Amber (pseudonyms)—as they navigate their first year in college.

In the early pages of the book, Tachine shares the Twin Warriors story with us. It is a story that one of the Navajo young people at the center of this book, Cecilia, shared with her during their research together. As Tachine writes:

> The Twin Warrior story highlights past vicious monsters that sought to destroy our Navajo people. Cecilia believes that today's monsters work to disrupt our way of life. Cecilia imagines a future where she (and others like her) journey toward college with hopes of returning home to help the people. (p. xiii)

Tachine continues by asking:

> How do teenagers like Cecilia make it into college? What are the present-day monsters that lurk and pull them back when they are desperately striving to attain a college degree, when they are trying to find a sense of belonging? And like the Twin Warriors, what weapons do they use? (p. xiv)

This book will help all who are ready to listen and learn and act to understand the answers to these and other pressing questions about Native students and college-going specifically, and, more generally, about the ways nation-state education and educators (pre-K through university) can divest from settler colonialism, white supremacy, and related cisheteropatriarchy to better center and sustain Native students. This means that this book holds lessons for families, youth, and educators—for all concerned with offering good and right educational paths for Native students. I should also mention that the lessons Tachine shares, though crucially centered on Navajo students and their lands, lifeways, and futures, also hold vital, broader lessons for Black, Indigenous, Latinx, Asian, and Pacific Islander journeys into and through college.

I would also be remiss to not share that as I write this series foreword, we are approaching the 2-year mark of the pandemic—2 years that have disproportionately impacted Indigenous, Black, Latinx, Asian, and Pacific Islander communities, affecting our elders and families in the U.S. nation-state and globally. This has also been a time of worsening climate crisis, emboldened white supremacy and, of course, massive ongoing struggles for racial justice and decolonization. It can sometime be difficult to make necessary connections between continued violence against the Earth, ongoing justice movements, the global pandemic, and the role of educators, schools, and colleges in working with young people and families toward more just and sustainable futures. Tachine takes on this confluence of unimaginable loss and concurrent deep ethics of care in Indigenous communities and beyond. As she shares about the devastating rise of COVID-19 and the simultaneous burgeoning uprisings for racial justice: "The year 2020 was erupting while I was writing this. Time and context were my teachers" (p. 9).

Tachine's explicit engagement with the lessons we are offered in the present as connected to the journeys of these 10 Navajo young people are so needed and welcomed. Indeed, this book provides layers of understanding that chart ways forward to bring pre-K–university Native education together with national and global policy implications that center Indigenous knowledges to combat the confluence of pandemic, racism, and climate crisis and shift us toward more just futures for all peoples, beings, and lands.

Toward the end of the book, Tachine asks, "What if institutions measured success based on how the Native communities measure success?" (p. 180). She then offers a series of recommendations for what that does, can, and should look like for colleges and for education broadly. Tachine's offerings grow from the powerful stories of Jessie, Lauryn, Joy, Chris, Mike, Cecilia, Sam, Sarah, Wesley, and Amber. Please join me in thanking each of them for these stories as we learn how they sustain Indigenous weapons to defeat systemic monsters.

—Django Paris, University of Washington on Coast Salish Lands

Navajo Twin Warriors

Dear sha'áłchíní (my children),

Stories of our people long ago teach us much of today and tomorrow. I am going to tell you a story that I heard as a young girl. I am telling you as it has been told. It is said.

Asdzáá Nádleehé (Changing Woman) gave birth to twin sons, Tóbájíshchíní (Born for Water) and Naayéé' Neizghání (Monster Slayer). They were very special babies. In a matter of days, the twins reached the ripe age of adolescence. As the twins developed and grew each day to manhood, they began to wonder who their father was. Various monsters were rapidly killing their people, and the twins desired to ask their father for help in conquering the monsters. Tóbájíshchíní (Born for Water) and Naayéé' Neizghání (Monster Slayer) decided to go on a journey to find their father. As they traveled, they were guided with favor by gods who created a holy trail paved with rainbows.

On their journey, they met Na'ashjé'ii Asdzáá (Spider Woman), who shared with the twins that their father was Jóhonaa'éí (Sun). To prepare them for their treacherous quest to find their father, Jóhonaa'éí (Sun), Na'ashjé'ii Asdzáá (Spider Woman) gave Tóbájíshchíní and Naayéé' Neizghání tools and prayers for protection and perseverance. The twins were grateful for Na'ashjé'ii Asdzáá and her loving assistance and so the twins continued on. As they traveled, they encountered four obstacles, and they withstood each barrier because of the powerful tools and prayers that Na'ashjé'ii Asdzáá provided.

When they finally reached their father's place, Jóhonaa'éí put the twins through four tests as a way to determine whether the twins were indeed his. Níłch'i (Wind) appeared and assisted the twins in passing each test. Jóhonaa'éí was pleased with the twins' achievements and knew that they belonged to him. He then inquired, "Now, my children, what do you ask of me?" The twins requested that their father equip them with weapons to slay the Naayéé' (Monsters) who were killing the Navajo people. Jóhonaa'éí smiled and offered weapons to his children. With immense appreciation, the twins thanked their father, Jóhonaa'éí, and went on their way to face the monsters.

The twin warriors first confronted Yé'iitsoh (Big Giant), who was said to be enormous and tremendously powerful. The twins waited for Yé'iitsoh (Big Giant) to arrive at a lake which they were told was a place the monster went to daily. As Yé'iitsoh approached the lake to drink water, the twins quickly came out of their hiding place and struck the monster with their father's weapons of lightning and arrows. Yé'iitsoh fell with a roaring thud. The ground trembled as thick dust rose and circled around Yé'iitsoh. As the dust settled, no movement came from the giant. It was said that Yé'iitsoh instantly perished. The second confrontation was with the Déélgééd (Horned Monster), who was known to be unbreakable. With the help of Na'azísí (Gopher) and the weapons provided by father Sun, the Déélgééd (Horned Monster) was shattered. The third conquest was with Tsé Nináhálééh (Bird Monster), and the fourth monster defeated was Bináá' yee Agháni (Who Kills With His Eyes).

After the twins overcame each monster, they returned home to their mother, Asdzáá Nádleehé (Changing Woman), to share the news. Asdzáá Nádleehé rejoiced with her two sons and told the brave story to the Navajo people. Through their valiant and courageous efforts, the twin warriors are considered heroes to the Navajo people.[1]

This story tells of a time when our Diné (the People) came from different worlds. Note that I will use Diné (the People) and Navajo interchangeably. The story places Diné peoples' coming to be as connected to the lands and waters, worlds before, worlds that our minds are too naive to comprehend. I started with this story because Cecilia (pseudonym) brought it to me. And by beginning with Diné storying, Cecilia centers Diné ways.

I met Cecilia when she was a freshman in college. She had a petite frame, with long, dark russet layers of hair. She regularly smiled coyly with closed lips and two full cheeks. Emanating from her walnut brown eyes was a depth of kindness that I later learned was a special gift she possessed. Cecilia frequently wore a fine-strung, turquoise-beaded necklace with a dangling, nickel-sized arrowhead and matching turquoise stone earrings. Navajo jewelry gifted to her. She told me once that she would rather wear jewelry made of silver and turquoise than of the gold and diamonds that most women desired to wear. When she told me this, I noticed a sense of pride as she gently touched the strand of her turquoise necklace while positioning herself a little bit straighter on the chair. This made me smile.

Cecilia grew up in a large urban city with her parents, aunt, five siblings (she is the second-youngest child), and their family cat. Her parents moved to the city to find work with a decent salary, enough to support their growing family. Much of Cecilia's life was living in a world alongside concrete, streetlights, and noise—city life. Because of this, she had street smarts. She knew her way around the city. And if there were times when she did not know what to do or if she was in a bind, she would figure it out. That was Cecilia, the figure-it-out type. Cecilia and her family lived in a modest two-bedroom apartment, where she grew up learning and respecting Navajo teachings taught to her by her mom and dad. Having been raised predominantly off the Navajo reservation lands, Cecilia confessed that sometimes she felt like it was hard to relate to being a Navajo, but she still knew she was connected to the land. Her experiences remind me of Tommy

Orange's (2018) description of urbanity: "An Urban Indian belongs to the city, and cities belong to the earth. Everything here is formed in relation to every other living and nonliving thing from the earth. All our relations" (p. 11). I interpret this as not separating ourselves from reservation and urban Natives. All land is Native land, whether it's a city or a rural town. We are all related and should treat each other as such. We must remember this. Another note: I will be using "Native," "American Indian," "Native American," and "Indigenous" interchangeably throughout the text.

In high school, Cecilia and a classmate gave a presentation to a group of urban Native community members on how alcoholism was ravaging the lives of Native Americans. She was actively involved with the urban Native community and took part in providing workshops to the group and newcomers who attended meetings. After their presentation, Cecilia told me, "One of the elders in the group stood up and said, 'You guys are like the epitome of the Twin Warriors. The Twin Warriors traveled from one world to the next to slay monsters and bring knowledge back to the people. You guys are just like the Twin Warriors, that's amazing; you are bringing knowledge back to community.'" Reaffirming being a warrior is reminiscent of Gus Bighorse, a Navajo man who survived the Long Walk in 1864, who told his daughter Tiana, "In Navajo, a warrior means someone who can get through the snowstorm when no one else can. . . . In Navajo, a warrior says what is in the people's hearts. Talks about what the land means to them. Brings them together to fight for it" (Bighorse, 1990, p. xxiv). There is strength exuded when we tell our young people that they are warriors. The elder told Cecilia and her classmate. Mr. Bighorse told his daughter Tiana. I am telling you. We are all warriors, in our own way.

When reflecting back on this experience, Cecilia smiled and explained to me that she believed the Navajo oral story of the Twin Warriors. She also believes that she is joining other Native warrior students who will go to college by describing that as many Navajo students journey to college, they (you) are re-creating a contemporary version of the Twin Warriors story. Cecilia sees herself and other Native students as warriors, capable of facing the snowstorms. The Twin Warrior story highlights past vicious monsters that sought to destroy our Navajo people. Cecilia believes that today's monsters work to disrupt our way of life.

Cecilia imagines a future where she (and others like her) journeys toward college with hopes of returning home to help the people. She shared this connection and referred to the Navajo elder's comments:

> He told us that we should be proud of who we are and that what we are doing is really good. "You are taking the knowledge from the elders as well as today's society and putting them together to make a better world for the Native community and the city as well as the reservation." That was something that impacted my life because I always felt like being able to go back to the city and bring knowledge

and bring it back to my cousins. After college, maybe I can return the knowledge back to the people and help them prosper. Having him tell me that was really inspirational, and just motivating, made me feel like I had a purpose to do something.

Knowledge, emphasized in Cecilia's statement, is important to highlight. What knowledges are specified? And what knowledges have always existed? Cecilia affirmed that elder knowledge is critical to advance the betterment of people and society. This distinction matters because for far too long, Indigenous knowledge systems have been erased and deemed invaluable and inferior to White settler knowledge systems. Rather, students like Cecilia are reinvigorated with a sense of existence, a reaffirming of "we are here," armed with an ontological and epistemological understanding that centers the richness and persistence of Navajo knowledge systems. This is an example of emphasizing Navajo sovereignty in education, in life, in our humanity. Yet, this process also does not mean the complete, binary opposite of western, Eurocentric knowledge.

A binary is having two parts. It's often used in mathematics to explain two elements such as 0 and 1. Binary thinking includes yes or no, right and wrong, good and bad, and beginning and end. Binary is also used to separate genders into male and female, falsely viewing gender as only two options. If we are not careful, we also use binary framings among ourselves, such as urban and rural, traditional and contemporary, Native language speaker and non–Native language speaker, and White world versus Native world (two-world framing). It's a simple categorization. Yet, simple also means reductivity to the complexities, in-betweenness, the grayness, nuances, beauty, messiness, paradoxes, and the multitudes of life of peoples. There are moments when a yes or no answer is important, but there are many more times when we may answer with "I don't know" or both a "yes and no." Lumbee scholar Bryan McKinley Jones Brayboy and Emma Maughan (2009) indicate, "Setting these knowledges in opposition to one another erases complexity and nuance, closing off spaces of potential and possibility" (p. 5). To reify knowledge systems as ideologies of dichotomy, binary, and two worlds dilutes the sophistication of Diné thought and ways of knowing. We are more than two-world, binary concepts. We have come from multiple worlds. We are in the beauty of the infinite dimensions of the glittering world. I will share more on this further during our literary time together.

Sha'álchíní (my children), how do teenagers like Cecilia make it into college? What are the present-day monsters that lurk and pull them back when they are desperately striving to attain a college degree, when they are trying to find a sense of belonging? And like the Twin Warriors, what weapons do they use? This book is a result of my journey to find out, for you, because ayóó ánóshní (I love you).

Introduction

We don't have to hide anymore
because now is the time
With forgiveness as my bow
and my prayers as my arrows
pulling back and let go and watch them fly like sparrows
Have hope
Yeah have hope
With compassion as my shield and
faith down to my marrow
I will walk the corn pollen path
even when it gets narrow

—Lyla June, "All Nations Rise"[1]

Belonging. It was a Saturday morning when I learned that police removed two Mohawk youth from a college campus tour. Thomas Kanewakeron Gray (age 19) and Lloyd Skanahwati Gray (age 17) researched potential colleges, saved up money, and drove seven hours to take part in a campus tour at one of their dream schools. This was the first time they took a road trip by themselves. That's a big deal. The Gray brothers displayed intelligence and determination, setting and sticking to priorities, and a heck of a lot of maturity in doing all the right things when searching for colleges and planning for the future. My social media feeds were flooded with thoughts of anger and frustration at the police, the institution, and the White woman who accused the boys of *not belonging*.

Their sense of belonging was called into question as soon as they arrived on campus. Shortly after the brothers joined the tour, a White woman stepped away and called 911. Audio clips of the 911 call revealed that she responded by describing that the boys were "creepy kids," "made me feel sick," were "definitely not part of the tour," and that "they don't belong." Police arrived. Thomas and Lloyd were immediately removed from the tour and questioned by the police. One of the brothers pulled out his cell phone, scrolled through his email, and showed the police officers their campus tour registration confirmation. They had to show proof of belonging to a place where Native peoples thrived long before Colorado State University was

1

even thought of or built. The irony. After police verified their campus tour registration, the Gray brothers were finally allowed to rejoin the tour, but it was nearly over by that time. Instead of continuing on the tour, they walked to their vehicle, turned the engine on, and drove seven hours back home.

In an article in *Indian Country Today*, one of the brothers, Thomas Gray, stated, "What happened was wrong in so many ways and we wish this on no one else" (Schilling, 2018). I'd like to think that most people are like Thomas in not wishing harm on others, but our historical and present reality is that many are not. Disturbance and disruption took place; it has and always been in motion against Indigenous peoples. Removal and dispossession of Indigenous bodies from land, places, and peoples constitute an experience that has been in motion for centuries, especially on campuses, and yes, even occurring on college tours (Minthorn & Nelson, 2018). I don't blame the brothers for leaving. I would have too.

The Gray brothers' story, as shocking as it sounds, is not unique for Native students and college environments, and quite frankly not unique at all for countless Black, Brown, and gender nonbinary peoples in society. After I heard about the incident through my social media feeds, Adrienne Keene, a Cherokee scholar and the creator of the blog *Native Appropriations,* and I texted back and forth with much anger, disgust, and pain. We understood that the Gray brothers' experiences were a recurring nightmare, and as Native scholars, we had to do something. We wrote an op-ed for *Teen Vogue* (Keene & Tachine, 2018) titled "Colorado State University Tour Incident Is Nothing New for Native Students." In our piece, we stressed the reality that the history of Native education is tainted with appropriation, theft, forced assimilation, dehumanization, and genocide through colonial colleges and government-run boarding schools. And as the incident at Colorado State University demonstrated, educational institutions continue to be sites of oppression that disrupt notions of belonging.

We live in a society where belonging is desired and needed. Brené Brown (2017), a scholar known for her work on vulnerability and shame, writes that "we want to be part of something," and in her book *The Gifts of Imperfection,* she writes, "Because true belonging only happens when we present our authentic, imperfect selves to the world, our sense of belonging can never be greater than our level of self-acceptance" (Brown, 2010, p. 26). There is truth and power to being authentic and accepting of one's self, yet the reality is that for many Black, Brown, trans, and queer peoples, there is a reckoning that authenticity may come with a violent price—especially in a pervasive whitestreaming nation (Grande, 2003). Whether grilling at a barbecue, selling water, wearing a hooded sweatshirt, going to kindergarten, staying at an Airbnb, sitting at Starbucks, attending a hockey game with classmates, jogging in a neighborhood, playing in a high school basketball or volleyball game, or taking part in a campus tour, Black, Brown, trans, and queer bodies are harassed and removed for being, doing, and simply living. In many cases, the police are involved in disrupting and reinforcing their removal and dispossession from a sense of self and personhood, fracturing again and again and again ideas and practices of self-acceptance and true belonging.

Some consider that there is a politics of belonging. For example, in Thea Renda Abu El-Haj's book titled *Unsettled Belonging: Educating Palestinian American Youth After 9/11*, she states that "feeling part of a collectivity—particularly a national collectivity—is never given, but instead is actively constructed through political projects" (2015, p. 5). Learning from Palestinian American youth after 9/11, she documents how young people in school settings are excluded from an American nationalism of belonging and antagonized as "impossible subjects" as they encounter everyday "disjuncture" in their lives (Abu El-Haj, 2015, p.3). Diné scholar Jennifer Denetdale also asserts that Native Nations are marked with constraints by the domestic dependent relationship to the United States and hopes that "we envision Diné belonging that cuts across the fabric of national and nationalism, that is inclusive, and holds all Diné as being valuable and inclusive" (Denetdale, 2020, p. 1054). I believe that we live in a society where belonging is desired and needed among our young people and across generations, and yet belonging does not look the same for everyone; it is contested.

In higher education, belonging is becoming a popular concept. More and more institutions are discussing and seeking ways to create belonging for their diverse student clientele. In higher education research, belongingness is defined as "the need to belong" (Alejandro et al., 2020, p. 680) and sense of belonging is often referred to as an "individual's sense of belonging to a particular group and his or her feelings of morale, associated with membership in the group" (Cabrera et al., 2016, p. 67). Frequently, "integrating" into the campus environment is viewed as a requirement for belonging (Tinto, 1987). The logic goes: if students integrate, they then have a sense of belonging, and *bam!* they will persist and graduate with a degree. That sounds simple enough. But what is at stake when our young people attempt to belong to a world that does not want them for who they are?

The White woman who called the police said of the Gray brothers, "They don't belong." Rereading those three words now gives me chills. *They. don't. belong.* She and others have made me then wonder: Who belongs in college settings? And who defines and sets the terms of belonging?

*   *   *

We are from Lók'aahnteel (Patch of Wide Reeds). We are Naasht'ézhí Táchii'nii (Red Running Into the Water, Zuni clan). You were born for the Tó'díchʼii'nii (Water's Edge) clan, while I was born for the Tł'ízí łání (Many Goats) clan. We come from a long lineage of strong matriarchs and ancestors who instilled in us to love one another and care for the people and the land as best we could. While I had the experience of growing up on our home(lands), you all learned to live in the city and also find your way back to our original home(lands). Diné scholar Farina King (2018), in her book titled *The Earth Memory Compass: Diné Landscapes and Education in the Twentieth Century*, places parentheses around (lands) when she writes "home(lands)" because she states, "I often consider home and homeland as entangled and synonymous" (p. 34). I agree with her statement and also include the parentheses myself to emphasize the simultaneous entanglements. I am writing from a Navajo matrilineal centeredness in hopes that these stories help you on your journey toward home. You will notice that I go back and forth through time; in a way, we are time-traveling together because it is important to see how history coexists with the present and future (Tachine et al., 2021). Take note of moments that make you pause (Patel, 2016). I encourage you to stop reading and wonder a bit, feel through the pausing, and possibly jot down your thoughts. See this as a shared experience between you, our ancestors, and the world around us. Know that woven through these words are my prayers, tears, anguish, remembrance, and love.

Most mornings, I have the pleasure of lying close to you, before you have the opportunity to greet a new day. If I am not rushing to start the day, I try to relax and embrace that precious moment. Today, I paused. I breathed in your sweet baby scent and gazed at your smooth cheeks, little nose, and bushy eyebrows. And then in that moment, I began wondering: What will your future look like? What dreams will you have? I then thought of all of you, sha'áłchíní, and wondered the same thing: What will your journey look like? A burning question stirred inside as I asked myself: Will college be in your pathway? And if so, will college be an accessible pathway? I'm sure these types of questions are common for many mothers, as most of us only hope for the best for our future generations, our babies. But I cannot deny the harsh reality that the course to college for most of our Native people is an arduous one. That is why I am writing to you. This book weaves the stories of 10 Navajo college students, bringing together their experiences of presence and belonging in educational settings. Monsters and weapons are important parts of their stories.

I started thinking more sincerely about monsters in 2020, a year of boundless anticipation. Then, you were a senior in high school, excited to embark on what was next. Our family was thrilled too, making necessary preparations for graduation, because graduations mean so much to us, a celebration for you, for the entire family, and even for the Tribal nation. One Native graduate is a celebration for us all! Your gorgeous, deep gray velveteen top and matching black sateen skirt were complete. You chose the colors and texture. In early March, we traveled home to get final items: buckskin moccasins, a wide sash belt woven with radiant red tones and an intricate white motif design of a spider woman, and hair ties for a tsiiyééł (hair bun). Your auntie volunteered to make the cake, and nálí lady (paternal grandmother) had many eager questions. They were saving money to celebrate with us. We felt their love and joy. I could see the excitement in your face, growing day to day.

Days later, after returning home, the state of Arizona instituted a stay-at-home order as news quickly erupted that COVID-19 was spreading. We took it seriously, at first thinking that the order would last for only a few weeks. In those initial weeks, we enjoyed sleeping in, leisurely going about our day, cooking from home, and staying inside. But weeks turned into more weeks. Then, more news that altered our rhythm occurred when schools changed from in-person to online. And we wondered more intensely: How long will this last? We knew what was coming regarding your graduation, but there was a part of me that didn't want to know. For the class of 2020, graduation was different. The typical graduation in the football field, with loud cheers, long speeches, and heartfelt hugs from family and friends, faded from our future outlook. Graduation had to be distant and online for the sake of our safety and health. COVID made the rules. We canceled the cake order with auntie. We made the difficult announcement to our family that graduation would occur online and we had to cancel the carefully planned reception.

You were strong during that entire time, she'awéé' (my baby). But mama knew that this was hard for you, difficult for many. On graduation day, I tried to do what your nalí lady would have done by wrapping your tsiiyééł (hair bun) tightly. When your másání (maternal grandmother) saw you in full dress, dripping with Navajo bling and pride, she smiled so big. I will cherish that smile. We piled into the chidí (vehicle) to take part in the drive-by graduation ceremony to celebrate your wonderful achievement. That day, I held back tears because it seemed as though tears were ever-flowing, unrelenting, and they started a month prior to your beautiful day. I did not want to confuse and stain this joyful day with the deep sorrow that many of us were feeling.

On March 17, 2020 the *Navajo Times* released an article titled "First Diné Tested Positive for Coronavirus" (Becenti, 2020). A month later, in April, COVID-19 rapidly roared through the Navajo Nation as the illness took the lives of many Navajo people, our relatives. By summer, the Navajo Nation had the highest COVID-19 infection rates per capita in the country, surpassing New York City. National media began highlighting our people as reporters traveled to Diné Bikéyah (Navajo land) to cover the story. While coverage increased, much of the storyline depicted the impoverished conditions of our home(lands), reproducing poverty porn imagery of our beautiful people, and broadcasting our lives throughout the world through "the White gaze." I learned about the White gaze from Toni Morrison, who was critiqued for writing books that did not cater to a White readership that centered on White lives, thinking, and doing. In the film *Toni Morrison: The Pieces I Am,* she explained the craft and purpose of writing from her Black experience, which made me see more expansively how I want to write. Many of us do not realize that we often write for and/or think about the White audience when we talk about our experiences, and by doing so, we do not realize the damaging views that they already hold for many of us and the reoccurring harm we do to ourselves when we satisfy the White gaze.

Navajo Nation leadership enforced weekend curfews and pleaded that people stay home for survival. Daily, Navajo Nation president Jonathan Nez tweeted the count of total positive cases, those in recovery, and total deaths. Numbers were increasing and increasing, and they became harder and harder to see and feel through each day.

Many of us were grappling with ongoing death in deep and profound ways, learning and desperately trying to find the strength to see the goodness in life.

In October of that year, President Nez delivered a keynote at the National Tribal Health Conference. He emphasized the devastating impact that COVID-19 had on Native communities. Navajos were not the only hard-hit community. Tribal Nations and Black/Brown people were overrepresented in daily deaths and positive cases. President Nez addressed the 900 Tribal leaders in attendance and emphatically stated, "Let us remind ourselves to use our way of life teachings, our culture, tradition and language to fight these monsters. Our ancestors fought hard for us to be here today—it is now our turn as tribal leaders, citizens to fight for what is right for the future of our people" (Nez, 2020). President Nez connected the twin warrior story to the COVID-19 pandemic and referred to the virus as the monster. I was moved by his declaration of asserting Diné ways as a powerful source of strength, as weapons. I agreed with him. Yet, as I read the article further that featured his talk, I could not help but think differently when he spoke about the monster as COVID-19. The monster is not COVID-19. Rather, COVID-19 is the hauntings (the preconditions) from the monsters, which I will explain further shortly. This is in no way meant to disrespect or to discredit President Nez—it's an alternative way of interpreting stories and making connections with our lives. That's theorizing (building off of knowledges), story sharing, and world-making.

You asked me about monsters while we drove through the desert city blasting Lyla June. That questioning was profound and a matter that is too often neglected in classrooms and households. I could not answer the question fully during that joyride, as I grappled with how much to share with your precious minds and hearts. But as COVID-19 erupted into our intimate lives over that summer, the world also revealed poignantly deep-seated racism as Black people and allies took to the streets with their fists up after George Floyd and Breonna Taylor were tragically killed by the police, and then in January 2021, White people with red MAGA caps and Trump flags stormed through the U.S. Capitol with hateful screams rooted in White supremacy. I began to wonder more deeply about the roles that power, race, history, story, and context play in shaping our Navajo livelihood. The context of COVID-19, the usage of the monster framing by Navajo leadership, and the ongoing presence of systemic racism pushed me further into understanding systemic monsters and their hauntings. Sha'áłchíní (my children), we have to learn about the systemic monsters and their hauntings.

SYSTEMIC MONSTERS AND HAUNTINGS

Systemic monsters[3] are the interlocking structures of power rooted in White supremacy, settler colonialism, racism, erasure, heteropatriarchy, and capitalism that disrupt sovereignty and belonging. Systemic monsters are shape-shifting, morphing in various ways with deep intentions to maintain power over the land and peoples. In the Navajo language, collective challenges can be referred to as "naayéé'," which translates into English as "monsters" (Austin, 2009). "Naayéé'" describes anything that disrupts hózhó, which is a significantly meaningful and profound concept that encompasses all that is consumed of peace, harmony, balance, and goodness (Austin, 2009). Monsters disrupt harmony. Monsters disrupt humanity. Monsters are connected to the Twin Warriors story and to the beginnings of our existence.

Let me be clear, systemic monsters show the groundwork of White supremacy and the construction of Whiteness. White supremacy secures White racial hegemony that maintains domination and the privileges associated with it in everyday life (Leonard, 2004). Groundwork is key here because it describes the foundation, where the roots of domination spring forth. The challenge with groundwork is that there is not much thought devoted to it among the general public; it's merely there, or even forgotten and unrecognized. Diné scholar Melanie Yazzie also suggests that "common sense" language is another indicator of the invisible ways dominance is secured (Yazzie, 2014). In many ways, that is how Western society functions—we do not recognize how much of our world is formed by White supremacy. I see how White supremacy and Whiteness are the foundation of systemic monsters, such that "whiteness naturalizes the existence of systemic racism" (Cabrera, 2019, p. 10). What I mean is that Whiteness is composed of normative constructions—rooted in White supremacy—that are everyday ways of being, actions, behaviors, policies, logics, and common sense that are taken for granted as "the way things are done," which devalues how we, as Diné, may think or act. Throughout this book, I will return to normative constructions of Whiteness to help point out the hiddenness or the everydayness of White settler ways, which reinforces and reaffirms the nation-state's (U.S.) ownership, control, and domination also referred to as "white possessive logics" over our lands, bodies, and minds (Moreton-Robinson, 2015, p. xii).

Black scholars have also used monsters in their framing of injustices. I want to thank Black thinkers for their brilliance in helping to push my thinking. You will see throughout this book the engagement of Black scholarship that shaped my understanding. We can learn a lot from those who are also being harmed by systemic monsters. For example, Christine Sharpe, in her book *Monstrous Intimacies*, defined monstrous intimacies as "a set of known and unknown performances and inhabited horrors, desires, and positions produced, reproduced, circulated, and transmitted, that are breathed in like air and often unacknowledged to be monstrous" (Sharpe, 2010, p. 3).

I appreciate Sharpe's definition because living in today's sociopolitical climate presents an onslaught of monsters and their torment of Indigenous peoples, that are "breathed in like air" and unacknowledged. Incarceration, missing and murdered Indigenous womxn,[4] lack of academic achievement, suicide, diabetes, racist mascots, systemic poverty, harm and dispossession of lands and waters, oppressive policies, and many more (too many to name) are tormenting Native communities.

Therefore, I think systemic monsters create(d) the "preconditions" for Navajo people (and many more) to suffer and die. I am using the term "preconditions" intentionally because health and political leaders stated that COVID-19 is more aggressive among peoples who have preconditions of poor health (heart disease, diabetes, and other illnesses), which individualizes death and dismisses the larger structural preconditions that exacerbated health disparities. For the Navajo people, structural preconditions include lack of running water and electricity, few grocery stores across Navajo land, weak healthcare and telecommunications infrastructure and support, and years and years of neglect from the federal government—a government that promised to care for the first peoples of this place in exchange for Indigenous land. COVID-19 is not the monster. The systemic monsters are the deep structures of power that make it easier for this virus to spread.

Octavia Butler (1998), in *Parable of the Talents,* wrote, "Beware: At war or at peace, more people die of unenlightened self-interest than of any other disease" (p.77). Self-interest, as indicated by Butler, is an example of the multifaceted ways that systemic monsters operate. We need to see and name the longstanding systemic monsters and build a resistance that destroys their pandemic power and hauntings. Systemic monsters are killing us, even more than COVID-19.

Hauntings are also critically important to understand. The Unangax̂ scholar Eve Tuck and C. Ree (2013) wrote about "the glossary of haunting," which foregrounds justice, and about "righting (and sometimes wronging) wrongs," which provide another way to understand settler colonialism and decolonization (p. 640). I take up the framing of haunting and build off their work by seeing the hauntings of systemic monsters from a complicated, multifaceted view in which we can see (and feel) through the opaqueness (and violence) of injustices and oppression brought forth by the systemic monsters, in hopes of not fearing what is right before our eyes and felt through our senses. To be clear, then, the preconditions are the hauntings, which I define as the ongoing everyday suffering and struggles that function to uphold the inferiority of people. Hauntings in this context are what Avery F. Gordon (1997) defines as "one way in which abusive systems of power make themselves known and their impacts felt in everyday life, especially when they are supposedly over and done with (slavery, for instance) or when their oppressive nature is denied" (p. xvi). The phrase "supposedly over and done with" is critical here because hauntings are not cast aside as some like to believe—they live in the present and cling to the now.

Dionne Brand (2006) wrote, "How imprisoned, we are in their ghosts," reminding us that in many ways, we can get trapped in the hauntings (p. 9). What I mean by this is that in many ways, we can blame ourselves and our people for the multiple everyday sufferings and struggles that we encounter and endure. I am ashamed to admit that I have done this, especially when I was younger and didn't know the depths of the White supremacy that was indoctrinated in me. I am still learning how harmfully we can treat ourselves and others when we get imprisoned in the hauntings. When we do, the systemic monsters continue to persevere and control our lives.

Lakota scholar Nick Estes gave an interview for the news organization *Truthout* in May of 2020. In that interview, he said, "The conditions of war are created by design to intensify these outbreaks of contagious diseases" (Litvin, 2020), meaning that although many of our relatives are in anguish and dying from COVID-19, much ongoing suffering remains from the conditions (prior, present, and future) of economic hardships, lack of basic living needs, social ills, and so much more brought forth from the systemic monsters. Many of us have been praying for our people, for their protection against COVID-19; we must also focus on protection against the systemic monsters of White supremacy, settler colonialism, racism, erasure, heteropatriarchy, and capitalism.

The year 2020 was erupting while I was writing this. Time and context were my teachers. I was able to grasp more clearly how systemic monsters influence belonging that continuously brought me back to the question I asked earlier: Who belongs in college settings?

Hauntings also linger in college settings. We must understand enrollment rates as an example of the hauntings, the conditions of injustices that maintain oppression among groups of peoples. When we look at the decreasing number of Native students entering college, we start getting a picture of who gets in (and who does not), already providing conceptions of belonging and the politics of belonging. While more Native youth are aspiring to go to college, college enrollment and first-year persistence trends tell a critical story. According to the latest available data,[5] between 1980 and 2002, Native 10th-grade students' expectations to complete a bachelor's degree increased by 19%, and by 26% for those aspiring to get master's and doctorate degrees (Freeman & Fox, 2005). An increasing number of Native students aspired to obtain a college degree, and yet nationally, only 17% of Native students who graduated from high school attended any college, compared to the national average college-going rate of 67% (Brayboy et al., 2012). For those who did enroll in college, in 2009, there were 205,900 Native students enrolled in degree-granting 4-year colleges; in 2010, the enrollment dropped to 196,200; and by 2014, the enrollment plummeted to 152,900, the lowest it had been since the year 2000 (Musu-Gillette et al., 2017). When compared to the overall Native population growth, the raw numbers of college enrollment are not encouraging.

The Native American population increased by 39% from 2000 to 2010 (with some tribes having the highest growth among young adults and youth), but the college enrollment rate stagnated at 1% during the same period. A closer examination of college persistence rates also reveal that 7 out of 10 Native students returned to college after the first year, demonstrating the importance of understanding what occurs during that critical first year (CRSDE, 2020). One may argue that just because Native students have a small representation in college enrollment numbers, that does not mean they do not belong. Yet, the reality is that enrollment rates are one serious marker of inclusion/exclusion that many look to, and when an enrollment stagnation crisis is unaccounted for over decades, that's because of neglect.

While all U.S. universities and colleges reside on Indigenous land, many deny and erase the fact that Indigenous lands and bodies were stolen (Lee & Ahtone, 2020). Genocide, dispossession, and displacement of Indigenous peoples, as well as the simultaneous enslavement and forced labor of Blacks, form the foundation of what is now the United States and many colonial colleges and settler universities (Carney, 1999; Lee & Ahtone, 2020; Nash, 2019; la paperson, 2017; Stein, 2020; Wilder, 2013). Policies such as the Morrill Act have served what Lumbee scholar Bryan Brayboy and I call the "immoral triad" of myths, erasure, and violence (Brayboy & Tachine, 2021). Myths, erasure, and violence are part of a larger story of what is called the United States. The irony of the triad is the contemporary reality that a college degree is becoming more and more costly, and many of our people cannot afford to attend an institution that benefits from Indigenous lands and lost lives. I will illustrate in this book that increased college costs are examples of the hauntings brought forth by the systemic monsters.

Most people do not know about us. We have been erased from memory or cast in a fixed and distant past, romanticized, and dehumanized. Even in educational research, we are often relegated to a footnote under an asterisk that justifies exclusion from research studies because of low numbers, or we are completely ignored, pushed from the language of underrepresented to invisible (Shotton et al., 2013). These types of exclusionary measures signify "statistical extermination," which are formulas sanctioned by the federal government that quantify the validation of the removal of Indigenous existence and presence (Jaimes, 1992, p. 137). A *Teen Vogue* (Nagle, 2018) article titled "Invisibility Is the Modern Form of Racism Against Native Americans" highlighted this structural violence. Emphasized in that article was a national study, *Reclaiming Native Truth* (First Nations Development Institute & Echo Hawk Consulting, 2018), which investigated how non-Natives perceive Native peoples. Findings revealed that a majority of respondents believe that the Native population is declining (which is empirically false—Native populations have been increasing steadily); and they do not think about Native people (affirming the pervasiveness of erasure). Their research confirms what Patrick Wolfe (1999, 2006) calls "the logic of elimination," which is the killing off, getting rid, of Native peoples in order to obtain access to land and territory.

Neglecting Native peoples perpetuates multiple harms in education. First, disregarding Native peoples perpetuates the status quo; our perspectives will continue to be marginalized or erased, and these discouraging trends will persist. Second, neglect maintains the pervasive deficit narratives about Native peoples, stigmatizing our place in society and in education. Third, Native peoples are combined with other minoritized populations, ignoring or erasing the sovereign status of Indigenous peoples of the United States and diluting the nuances of distinctive cultural life ways. Fourth, those who seek to resolve inequities by enhancing access and the success of Native students in higher education are left with little to no guidance. Finally, this absence of representation limits the "possible selves" imagined by and for Native peoples. Possible selves, as researched by the Tulalip scholar Stephanie Fryberg and Hazel Rose Markus (2003), are the social representations (ideas, images) of how to be a person that people use to orient themselves in their social world.

These statistics and realities are difficult to swallow, alarming, and worrisome. It is too easy in our minds to start an anxiety-inducing list of hardships impacting our people, our family, and our own lives. The Unangax̂ scholar Eve Tuck (2009) frames this as "damage-centered research," such that a pathologizing approach is enacted to address oppression as a singular definition of Native communities (p. 409). We cannot deny the harsh realities that our people are facing, but deep down, we also know that much beauty and wisdom lie inside all our Native peoples and communities. Tuck calls on educational researchers to move away from damage-centered research to desire-centered research, which "understands complexity, contradiction, and the self-determination of lived lives" (2009, p. 416). This reminds me of the Navajo concept of "walking in beauty," which accentuates the capacity to move forward in and with beauty and balance, knowing and recognizing the monsters that are present and the powerful teachings that we have been equipped with, which I refer to as "Indigenous weapons."

INDIGENOUS WEAPONS

Indigenous weapons are knowledges and ethical engagements that are rooted in Navajo ways of knowing of k'é (kinship; relational-based) that build survivance and reawaken the power and sovereignty of Indigenous presence and belonging. Minnesota Chippewa writer and scholar Gerald Vizenor (1994) gifted us with the concept of survivance, which is described as "moving beyond our basic survival in the face of overwhelming cultural genocide to create spaces of synthesis and renewal" (p. 53). Survivance is a semantic combination of "survival" and "resistance" that signifies the force that both terms form when placed and enacted together. In these spaces of synthesis and renewal, we can "imagine education otherwise," as Alutiiq scholar Leilani Sabzalian (2019) has shown us, by documenting the nuance, beauty, love, courage, intelligence, fear, and survivance of Native students and their families.

What makes Indigenous weapons so powerful is that they are centered and balanced on Diné philosophies of k'é. The Navajo term "k'é" is a belief system based on a matrilineal society that deeply recognizes and honors relationality and kinship through clans. Diné scholar Hollie Kulago (2016) stated that "the concept of k'é speaks directly to the way relationships of respect and interdependence should exist between people and nature" (p. 4). In this way, k'é is not a static concept, but an abundantly dynamic way of life that regards and respects our relationship to all beings in order to construct social harmony and beauty of hózhó (balance and beauty). Diné scholar Lloyd Lee (2020) further explained:

> K'é does not emphasize independence, self-reliance, and separateness; rather, people connect themselves to all entities in this world. This relation creates a bond in which the individual understands that they are not alone and have family in places. . . . Fulfillment comes from the social and affective acts and bonds, which helps the person unite and harmonize with the social universe (p. 53).

K'é is a knowledge system that has been passed down from generation to generation since time immemorial. We are alive today because of k'é. We must then see k'é as our superpower and the force flowing through Indigenous weapons!

In Django Paris and H. Samy Alim's (2017) book *Culturally Sustaining Pedagogies*, they begin the pages with five powerful words gifted by Gloria Ladson-Billings, "We teach what we value." Diné peoples follow that same logic by imparting values to the next generation that have been taught by our ancestors and their ancestors, which emphasizes that knowledge is multigenerational, relational, and sustaining. These knowledge systems (pedagogical, epistemological, ontological, and axiological) are rooted in love, life, sacredness, and sovereignty that are in relation to the evolution and fluidity of spatial, temporal, and spiritual dimensions and worlds. Indigenous weapons are connected to and build off of k'é that has endured over and beyond time. Indigenous weapons are in community and in solidarity—locking arms and hearts—with culturally sustaining pedagogies (Paris & Alim, 2017) that critically ask, "What knowledges must we sustain in order to overcome and survive when faced with a power that seeks to sustain itself above and beyond—and sometimes shot through—our bodies?" (p. 14). We must teach what we value for survivance.

I want to be clear that Indigenous weapons are not an attempt to reproduce tropes of healing through essentialist culturalism that separates Nativeness into binary divisions of traditionalism versus nontraditionalism, that in turn can often dismiss and distract us from the systemic monsters that are actively at play to maintain their power. Rather, Indigenous weapons are action and processual oriented and involved remembering, repositioning, and resurging against systems of domination. Diné scholar Valerie Shirley (2017) asserts that "when Indigenous youth are provided with the necessary knowledge, skills, and analytical tools to navigate this future undertaking, they will be prepared to be protectors and change agents for their Indigenous communities; which, in turn, contributes to nation building" (p. 163).

INDIGENOUS WEAPONS AND SYSTEMIC MONSTERS IN EDUCATIONAL SETTINGS

Ten Navajo teenagers know that they will go to college. Jessie, Lauryn, Joy, Chris, Mike, Cecilia, Sam, Sarah, Wesley, and Amber (names are pseudonyms) shared, with permission, their stories as they navigated through and negotiated their first year in college. They are the top academic students in their class, connected to family and home and full of hope that they will rise above daily struggles. These students see college as an opportunity to better the circumstances for themselves, their family, and their Native community. As they confront college enrollment and then navigate through their first year, they face systemic monsters that are entrenched in historical and present-day policies and a world where many do not understand Indigenous ways of life. Through their journey, we may get closer to learning about the contentious ways that belonging is shaped in college settings. The experiences of these 10 Navajo students are not unique; many Native people across the nation can relate.

As a Diné scholar and mother, I share stories from a place that centers on Navajo ways of knowing. I foreground the students' experiences by connecting their lives to the Twin Warriors story when twin brothers defeated monsters including Yé'iitsoh (Big Giant), Déélgééd (Horned Monster), and Bináá' yee Aghání (Who Kills With His Eyes) that were destroying the Navajo people. Today, systemic monsters attempt to thwart these 10 Navajo students' ambitions to get into college and succeed during their first year. Much respect and gratitude is given to Cecilia, whom I mentioned earlier, for linking her and her classmates' experiences with the Twin Warriors. The Navajo oral story not only helps frame these students' stories, but also acknowledges the powerful role that oral stories have on existing realities and experiences among Indigenous peoples. We have much to learn from stories.

What are the systemic monsters that attempt to derail Navajo students? What Indigenous weapons help students to persist despite the systemic monsters attempting to work against them? And how do answers to these questions help us to better understand belonging in college settings?

This book is divided into two sections to address these questions. The first half of the book, titled "Fight to Enter College," details the 10 students' experiences while they were seniors in high school. They encounter two systemic monsters, including the *financial hardship monster*, rooted in settler colonialism; and the *deficit (not enough) monster*, rooted in assimilation. Each systemic monster generates *monstrous internalization*, which I define as the internalized beliefs, behaviors, attitudes, and feelings that diminish our brilliance and sacredness. For example, the financial hardship monster and the deficit (not enough) monster reveal the harsh conditions and realities of Navajo students' financial and academic experiences, which in turn (monstrous internalization operating) conjure fears of college affordability and damaging perspectives about college possibilities. Yet what is also shown is that the 10 teenagers—like the twin brothers—activate powerful regenerative Indigenous weapons of *resurgence* (love-centered) and *continuance* (life-centered) that strengthen them to withstand and challenge the monsters.

The second half of the book, titled "Surviving the First Year," continues their journey as they enter and transition into their first year in college. In this phase of their lives, they encounter the *failure monster*, rooted in meritocracy and capitalism; and the *(in)visibility monster*, rooted in erasure and racism. For example, students share the costly expenses of attending college and also discuss racist encounters in the classroom, residence hall, and in everyday experiences on campus. Monstrous internalization then occurs as students in turn question their academic talent, ability to afford college, and problematized ways of being and belonging. Indigenous weapons of *reverence* (sacred-centered) and *refusal* (sovereignty-centered) equip these students with the courage to face, look away from, and see themselves as sacred and sovereign.

Each of these systemic monsters is entrenched with White supremacy and heteropatriarchy, which are too often normalized or hidden from view by a society that ignores the inequities in higher education by maintaining the status quo of Native people in the United States. In these stories, we see how systemic monsters shape belonging. We must then examine conceptions of belonging by questioning who determines belonging and who sets the terms of who belongs and does not belong. We must contend with the ways that campus environments are sites of what I call "monsters' sense of belonging," which is assimilating, erasing, diminishing, and harming those whose worldviews are not rooted in White supremacy, heteropatriarchy, capitalism, racism, and erasure. These students show that there is a process of (un)belonging, a recognition of the politics of belonging and a repositioning against systemic monsters. They then remember and resurge to create what I see and define as "relational–sovereign belonging," the moving through and honoring of self-determination while intricately woven to relations (ancestors, more than human relatives, land/place, and even to monsters) that are complex, contradicting, and nuanced.

We represent an array of beauty, brilliance, and endurance. Many of us are deeply connected to the land and waters of what is now the United States and the world around us. We see ourselves and our people as strong and resilient, knowing the harsh history that our ancestors and relatives endured, and we continue to persevere, resisting injustices with hopes for the visions of a beautiful future. These stories are about love, "a love that can help us see our young people as whole versus broken when they enter schools, and a love that can work to keep them whole as they grow and expand who they are and can be through education" (Paris & Alim, 2017, p. 14).

METHODOLOGICAL NOTES: THE STORY RUG AS METHOD

In 2013, I started the weaving process of developing the methodology of a story rug. I received approval from the Institutional Review Board (IRB), as well as consulting with the Navajo Nation IRB, and was approved to start the story-sharing process for this dissertation. Research that follows Tribal protocol is extremely important, as there have been devastating circumstances impacting Native peoples that resulted from abusive methodological practices. With that knowledge, as well as respecting Tribal sovereignty, I connected with members of the Navajo Nation Human Subjects Board. I learned that because this research would occur off of the juridical boundaries of the Navajo Nation, Tribal approval was not warranted. I share these details because many people are not aware of the fact that if research is conducted with our people on our home(lands), there is another layer of approval to ensure that the research is completed in a good way. It's important to know that.

Ten full-time, first-time Navajo freshman students shared their stories with me and gave written consent as required by IRB. We met for several hours and at four different times throughout the spring 2013 semester. With their permission, I audio-recorded each meeting, and then after each interview, the audio recordings were transcribed. I shared the full transcripts with the students in order to ensure, for accuracy, that they would have the opportunity to edit, delete, add, and tell me what they did not want to share publicly. In addition, throughout different phases of analyzing and writing, I sent drafts to the students, and they were invited to make changes and again tell me if I was misinterpreting their stories. It is important to me to share stories in a good way.

Stol:lo and Coast Salish scholar Jo-Ann Archibald (2008) gifted us with her beautiful methodology of *Indigenous Storywork*. Because from her, I was inspired to see this evolving methodological work as a story rug. In Robin Starr Minthorn and Heather J. Shotton's (2018) edited book *Reclaiming Indigenous Research in Higher Education,* I wrote a chapter about the development of the story rug as an Indigenous research framework. I described setting up the loom, gathering the weaving tools, the warping and weaving process, and taking the rug off of the loom. While I described the broad phases of weaving, I connected that process to setting up a research design that included writing the literature review, framing the methods, gathering the data (stories) into findings, and providing discussion and implications. Combining Diné weaving to research design asserted Indigenous ways of knowing in methodology, while also giving space for creativity and freedom from the confines and rigidness of Eurocentric research methods. Since that publication, I continue to learn, write, and work my hands through the warps and wefts of the weaving loom to expand on the story rug not only as a framework, but as a rigorous analytical tool, as methodology.

Within Diné society, weaving has been a sustaining practice and teaching passed down through the generations from Spider Woman and the Twin Warriors as a vital tool and laborious process for protection, sustenance, healing, solving problems, and resistance. When I sit in front of the loom, I often feel, see, hear, and think about weaving as research. I pick up my weaving comb in my right hand and feel the sturdiness that the comb offers. I try to remember to go into weaving with a positive mindset, with an understanding that my thoughts go into the loom and rug. Yet, there have been many times when I entered into weaving with a heavy heart, pain, impatience, frustration, and uneasiness. We are human after all and carry the many burdens in our hearts and minds. The loom is ready for me with no judgment, no matter how I come into practice. I get my body situated to ensure that I am ready for the laborious task ahead. Then, I look closely at the detailed patterns in the textile and find where I last left off in order to remember where and what I need to do to proceed. I locate that point, set the male shed rod in place, strum my fingers across the warp strings and hear the rhythmic music of the loom, and then, with my left hand, I grab the female heddle rod toward me, and with my right hand, I insert the batten through the separation of the female and male warp strings. I then set the batten in place, grab the significant single strand of yarn, and pull the strand through the warp strings. Once the single strand is in place, I use my left pointer finger to push the strand down a bit and then, with the weaving comb in my right hand, I tamp it down. The batten is removed and replaced for the next turnaround. My body and mind get into a steady rhythm of repetition as I enter through the female way and pull individual weft threads through the rains of the warp strings. A steady back-and-forth or turnarounds are set into motion, such that threads join other threads to tell stories of interrelatedness and relationality. As I move through the weaving process, the stories become more expansive and intricate as the overall design takes shape, and they form in relation to one another and the environment. The warp and weft need each other for wholeness and strength as I see how individual threads are intimately hugging each other to create a dazzling beauty.

Weaving has helped me to be a better researcher. I give credit to the beauty of the loom for teaching me that research is active, that it requires movement and rest, that it is not solely from human knowledge, but also includes more than human (land and Spider Woman) wisdom and knowledges and is often tangled and twisted, which requires our utmost presence, patience, and humility. I am inspired by the Pueblo researcher Anya Dozier Enos (2017), who also used spider webs as methodology:

> To think through gathering information, how relationships and concepts interrelate and then how those ideas are shared and used, meaning going back and forth between how to gather information, and then how to analyze, present and use the findings with the goal of benefitting Pueblo community. This is not neatly predictable or organized; it is the messiness of research that results in something powerful. It is the spider web. (p. 42)

Spider webs are much like weaving textiles, especially given that Spider Woman taught us how to weave. These teachings helped me to develop the analytical process of weaving stories and display them in a patterned way.

The story rug, then, is an Indigenous mixed-methodological weaving approach to storying that interconnects multiple story threads, from various contexts, time periods, and experiences into a cohesive patterned whole. It is qualitative in nature through the collection and analysis of multiple stories. Each thread is a story. For this book, the story rug includes the 10 Navajo stories, the oral story of the Twin Warriors, and my (our) personal story. The story rug is also quantitative because there is a natural numerical counting and formula in the development of a loom and in the weaving patterned process to help maintain balance and symmetry in the design. In the story rug, there is a numerical pattern (formula) developed through the interweaving of multiple stories.

To be honest, while I was forming the story rug, I struggled to find a rhythm, a pattern connecting multiple stories from different time periods (history and present) into a cohesive written textile. Also, I was thinking about you. Therefore, I carefully and intentionally thought about the content and structure of storytelling that was accessible and that not only shared the students' experiences, but relates those experiences to historical and contemporary structures and realities that interplay in our lives and are too often unnoticed or not taught in schools. In Diné ways, we also understand the preciousness of one person's story; therefore, it was critical that I cared for and respected each individual I had the honor of interviewing and the stories that they shared. The story rug allowed me to bring history into the present and demonstrate that they are not easily separated but tightly woven together. I began to see the pattern as I continued to work through various story threads. The story rug then became a patterned, repetitive style of telling a story.

Figure I.1. Story Rug as Method

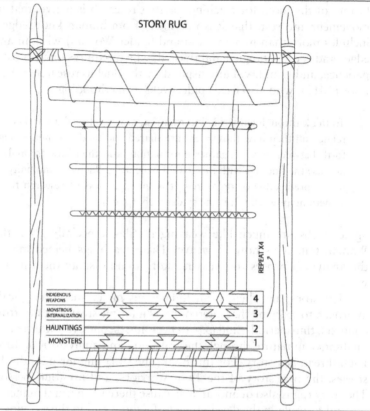

Story rug artwork by Lynne Hardy

This book is a story rug. Let me take a moment to explain the overall pattern of the story rug. Its design is divided into two sections (halves) that include the sections on "Fight to Enter College" (before college) and then "Surviving the First Year" (transitioning into college). Within each half, there are an additional two parts. Possibly visualize the entire story rug as having four sections. The four parts in the entire story rug follow an even finer detailed pattern. And that is the case with woven textiles—the closer you look at a rug, the finer the intricate patterns become. You become aware of the layers of patterns woven throughout. Thus, each of the four parts are further divided into four distinctive chapters that are in numerical order in our Navajo language.

I am a visual learner, so in order for me to understand patterns, I have to see it to better understand. Therefore, in Figure I.1, I provide a visual depiction of the pattern that emerged. Each part begins with a student story (an individual thread), a biographical sketch of who the person is and where he or she comes from. Then the story rug moves into historical stories that bring in the development of the systemic monsters. After I weave that section, the next pattern of the story rug is the stories of hauntings, which are the current conditions and everyday experiences that perpetuate suffering. Then, the pattern develops into how students internalize the systemic monsters and hauntings in their lives as monstrous internalizations. The pattern then moves into stories of Indigenous weaponry, which are activated to guide and strengthen students. This same pattern is repeated four times: monsters, hauntings, monstrous internalization, and Indigenous weapons. There is a design guiding when stories enter. I provided visual cues throughout the pages to demarcate the pattern transitions. I hope that helps you to see the analytical pattern of the story rug.

The story rug has taught me about the power of presence. In research, we often think about the visual and auditory aspect of knowledge through text/pictures and storying. Yet, knowledge is also created through multiple senses of touch, taste, and felt, as well as through kinetic movements. Sitting in front of the loom, I can feel the rigors of my body warping and then weaving thread through wefts. In the same way, I felt in my body the stories as they were revealed to me. The story rug is more than a methodological shift—it is an ontological shift as well.

I'm going to tell you a story, and it's going to be woven like a Navajo rug. Like a rug where single strands of yarn help to create and strengthen the complete design, individual stories will be interwoven throughout to construct the whole story rug. Those distinctive storylines will include a traditional Navajo story of the Twin Warriors, and will distinguish the stories of the lives of 10 Navajo students. The students' stories will be intertwined as a way to maintain the integrity and unique strand that each student offers to create the overall tapestry. These stories reveal the beauty of their lives, the tough struggles that they faced, and the powerful threads that guided them to move forward. And just like a rug, where designs are formed through a process of gathering single strands, I will connect these individual stories to construct collective themes that provide a picture of salient views that students share. As I am writing this, I am thinking about you and the brilliant Native youth and college students who may open these pages. When I started writing this, I prayed to the Creator, asking for guidance on what to do, what to write about, and the strength to write. Know that this book is meant for you. My prayers are that these stories equip you, just as Spider Woman equipped the twins. Also, know that the 10 Navajo students gave me permission to share their experiences with you in hopes that their stories will inspire and empower you to persevere.

FIGHT TO ENTER COLLEGE

Part I

RESURGENCE: RISING ABOVE THE STRUGGLE

Financial Hardship Monster

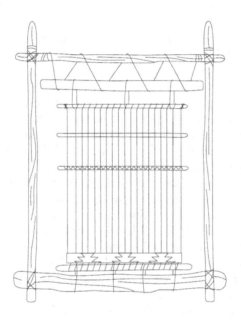

There is much freedom on Diné Bikéyah (Navajo land), our beloved home(lands). Sarah loved to roam and ride her horse freely on Diné Bikéyah. She and her horse would often spend an entire day traveling to visit friends and family and occasionally stopping by the general store. At the tender age of 17, Sarah already had a deep connection to the land, her more than human relatives, and the expansive universe. Sarah explained:

> The best days are on a summer day, when you wake up early, you go for a run, it's so nice and cool. You hear like the birds, you know you hear the bus coming down the road for other kids. You hear like just little things. And then the smell also, if it's a cold morning, you can always smell the smoke from the stove, you can smell grandma's cooking, you can smell the sagebrush and just like the wet dirt, and stuff. I would wake up, cook if I have to, clean, and then before it starts getting hot, I would saddle my horse. I would meet my friends

and we would ride to the lake and do some open-range roping or just ride anywhere, and we would ride all day. And then come evening, we would unsaddle, feed the animals, and we would just kick back. On a perfect, perfect summer day, you can sit there, anywhere on the dirt, it's not too hot, it's not too cold, it's just perfect, and you can hear everything like the, what are those bugs called? The crickets, yeah you can hear that, and the stars are so bright.

Sarah had long, dark brown hair that was usually coiled in a large, tight bun. She often wore faded-wash blue jeans, a short-sleeved T-shirt with a black Nike zip-up sweatshirt and worn running shoes. Her black-framed glasses sat comfortably on her face. She had an infectious expression that naturally formed into a warm smile. Even now, when I think of her I can't help but smile. Sarah was born and raised on the Navajo Nation, in a small rural town called Purple Hills, with roughly 1,200 residents. (Note that all Navajo reservation towns/places mentioned in this book are pseudonyms.) Three gas stations, a post office, a small hospital/clinic, a school campus, and a handful of state/tribal offices are sprinkled throughout Purple Hills. Modest homes, mobile trailers, and hooghan (homes) are nestled through-out the maroon and tan mesas that surround the little town.

Sarah has fond memories of living in a cozy, one-room, octagon hooghan (home) with the sturdy wooden door facing ha'a'aah (east), a teaching to honor the east, the opening to all living things, including the place where Diné people came from. She smiles, remembering evenings squeezing into their full-sized bed with her mom and siblings. Their home provided essential comfort and protection. Sarah told me that what makes a home is not the amount or types of amenities within the home, but the family who make up the home because "family is the backbone of everything."

The youngest of four children, Sarah was raised by a "strong" single mom, "loving" maternal grandma, and a "tough" maternal grandpa. Until she was 10 years old, she lived in a hooghan that had no running water or electricity. Sarah and her family's living situation is not unique, especially in the Navajo Nation. Many Native families living on reservations lack basic needs. Approximately 40% of reservation homes do not have running water (Conover, 2013). While the average American uses about 100 gallons a day, Navajo residents on average use 7 gallons a day. Many Navajo people know what to take (not too much, just enough) and give to Nihimá Nahasdzáán (Mother Earth).

There was a story on National Public Radio that featured Darlene Arviso, also known as "the water lady," who delivered water to 250 homes each month (Morales, 2015). Every day, Darlene loads up her big yellow truck and delivers water to homes that do not have access to running wa-ter. Many of those homes house the most vulnerable: the elderly, children, and the disabled. The once-a-month water delivery is not always reliable due to impassable muddy roads during the winter months. People in those situations must utilize other strategies, including hauling water or melting snow during the winter months to acquire the daily water needs for survival. Sarah told me that her mother would go and haul water for the family. After a full workday or on an early Saturday afternoon, she would drive to the nearest water hole, climb to the back of the truck, and fill up large water canisters. Blasting country star George Strait from the KTNN radio station, Sarah's mom would return driving the chidí (vehicle), hauling enough water to last for a few days.

When evening approached and the darkness from outside was thick, the stars and moon offered a soft glow, providing a hint of an outline of the distant mesas surrounding Purple Hills. Sarah's mom or older brother would start a fire in the hooghan to offer warmth in the home and also provide some light. Growing up without electricity meant that Sarah learned not to waste the daylight and to find ways to see in the darkness. For many of us, it's hard to comprehend what life would be like without electricity. How would we charge our cell phones or laptops? Kerosene lamps, fire from stoves, generators, and natural light from the sun provide some relief to families who are unable to simply watch the evening news, indulge in Netflix and YouTube shows, or complete schoolwork in the evenings. Sarah and her family are not alone in figuring out ways to adapt to basic needs that many of us take for granted and often use in excess. There are 16,000 Navajo households that do not have electricity (Shone, 2010). The Navajo Tribal Utility Authority (NTUA) strives to connect 400 to 450 homes a year. At that rate, it is estimated that it would take 35 years to get electricity to the homes that currently do not have access (Fonseca, 2019). Walter Haase, general manager of NTUA, indicated that it could cost up to $40,000 to hook up electricity for a single home. With an estimated 16,000 households without electricity, the cost could reach as high as $640 million. That estimation is based on the assumption that the population and needs will not grow—but they will.

What is now called the United States is one of the wealthiest countries in the world, and 16,000 Navajo people have homes with no electricity and 40% of homes in the Navajo Nation do not have running water. I emphasize "what is now called the United States" to remind you that before the United States was born, our ancestors lived and thrived here. We were here before the United States came to be, which I will explain further as you read on. These challenges of lack of water and electricity are not the fault of people like Sarah and her family, but an Americanized system that at its origin stole land and lives from the Diné people and then continuously make existing tough for them. No electricity typically means no running water, illuminating a lack of overall economic development and an impoverished infrastructure. They are the hauntings brought forth by systemic monsters. While the United States benefits from the taking of Indigenous land, we can see the first monster emerge, which I refer to as the *financial hardship monster,* which crept into the lives of the original peoples and caretakers of the land, our relatives.

Now, my children, bear with me. Throughout this book, I will tell you aspects of our history that may be difficult to hear. Yet, we cannot look at ourselves as the White settlers have, and sometimes how they still look at us today. We must resist the White settler gaze, the bilagáana (White person) gaze. Our history is a part of us, and we are a part of it. During the pandemic, I attended a writing symposium titled Saadtah (Among Words) that was hosted by the Diné poet Jake Skeets, who is also a professor at Diné College. In that webinar, the Diné writer and literary scholar Manny Leloy talked about sa'ah naagháí bik'eh hózhóón, a powerful teaching of life that has sustained the Navajo people since time immemorial. Leloy remarked that Diné thought is ongoing, goes beyond time, and engages in loops that thread history to the present and into the future. In this way, time is not linear but related, everlasting, and dynamic to something greater, and in omnipresent beauty.

The Navajo Nation is the second-largest tribal group in the United States, with a population count at 340,000 in 2015. A large portion (33%) of our Navajo members are under the age of 18: young people, teenagers, children, the future. College is one influential way that tribal leaders, family members, schoolteachers and basketball coaches, and many of the rest of our people have expressed the sustainability and growth of the Navajo Nation, our families; this is called "Native nation building" (Brayboy et al., 2012). Navajo people call this Sihasin (hope). Hope that has been passed down from generation to generation.

I heard and felt that message when I was a teenager. And I can hear myself restating that same message to you. I am sure that you will echo those words to your children. Much hope lies with our young people. Hope because the history of Native peoples in what is now the United States has been stained with distrust and devastation. Looking to the beauty of the next generation is centered on a Diné philosophy. It has helped many of our people to survive and is what still today gets many of us up each morning.

Many people forget that our ancestors came into being on this land, long before settlers came and started calling it "America." We do not own the land, but we do come from the land. The Navajo Hataałii (singer/medicine man) Avery Denny explained that "the land wasn't drawn to be somebody's property . . . the land itself was sacred that we belong to the land" (p. 8). The sacredness and belonging to the land are based on knowledge systems passed through oral stories that tell us that we are in the fifth world, the glittering world. It is said that our ancestors emerged from worlds to the present land that we now call Diné Bikéyah. The Diné scholar Farina King (2018) explains that Diné have a knowing that she calls an "earth memory compass," which is "embedded in the lands and waters—the earth memories—to guide them [Diné] home toward one another as a people" (p. 1). The earth memory compass represents reciprocity between Navajos and our home(land). She explains that there are engrained memories passed down through generations in the land, and the land leads us home.

As I write this, tears are welling in my eyes as I think about the sweet beauty and protection that I felt (and still feel) about our home(lands). When I was a teenager, I used to go on long runs on winding dirt paths along the edge of hills near shimá sání (my maternal grandmother) house. My feet felt strong and supported with each step on rich shades of mauve, maroon, cinnamon, and blue-gray soil. And in some tougher terrain, my legs and the wind guided me through coarse clay in stains of crimson and bronze. Often, I lost track of time while on runs. It's easy to do when you are in complete presence with the land, connecting to her knowledge and wisdom. There were many runs where I cried and prayed, asking the Creator for strength and love. Those runs are an example of what helped me to know the divine relationship that we have to our home(lands) because I felt the connection. There are many more experiences and treasured stories of our connection to the sacred mountains, the sun, the wind, the horned toad, the coyote, and more that are shared in songs, prayers, meetings, stories, and sacredness. We have a belonging to the land, a respectful divine connection, and a responsibility to care for her. In the stories that I share, historical and present-day, the relationship between our people and the land is woven throughout. The story rug reminds us that stories are intertwined tightly together from the past and the present, and into the future.

Learning the relationship between Navajo people and the land helps us to understand why our people's hearts were then crushed and in deep sorrow when settlers arrived, especially when their intent on coming was shown.

Countless of our Native relatives were brutalized and dehumanized on contact with European settlers, largely due to the settlers' overpowering desires to acquire and have power over your ancestors and our Indigenous relatives' land. Those destructive and coercive yearnings—the violent killing of bodies and stealing of land—have not ended. Many call this "settler colonialism," which means the *ongoing* structure (like a relentless machine) to occupy and maintain control of Indigenous land (Wolfe, 1999). Much gratitude to Patrick Wolfe (1999) and Kānaka Maoli scholar Huanani-Kay Trask (1993) for providing a name to something that we experience and feel (and felt) through the generations. Settler colonialism is the root of the first monster identified, the financial hardship monster. It is also what keeps the financial hardship monster alive. I define the financial hardship monster as having its roots in settler colonialism, which functions to maintain and reinforce impoverished conditions among Native peoples, which in turn threatened the dreams of attaining a college degree for them.

Much of the early European contact with Native peoples occurred on the eastern shores. On the western end, our Navajo people were on guard against Spanish and Mexican attack beginning around 1540, and subsequently endured continuous raiding for another 200 years (Roessel, 1979; Iverson, 2002). Spanish and Mexican settlers intended to develop and pursue the land, fueled by tales that our ancestors owned gold. Warfare erupted. Many of our Navajo people died, and the Spanish stole women and children to use as slaves. The Spanish and Mexican governments viewed Navajos as an enemy. Our people were known for reprisals as they fought for the return and well-being of the young girls, women, our people (Kluckhohn & Leighton, 1962; Locke, 1992). We still need to fight for the well-being of our women, girls, and I would add our lesbian, gay, bisexual, trans, and queer relatives. This is survivance.

As this was occurring, White settlers were establishing the U.S. government. Systemic monsters were also being formulated that would work to diminish sovereignty, presence, and belonging for the first peoples of the land. Fundamental changes followed in the government's relationship with Natives. The United States seized ownership of southwestern territories from Mexico in 1848 with the signing of the Treaty of Guadalupe Hidalgo, which ended the Mexican and American war. After this transfer of ownership, the Navajo and other tribal groups were perceived as threats to the United States. General Stephen W. Kearny commented in 1846 that the United States would "protect the persons and property of all quiet and peaceable inhabitants with its boundaries against their enemies: The Eutaws, the Navajoes, and others" (Iverson, 2002, p. 34). We were considered enemies of the United States. Warfare continued as the federal government's plans to expand westward intensified, with rumors of gold and riches to be had along the ocean shores of the West. Greed and capitalism from settlers birthed hardships for our Navajo people.

In 1864, led by Colonel Kit Carson, 11,000 Navajo people were forced to walk 300+ miles from their homes among the four sacred mountains to an area called Hwéeldih, also recognized as Bosque Redondo, a trek known as the Long Walk. Thereafter, Navajo people were held captive in prison camps for 4 years. As the Diné historian Jennifer Denetdale stated in her book *Reclaiming Diné History: The Legacies of Chief Manuelito and Juanita,* "The people still remember those dark years with pain and bitterness, and many refused to speak of the nightmare for decades afterward" (2007, p. 77). Oral accounts from Navajo people call Carson's plan "t'áá altso anaá siljj" (when everything—humans, plants, and animals— turned enemy) (Austin, 2009. p. 2). An estimated 2,500 lives were taken during this time due to malnutrition, starvation, disease, sexual violence, forced labor, homesickness, and broken hearts (Denetdale, 2007; Iverson, 2002; Roessel, 1979). These are only estimates because many more deaths have been unaccounted for. Counting those who journeyed on due to inhumane violence is in and of itself traumatic and horrific for the Navajo people. And I doubt that most federal agents cared much about counting those whom they killed. These stories give us time to pause, to remember the lives lived and taken. I must remember that our existence of today is connected to their strength and love for us. We must remember the strength of our Navajo people.

While our Navajo people were dealing with an onslaught of war and then captivity, the federal government initiated treaties and policies that placed a binding contractual agreement between the federal government and Native tribes (Canby, 1998). From 1787 to 1871, hundreds of treaties were signed between the federal government and various tribes (Deloria, 1988). The treaties differed widely, but common points written into most treaties included a cession of lands (settler colonialism) to the federal government in exchange for the guarantee of peace and protection governed by the United States (Canby, 1998). By negotiating contractual agreements with tribes, the federal government implied that tribal nations were sovereign, with the rights to make decisions and govern. Tribal rights were further affirmed by the U.S. Constitution, which stated that Congress had the power "to regulate commerce with foreign nations, and among the several states, and with the Indian tribes" (U.S. Const., art. I, § 8). Although fundamental federal cases and laws recognized Tribes as having sovereign rights, Tribal nations already believed that sovereignty was inherently derived from within the people (Kickingbird, 1977). The Diné scholar Lloyd Lee (2017) refers to sovereignty as follows:

> To have the absolute freedom to think freely, to believe and practice the ways we choose, to fend for our family and people on our own terms. Sovereignty is a matter of life and soul. It is a matter of attitude; it is what we make it. Defined by the here and will of the people. (p. 163)

For the Navajo people, we knew that before White settlers arrived and the United States was established, the Creator gave sovereignty to us. We were born with sovereignty. It is "a matter of life and soul," which signifies the expansiveness and depth of sovereignty that is within us. We are sovereign, but it is not a normative construction of sovereignty that is premised on control, domination, rule, imperialism, and capital. That type of sovereignty is how the bilagáanaa (White people) think and act.

Navajo leaders including Chief Manuelito and Barboncito signed the Navajo Treaty of 1868. The provisions of the treaty stated that Navajo captives would be freed from Bosque Redondo, land would be held in trust by the United States and allocated to the Navajos, education would be provided for Navajo children, annuities would be paid for 10 years, and sovereign status would be assured (Austin, 2009; Denetdale, 2007; United States–Navajo Tribe, 1868). The Navajo people, similar to those of many other tribal nations, "linked arms" (Williams, 1999, p. i) with the federal government, as they viewed treaties as "a binding sacred agreement" (Austin, 2009, p. 6) that was to be respected and honored for the future of their people. Those linked arms have been broken and reunited time and time again, resulting in a deep sense of distrust toward the federal government and settlers. These treaties have formed the foundation of policies that on one hand provide for the protection of Navajo people, but on the other hand restrict and oppress the daily life of Navajo people.

The financial hardship monster, rooted in settler colonialism, maintained and reinforced impoverished conditions, which in turn threatened the dreams of attaining a college degree for Navajo teenagers. Sarah, Joy, Jessie, Lauryn, Wesley, Amber, Mike, and Chris (8 of the 10 students looked at in this book) grew up and lived a majority of their lives on the rez. All knew too well what life was like living paycheck to paycheck. Despite the financial hardship monster lurking in their lives, they each held tightly onto a sense of optimism, a deep respect and unyielding love for their family and the land from which they came.

Hauntings

Joy was strong in body, mind, and spirit. She lived about 80 miles from Purple Hills. At first glance, she seemed timid and quiet. She was petite and slender, often dressed in stonewashed jeans, a fitted top, and black sneakers. Her jet-black hair was midlength and often pulled to one side and draped over her shoulder. She had a poised, elegant stature as she sat comfortably in a proper, upright position: back straight, one leg crossed over the other, and hands folded softly on her lap. When I sat with her, I found myself adjusting my position to sit a little more upright. Although she appeared to be shy, that was far from the truth. Joy was a self-assured, natural leader. When I asked her to describe herself, she immediately stated that she was strong and smart. She explained strong as, "It's not just the physical part, but being able to be strong mentally, emotionally, and just to be able to hold myself together." She felt like her life experiences and Navajo teachings shaped her to become a stronger person, a Diné asdzą́ą́n (Navajo woman).

Her mom was a teenager when she gave birth to Joy. Because her mother couldn't financially support Joy, her másáni (maternal grandmother) and cheii (maternal grandfather) raised her until she was 10 years old. They lived far from the reservation, away from the four sacred mountains, and yet her grandparents taught her to speak fluent Navajo, and she learned from them about Navajo teachings and to respect the simplicities in life. These teachings demonstrated that much of our ways of life can be learned anywhere, even outside the sacred mountains. Her grandparents moved away from Diné Bikéyah (Navajo land) for employment and to support their new granddaughter. Joy shared affectionate memories of holding her grandfather's hand as they took regular walks together to nearby shopping centers and neighborhood craft fairs. Then, when Joy turned 10, she returned to Diné Bikéyah (Navajo land) and moved in with her mom and younger siblings (one brother and one sister). Surrounded by rolling hills and fragrant juniper trees, Joy's new home was located in the town of Juniper Mountain, with a population of roughly 1,700 people.

While living with her mom and younger siblings, Joy resided in a modest home that did not have electricity or running water. Her mother did not complete high school and was often unemployed. Joy could tell that her mother desperately wanted to provide for them, but gainful employment on the Navajo reservation was hard to come by. Life was hard, as her mother battled depression and a deep sense of inadequacy over being a financially unreliable mother to her three growing children.

The Navajo Nation covers 27,413 square miles, including roughly 17,544,500 acres of land in Arizona, Utah, and New Mexico. Diné Bikéyah is the largest reservation in the United States, with an array of geological beauty that encompasses majestic mountains, deep canyons, breathtaking mesas, and colors of every palette imaginable, from the earth to the skies. Yet, juxtaposed against the splendor are systemic injustices rooted in settler colonialism that include a 56% poverty rate and 44% unemployment rate: hauntings of the *financial hardship monster*.

At a national level, the median household income for Native populations was $39,719, compared to $50,448 for Arizona and $57,617 for the United States in general in 2016 (U.S. Census Bureau, 2017). For the Navajo Nation, the median family income is $11,885, and the per capita income is $6,217, which situates the Navajo Nation as having one of the highest poverty rates in the United States (U.S. Census Bureau, 2011). When I present these facts to non-Natives, I often hear comments from people such as: Why can't you all just find a job? Or why can't you all just start businesses? At first, I did not fully recognize the blame connotations (why can't *you?*) that people were imposing on us/me. I started asking myself those same questions and remember questioning myself: Why can't we just get jobs? But before I got sucked into normative constructions of the "American dream" that often tell us that hard work and determination enable you to "pull yourself up by your bootstraps," I learned that people were wrong to solely place the blame on us. There are deep-rooted reasons why unemployment and poverty rates are high among our relatives in the Navajo Nation. And those reasons are entrenched in settler colonialism, linked to the possession of Navajo land, and tethered to normative constructions of who belongs and who does not belong to the lands that our ancestors came from. That is why in this book, a story rug weaves historical context and present-day conditions back and forth so we understand that much of the hauntings of today are because of systemic monsters that are centuries old.

Let me explain further the hauntings of the financial hardship monster, which are rooted in settler colonialism and help to illustrate the impoverished conditions that many of our people are trapped in. Land impacts much of the life and economic growth for a society. Take a moment and think about where you go shopping, the place you live, the locations where you get gas for your chidí (vehicle). They all are established on land. We cannot deny that the land across what is now the United States was once freely occupied and utilized by Indigenous peoples. A policy report conducted by the Diné Policy Institute (2018) states, "Over the last century and a half of Anglo-colonialism, the U.S. has reduced our land size, settled it, privatized it, polluted it, and placed difficult restrictions around it" (p. 5). Most people in the United States do not realize that today, they benefit from the land, they benefit from Indigenous land.

In 2018, I attended a forum in Phoenix, Arizona, where several potential candidates spoke to a crowd in hopes of garnering the votes for the Navajo Nation presidential seat. Tom Chee, a candidate from Shiprock, New Mexico, discussed how land was a huge concern for the present and future of the Navajo people. He emphasized that "Navajo land is rented land," and that as a people, we must fight for our sovereign rights for the sake of our future lives and Nihima Nahasdzą́ą́n (Mother Earth) (T. Chee, personal communication, July 17, 2018). I agreed with him and noted that that was the first time I heard the idea of Navajo land as rented land. There is a piercing irony in renting land that you belong to.

More than 90% of the Navajo reservation is overseen by the U.S. Bureau of Indian Affairs, creating a "perpetual colonial status of our land" (Diné Policy Institute, 2018, p. 6). Because reservation land is held in trust by the U.S. government, individuals and companies are not allowed to purchase land on the reservation, making it nearly impossible to not only mortgage a home or secure a loan to start a business, but also to develop and expand strong and sustaining economies. This reality connects with Tom Chee's statement that Navajo land is rented land. With that understanding, we can understand why reservation rural towns have fewer businesses compared to states in the United States. For example, the Navajo Nation is comparable in size to the state of West Virginia. In 2014, the state of West Virginia had 90,403 businesses within its boundaries (West Virginia Secretary of State's office, personal communication, 2014). As of 2010, there were only about 636 businesses in the entire Navajo Nation, of which only 13 are grocery stores (Division of Economic Development, 2010). The U.S. Department of Agriculture labeled the Navajo Nation a "food desert" due to the lack of availability of healthy foods (Morales, 2015). The Navajo students contextualized these challenges, which helped me to make connections between how context matters in shaping the financial hardship monster. For example, Amber[1] from Red Sands expressed her frustrations to me about not having fresh produce: "There is only one grocery store, which is not the best grocery store. I love fruits, and they are like six bucks for strawberries, which they look disgusting. And the meat is not the best meat. So we had to travel to Flagstaff, which is two hours away, just for like good foods like fresh fruit." Reservation grocery stores are closer to home, offering some travel relief to families. However, as Amber described, those stores often provide low-quality food items and come at a hefty price. For families who do not have their own gardens or vegetable fields, they are left with the options of purchasing items at local grocery stores or driving long distances.

Wesley[2] and his family shopped at Gallup, New Mexico, which is located off the border of the Navajo Nation and is a highly populated hub for Navajo people. Although Gallup is generally viewed as off the Navajo reservation, it is on Diné land situated within the four sacred mountains. Referred to as a "bordertown,"[3] Gallup often doubles or even triples in population size on weekends due to the influx of Navajo shoppers. Westley traveled to Gallup and described the distance and the ongoing cost that it takes to travel to and from Gallup: "Purple Hills is isolated. Gallup is about 50 miles away, and Flagstaff is like 130 miles or so. You need money to get from one place to another. You need a vehicle, which costs money. You need gas, which costs money. You need food, which you get from Gallup, and it costs money to go to Gallup." The Diné Policy Institute (2018) conducted a thorough analysis of several communities on the Navajo Nation and found that 81% of their respondents spent between $0 and $150 on gas in a week, and 19% spent between $150 and $450. Many of us can relate to the cost of traveling just to purchase necessities, especially for those who live in rural settings. Yet, what makes these students' experiences unique is that there are systemic monsters—the financial hardship—that maintain the lack of businesses on the Navajo Nation, which forces Navajo people to spend more money just to travel the long distances.

The process to receive a business site lease in the Navajo Nation can take years, which is far longer in time when compared to receiving approval at Flagstaff, Arizona (a nearby city off the reservation), for example, which can take about three days (Navajo Nation Division of Economic Development, 2010). There are at least 13 different procedures needed to acquire approval, and one important detail is securing a lease to the land.

Contrary to common belief, obtaining permission to lease the land is a bureaucratic and lengthy process, with mandatory requirements from multiple federal and tribal departments including but not limited to the Historical Preservation Department, U.S. Environmental Protection Agency,

U.S. National Environmental Policy Act, and the local Navajo government. Also, only 10% of Navajo land is available to lease, with 90% of land tied to individual and family grazing permits, meaning that they are utilized by a family's livestock. To utilize grazing-permitted areas, you must seek approval from families that hold the permit, and most families are unwilling to approve. The regulation of grazing permits was imposed on the Navajo people by federal law and policies in the 1930s in an attempt to forcibly reduce livestock, break up communal land tenure, accommodate nearby non-Navajo ranchers, and usher in the advancement of railways and large-scale development projects. Grazing permits do not provide "ownership" of the land, but rather the ability to graze in a certain area. In other words, grazing permits were the hauntings of the federal hardship monster, rooted in settler colonialism, that restricts the ancestral ways of Navajo matrilineal land practices and subsistence.

There are many other obstacles that hinder economic vitality on the Navajo reservation. Lack of infrastructure and resources such as water, phone, electrical power, roads, and sewer systems have high costs and exacerbate the challenges of starting a business. Not surprisingly, as Amber mentioned earlier, 64% of money is spent at off-reservation communities (Navajo Nation Division of Economic Development, 2010). Amber and her family shopped in Flagstaff, Arizona; Wesley and his family shopped in Gallup, New Mexico. My family and I also shop in Gallup, a place where we stock up on items to last the week (or more), thereby releasing money to flow off the Navajo reservation, a place where the city thrives and relies on the bleeding wallets and hearts of Navajo people.

Gallup has been referred to as "drunk city" (Haederle, 1990) and "drunk town, USA" (Estes, 2014). Gallup's liquor industry is notorious for distributing alcohol with 39 liquor licenses and 19 alcohol-selling establishments within its vicinity—higher than most major cities (Estes, 2015). These liquor establishments profit from Navajo people while intensifying destructive addictions. Bordertowns also have high-interest, predatory payday loan sources (Wessler, 2014). Gallup has at least 45 such loan establishments, such as Cash Man, Sun Loans, and New Mexico Title Loans. Take a drive south on Highway 491 from Gamerco entering Gallup, and count how many loan places are eagerly waiting for you to stop by. Last time I counted, there were 9 loan establishments in a 1.5-mile stretch, and that is just on one side of the road. I could find a loan faster than finding a place to get a cold soda.

According to NBC's analysis of public data on state-licensed lenders, those lenders issued more than 52,000 loans worth 27.5 million, with interest rates of at least 175%, in 2012 (Wessler, 2014). Charges were filed by the U.S. Consumer Bureau and the Navajo Nation against companies and executives who used H&R Block franchises to operate an illegal tax-refund scheme (Lynch, 2015). The Consumer Financial Protection Bureau sought $438,000 in civil penalties and additional compensation for victims, many of whom were Navajo people. The complaint alleged that short-term, high-interest loans were allocated using individuals' anticipated tax refunds. Tax preparers received bonuses based on the number of clients who took advantage of those loans. On top of the onslaught of liquor establishments and predatory high-interest loan establishments that initiate illegal tax-refund schemes, bordertowns have high rates of Native arrests (Estes, 2015) and high incidences of racist attacks (Donovan, 2015). Denetdale (2016) stated, "For the most part, settlers remain innocent in the narratives that are created about their relationships with Navajos in border towns" (p. 112). There is a paradox at play: bordertowns provide essential items for living, but at the same time, they are stealing money and lives. The financial hardship monster thrives when bordertowns continue to operate in ways that maintain the financial status quo of Navajo people.

Do not get me wrong—there are some businesses on Navajo land. But for many of those businesses, dual taxation takes effect, squeezing out more money from the people living on Navajo land to help support people living off of Navajo land. Dual taxation is when two different taxing jurisdictions tax the same transaction. Tribal nations have the right to impose various taxes, but what gets complicated and costly is when states also impose taxes on top of the tribal taxes. Because of dual taxation, many businesses do not want to start enterprises on Native land. If a business is underway, it has to pay both taxes, which in turn often increases the cost of its products. Although tribal tax dollars support state revenue, states rarely allocate their tax monies to support and sustain tribes. This is in addition to the land that states benefit from, and Native business owners have to pay to lease the land—land that was stolen from Native peoples, the ongoing irony.

For Joy's mother, the toll of having unreliable income to support her family weighed heavily on her mind. Joy had a deep respect for her mother. She told me how much her mom had been there for her and how much her mother pushed her to do well in school and in life. Her mother listened to Joy when she needed someone to talk to. Joy also listened to her mother and knew that when wintertime came around, depression increased for her mother. The winter season was often the hardest because stress intensified due to the pressure to figure out how to get wood to keep the home warm, as well as to haul water on the treacherous, muddy roads.

Having to rely on others to help support their basic living needs was difficult for her mother. Joy and her siblings wished that their mother would start seeing a counselor to help with her depression. Yet, counselors on Navajo land are scarce, and people can't always be forced to do something that they are not ready to do. The struggle is real when you are broke and living in a home with no water or electricity. Struggle generated by the financial hardship monster was a result of settler colonialism that was formed long before Joy and her family's lifetime. And it is a struggle that still exists today and is intensified by settler colonialism's mission to take land and livelihood away from Indigenous peoples.

Joy told me that sometimes she tells her mom, "I'm trying to help you and I'm trying to do the best I can, but all I can really do right now is wait until I actually get my education. And then I can start helping you more." A college education for Joy represented a ticket out of the struggle, as it was for the rest of the 10 teenagers discussed in this book. I agreed with Joy and all these students in their determination to seek a college degree, but I could not deny that I also worried about how she (and others) would afford the cost of going to college.

Monstrous Internalization

College is not free for Native students, yet many folks like to think and believe that we do not pay for college. Ironically, there is an assumption, a stereotype, a "sincere fiction" that Native students go to college for free (Nelson & Tachine, 2018). Sincere in that the general public believes these myths and fiction because they are empirically false (Feagin & O'Brien, 2003). A report released in 2018 investigated the opinions of Americans in general and found that the most persistent and toxic narrative among the general public held that Native peoples received government benefits and are "getting rich off of casinos" (First Nations Development Institute & Echo Hawk Consulting, 2018). Those findings were reminiscent of documents and discussions during the 1930s that addressed "the Navajo Problem," which included that Navajos were problematic because of their dependency on government welfare and entrenched poverty (King, 2018, p. 81). Nearly a century has passed, and these persistent damaging narratives have not changed. The general public view of Native peoples as living off the government while simultaneously rolling in wealth from casinos is violent and harmful. They erase the ongoing presence of Native peoples and the systemic monsters generating the conditions of financial hardship. Brayboy and Chin (2020) refer to this as "terrortory," defined as "the simultaneous presence of the imaginary Indian and the absence of an actual Indigenous person" (p. 24).

The financial constraints that each student and their families experienced in their daily lives evoked inescapable concerns and fears over not having enough money to pay for college. And when students thought about paying for college, it was not just about finding resources for tuition; it was about finding resources to survive. The *financial hardship monster*, rooted in settler colonialism, maintained economic conditions that in turn made it difficult for Navajo students' to afford attending college. "In turn" is important because the financial hardship monster constructed the conditions and internalizations of exclusion. And these internalization mechanisms were not simply in the minds of these students, but also based on oppressive lived realities that have been woven into today's experience since settlers arrived and are "breathed in like air" as everyday ways that the financial hardship monster, rooted in settler colonialism, continues to function.

Sarah applied to many scholarships. She knew that her family could not afford the cost of attending an in-state public university. She told me that she was not just searching for funds to pay for tuition. She was finding funds to pay for living. She unpacked the total calculations that she was planning for: "You know, finding the funding also is a huge obstacle to overcome because books are not cheap, the dorm isn't cheap, how are you going to eat? Where are you going to sleep? Just little things if you need toiletry, how are you going to get that? . . . That was the major things you know, doing scholarships, left and right . . . it's a lot of work." Sarah was not alone in worrying about funding. All the students worked diligently on scholarship applications, hoping and praying that they would be able to receive funding to attend college, to survive while in college. They researched, applied, and did everything they thought was needed to secure financial support.

Then, one by one, they were denied scholarships. The grip on attending college began to slip away, especially for Mike, as he felt that maybe college was not in his foreseeable future. He told me, "Just like financially, I think that's the one thing that I really was scared of because especially getting out of high school, during the mid-second semester of my senior year, filling out so many scholarship applications and getting rejected by so many of them was really, it was maybe [state's university] is not something I can do right now." As we learned, the financial hardship monster created the conditions to maintain impoverished situations for many of these students and their families. *Hauntings.* Therefore, it is not surprising that scholarships are instrumental to their access into college. Financial support not only eased their minds but lifted the burden off of them and their families. Then when denial notifications from scholarships were received, some students, like Mike, began to doubt whether college was even possible.

Sarah, Jessie, Lauryn, Chris, Amber, and Joy applied to the Gates Millennium Scholarship. The Gates Millennium Scholarship was founded in 1999 with a large investment of $1.6 billion from the Bill and Melinda Gates Foundation. One of the few national scholarships awarded to students from racially marginalized backgrounds, Gates is awarded to high-achieving, low-income students. Students awarded receive funding throughout their schooling, from their bachelor's to the doctorate, which makes this scholarship a highly sought after source. Annually, 1,000 students are awarded the scholarship with 150 allocated to Native students (Youngbull, 2017). I was sad to hear that five out of the six Navajo teenagers who applied were denied funding from Gates. Each of their stories on receiving the denial letter brought forth mixed emotions of sadness, confusion, fear, and frustrations. Chris told me what he thought after receiving a denial notification from Gates. "The day I found out that I didn't make it to the recipient round was a huge blow to my educational confidence." In fact, Chris almost quit pursuing plans to go to college. And he was not alone in those thoughts, as Sarah, Jessie, Lauryn, and Joy were also concerned whether college was a possibility.

Amber was the only one of the six who applied that received the Gates Millennium Scholarship. She and several of her classmates applied and waited daily for the news on whether or not they received the scholarship. On the day that they learned about the decision, she shared with me what she felt and experienced:

> The final round came, that's when a lot of my friends packed in a small car. We went to the post office. We sat in there. We prayed. We were like, "Okay it's real life. Guys, this is real life. This is no joke." We walked inside. I saw the big packet. I couldn't believe myself. I just ripped it out, ripping it up. I really ripped it apart. I opened it. It said congratulations and I just screamed. I was holding it out, just so happy. I was crying. In my mind, my family doesn't have to really worry about me.

Amber was an exception in securing enough money to cover most of her college expenses. Although she was excited, a big part of her also felt for her friends who did not get the scholarship. She elaborated:

> We're happy, but at the same time, we knew in the back of our heads that our other friends didn't get it. My friend, she said she doesn't know what she's going to do. It was really bittersweet. I was just holding her. I was crying, but I was crying for them.

For Amber, she was grateful and relieved that she received the scholarship, but she also felt for her friends who did not receive it. Her heart ached for them because she knew how hard they worked and understood the burden that the cost of college would have on them and their families. Why couldn't they all receive funding? Why can't these students actually go to college for free, especially given the dark history of this country toward our relatives?

Sarah worked carefully and spent many hours on her Gates Millennium application. Yet, she did not make it through the competitive rounds. When she found out that she did not receive Gates, a sense of worthlessness came over her. She sat with that feeling, but she remembered why she needed to go to college—for her grandparents. So she became extra motivated and "applied to scholarships like crazy," submitting "10 times more" applications to various financial sources. Her persistence paid off, as she shared with me her story of earning scholarships:

> I slept in the living room and I was so tired. I woke up and my mom was cooking. She was like, "Sarah, you got a letter from [state's college]" I was like, "What?" Then I got up. I looked at it. I was like "Oh my gosh." I went to my room and I was like, I won't get denied. This can't happen, and I was scared, I was so scared. My heart was beating. I felt like throwing up. I was like, "No." I opened it and they leave, when they fold it, they leave a little part and I saw a congratulations and I was like, "Oh my God." I was jumping around. I ran down the hallway and I jumped on my brother's bed. He was sleeping. I was like, "I got the scholarship!" And then I told my mom and it was the best thing ever. Oh my gosh, it was totally awesome. My first scholarship. It felt really good. After that point, I just felt like I was invincible, even though it was just one scholarship, it was awesome.

Sarah continued to accumulate award letters, and with each financial award, her confidence grew. She acquired $21,000 in scholarships from multiple sources. Her goal of attaining $25,000 (the cost of attending an in-state university for one year) was nearly reached. She was relieved from placing an added encumbrance on her mom's limited income, and she was on her way to entering college. I point out Sarah's story because she (like the other students) first conveyed a sense of worthlessness after receiving the news of rejection from Gates. Yet, she thought about her grandparents and remembered that her desire for a college degree was to help and support her elderly grandparents. Sha áłchíní (my children), these lessons teach us that Sarah and the other students were feeling the wrath of the financial hardship monster, but they remembered why they were pursuing a college education, and that remembrance was rooted in Diné philosophy and values. This act of remembering your purpose is critical. When you are questioning self or feeling defeated, remember your purpose. And then activate the Indigenous weapon of resurgence, which I explain next.

Resurgence as Love-Centered

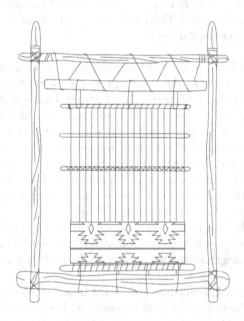

Sarah lived and sustained in ways of Navajo beauty. Since Sarah was a young girl, her four older siblings jokingly teased her by calling her "the baby" because she was always with their mother and grandmother. The youngest grandchild in a large family, she confessed that if she did not devote time with grandmother and mother, she could potentially miss a learning opportunity. This sensibility is what made Sarah special—a deep understanding and respect in Diné teachings shared by matriarchs: connection, love. Her siblings teased her, but if Sarah needed them for any reason, she knew that they would be there for her. They protected and supported her. That was the Navajo way, and Sarah knew and treasured that.

When Sarah turned 10 years old, her family moved to a home with running water and electricity. The move not only relieved them from constantly having to haul water and run the generator; the move also brought them closer to family. Just a few steps from their new home, their grandparents smiled with excitement because their children would be living closer to them, and that closeness was priceless. Every evening, Sarah walked to her grandparents' home to make sure that they had eaten and to check whether or not her másání (maternal grandmother) took her insulin. Her grandma was diabetic, and at an early age, Sarah already knew how to inject insulin shots, knew every single pill her grandma took, and traveled with her grandma to her doctor's appointments. During the wintertime, Sarah would help her grandpa by chopping wood, building a fire, and doing whatever else was needed to care for her másání and cheii (paternal this should be maternal grandfather). She had a deep, heartfelt love for her grandparents. Deep in a sense that it was consciously embedded into all of her being.

Whenever she spoke of másání and cheii, tears welled in her eyes. Her face would soften. With a smile, she would take a deeper breath, wipe away her delicate tears, and then continue telling me stories about her and her elderly grandparents. In listening to her, I wiped my own tears away, which were quickly and gently falling from my eyes like female rain. I understood the love and devotion that she carried for her másání and cheii. Sha'álchíní (my children), I think you understand too. Affection and respect for our elders are part of our Diné teachings. We have been raised to appreciate our elders, to ensure that they eat first when food is served, to make sure that they have a seat to sit on, to take care of them. We do this because we recognize that our lives would not exist if it were not for them. We do this because we recognize that they continue to teach us, shape us, pray for us to develop into who we are. They deserve respect and care. Those values, or axiology, to love and tend to others (our elders) are embedded into our ways of knowing, ways of being. As Diné, we seek love above all things. That is what makes us Diné, a belief system in thinking of others more than ourselves. And this teaching of ayóo'ó'ní (love) has been passed down from our ancestors to share unto the next generation.

Sarah's grandma told her, "Nizhónígo [in a beautiful way], Nizhónígo, you're going to school, keep at it!" Sarah was determined to be the first in her family to go to a university. She knew that if grandma believed in her, she could do it, because grandmas seem to always know all things, even the things we do not want to listen to. Although the finances were going to be tough to come by, Sarah was armed with a purpose in going to college. Her purpose was to one day return to Purple Hills and take care of her grandparents and mom because they, as she said, were "everything to me." The weapon of *resurgence*, rising up to enact the Diné axiology of love for family, a love for others, was inside Sarah. Resurgence is love-centered that instills the action of getting up, or rising up in deep respect, to care for elders (family) and carry on their teachings.

Leanne Betasammosake Simpson, the Michi Saagiig Nishnaabeg storyteller, scholar, and activist, stated, "Indigenous resurgence in its most radical form is nation building, not nation-state building, but nation building" that is grounded in Indigenous thought and practices (2016, p. 22). Indigenous resurgence is a flight from the violence of the *financial hardship monster* that is rooted in settler colonialism. In this case, flight does not mean to leave or disregard the financial hardship monster, but to face the monster and not get diminished by it.

Students viewed college as a strategy to defeat the financial hardship monster, to acquire a degree and help support their families and build an Indigenous future for their people. These students showed me that the weapon of resurgence was deep-rooted in love for family and hope for the future. Resurgence was passed down to us from our ancestors when they faced captivity, kidnapping, abuse, and horrendous violence. Resurgence is a generative and multigenerational process. Our ancestors rose up each day for us. That is why we are here today. We must keep enacting resurgence for our future.

I was amazed at the power of resurgence that all the students exhibited. I could tell that they did not want to get trapped either constantly battling or being defeated by the financial hardship monster. They did not want their families to live in the struggle. A college education was a means to a communal good (not solely an individual good), emphasizing the value they placed on family and community: ayóo'ó'ní (love). They represented Pablo Freire's (1970) visionary words: "A deepened consciousness of their situation leads people to apprehend that situation as a historical reality susceptible of transformation" (p. 85). They had a deepened consciousness of experiencing the struggle. Embedded in their knowing was a sense of transformative resurgence rooted in the Diné axiology of love for family, love for the larger community, love for their home(lands), love for future possibilities. They inspired me. The Indigenous weapon of resurgence was also shown to us by the Twin Warriors.

Naayéé' Neizghání (Monster Slayer) and Tóbájíshchíní (Born for Water) embarked on a journey to defeat the monsters that were killing the Navajo people. In essence, a burning desire to save their people from being destroyed was instilled in the twins. That burning desire is resurgence. The 10 Navajo teenagers followed a similar yearning. Collectively, attending college was a practice of resurgence, an embedded benevolence and love for their peoples:

> "I just want to be able to help in some way to contribute to again, people like me, Native Americans," Jessie shared.

> "I want to go back to the Indian hospital on the reservation to help my people. . . . Yeah, I have to come back," Lauryn stated.

> "I decided to come here [college] to pursue an education to advance myself so I can help advance other Natives and really help our people," Sam conveyed.

> "My whole goal is to give back to my communities. . . . When I think about that, that's what really makes me happy is just helping other people," Amber said.

> "I want them to see that I'm always going to be that individual who will go back to the reservation and to push for understanding of our language, and our culture, and of our tradition," Joy stated.

"I want to go back to the reservation and make it a better place," Mike commented.

Cecilia said, "That really keeps me going because like someday, I want to work for the tribe, maybe even be the first female president. That's something like I really want to do."

"I wanted to go to college to help my community. I feel like every community has their own leader, and I feel like my community needs a leader," Chris conveyed.

"I want to get my degree, learn, get an education and go home and help my people, so that's why I want to come to college," Sarah offered.

Regardless of whether they were raised on or off the reservation, whether they had electricity in their homes or not, whether they were first in their family to go to college or not, these Navajo teenagers knew that they were meant to advance the well-being of the people and the land from which they came. They employed what the Diné scholar Tiffany Lee (2006) describes as "Indigenous consciousness," such that Native college students embrace the role of Indigenous leadership in providing service to their community and people (p. 1). The Quechan scholar Jameson Lopez (2021) has also found that giving back (in advancement of community well-being) should be considered as a measured outcome for persistence among Native students. That is love, decolonial love (Simpson, 2013). What I mean by "decolonial love" is love that is not emptied by a culture that commodifies, flattens, and privileges systems of capitalism and heteropatriarchy. Decolonial love is an intimate relationship with relatives (past, present, and future), home(lands), the divine, and a deepened consciousness of connection and futures. For Diné people, love is grounded in k'é. The Muscogee scholar Joy Harjo described this concept by stating, "I have a home in the world. I feel there is a root community that I have a responsibility to nurture and help move in a good direction. It's very, very precious. It is the central source of meaning, the root, the template" (Mankiller, 2004, p. 146). These deeply embedded axiological orientations, or roots as Harjo indicated, are the weapons to help us rise. Resurgence.

Cecilia, who was raised in Phoenix more than 200 miles from the Navajo reservation, expressed how Navajo ways of knowing and being connected to home(lands) contributed to a longing to return and protect "home." Even though Cecilia did not grow up on the reservation, she still considered the reservation her primary home. She said:

Well when I was little, like growing up, my mom always told me that when a baby is born, the umbilical cord is buried outside of your home. It's just to show you're home and that you will always go back to it. So growing up like that, I just believed that it was my home, because it is my home. . . . That is where the life is. You have to always go back to where the starting point is, where life is.

There is a Navajo teaching that where an umbilical cord is buried signifies a place of importance, a place in which the family sets in motion the future of the child, and an example of an earth memory compass, as introduced by Farina King. When a baby's umbilical cord leaves the baby, many Navajos will bury the dried umbilical cord within the ancestral Navajo lands encompassing the borders of the four sacred mountains. Some bury the umbilical cord near the fields or corrals to instill in the little ones that they have a connection to cultivate the land and care for the livestock. Some bury the umbilical cord under a weaving loom to establish a lifelong appreciation for creating beautiful and intricate textiles. Some bury the umbilical cord near a school to ensure that the little one grows up to be educated. That sacred process is a way, as Cecilia discussed, to secure Navajo people to their home(lands), and also toward the future. College aspirations for many Navajos have been planted into the land, making a divine connection between place, person, and future. This sacred relationship occurs before a baby begins to walk. Cecilia acknowledged that she would return to Navajo land and assist in what was already planted for her, to protect her home(lands).

In our Navajo value systems, as the baby grows and develops, girls are often trained to keep up the home and care for younger siblings. Boys are taught to be attentive to the external aspects of the home by hauling wood and looking after the livestock (Yazzie & Speas, 2007). Girls may also help with outside chores such as tending livestock (not all families have livestock, but there are many other forms of outside chores, such as taking out the trash or cleaning the yard); and boys may also assist with chores within the home. It's critical to remember that gender roles are fluid, especially as the world changes around us (Lee, 2013). Tied into all these teachings is the essential teaching that we should not be lazy; instead, we should contribute to the family by working hard. These teachings nurture disciplining the mind and acknowledging that we are not in this world alone—we have a role in helping the world around us.

Jessie, Lauryn, Sam, Joy, and Amber were the eldest among their siblings and among their cousins. As the eldest, they each felt a heightened responsibility to model possibilities for their siblings and their younger cousins. Lauryn explained to me how she saw her role as the older sister: "I know they [siblings] are looking up to me, every day. I just try to watch what I do and stay good, show them how to do it, be a good mentor, be a good sister, someone they can look up to and footsteps they can follow. I just try to be the best that I can be, to show them that they can do it." Lauryn had a sister who was 14 years old and a brother who was 7 years old. They looked up to Lauryn, as she was not just a star athlete and a young leader in their small community, she was a loving sister. She took time to teach her younger sister how to spike the volleyball, carefully rotating her arm in a powerful position and encouraging her little sister to jump toward the sky as she hit the ball over the net. Lauryn loved her younger siblings and wanted them to make positive choices in life and "not go through the ups and downs . . .

because I love them that much." Therefore, Lauryn worked hard to excel in sports and academics, not just for herself, but for her brother and sister. She wanted to pursue college in order to create a possibility map for them.

Joy believed that there were others not on earth who were also observing her. She stated, "I keep in mind that there are people that are watching me, and that there are people who are not on earth that are watching me, my uncles that have passed away and my great-grandma who passed away." Joy believed that her family members who journeyed on from this world were still watching over her. She wanted to show them that she was making wise choices. They were choosing college for family, past, present, and future. *Resurgence.*

Earlier, I mentioned Chris, one of the students who was denied the Gates scholarship. He questioned whether college was in his future. What helped him get through that time was the weapon of resurgence, the act of rising again when he learned that he was setting an example for others to follow. Chris attended a high school off the reservation. For most of the school year, he lived in a student dormitory with other Native students. His close friends became like family members to him, like his best friend, Morgan. They were similar in a lot of ways. Both excelled in the most challenging courses available at their high school. One day when Chris and Morgan were studying together in the dormitory, they overheard a staff member talk about them. This was a turning point for Chris, as he discovered the power of resurgence:

> I remember one time we [Chris and Morgan] were in study hall at the dorm. We were studying and everything. The RA, the residential assistant, they came in and they were preaching to the underclassmen on why they were having bad grades. But us seniors, we were graduating, so we had good grades. And then the RAs were talking and surprisingly they were like, "You need to look up to Morgan and Chris because they are like your role models." That was a huge turning point in my educational career. People look up to me.

Chris told me that later that evening, a sophomore student who also lived in the dormitory approached him in private. He was surprised with the encounter because he had not talked to her before. She was timid when she spoke to Chris. He was too. Then she told him that she hoped to be like him. Chris was shocked. Her words awakened something in him. He realized that the decisions he was making, the acts he was undertaking were inspiring others—like her. She proceeded to tell Chris that she was struggling in life. Recently, her grandfather left this world, and she was finding it difficult to focus on school because she missed him. Chris remembered the beautiful relationship that he had with his grandfather. His sweet grandfather had also crossed over. After his passing, Chris longed for their long walks, and he missed the stories that his grandfather told him about growing up and about loving relatives, more than human relatives, and the sustenance of the land. His grandfather was a great man.

As the sophomore girl confided in Chris, he could not help but think of his grandpa and relate to her feelings. He knew that he was meant to offer some advice to her on how he got through. That moment, that exchange, combined with the kind words that the RA spoke about him and his friend, awakened Chris to the realization that he was creating possibilities for others. Excelling in education was no longer just for the sake of getting a good grade; it was for the benefit of classmates who needed hope and encouragement. He no longer felt like a failure. He knew that college would be in his future. This was his resurgence. He had embodied an awareness to rise up, pursue college, and be a possibility for others.

The financial hardship monster was present and overwhelming. What strengthened these young students was to look beyond the monster, to set their sights on serving as a caretaker and a possibility to family present and past, friends, and the broader Native community. Resurgence instilled purpose. Rising again and again meant that the discipline that they were taught at such a young age was within them. The Diné axiology of love for family, community, and the land activated the weapon of resurgence, which underscores the compelling prominence that interconnectedness with community and family have on Native students' college attainment.

Ayóo'ó'ní (Love). Caring for others is the foundation for a collective sense of justice. Santa Clara Pueblo scholar Gregory Cajete (2000) stated, "Ultimately, Indigenous leadership was about commitment to nurturing a healthy community. . . . Leaders were predisposed to care deeply and imagine richly with regard to their people" (p. 90). These students were leaders. Rather than personalizing tough experiences and circumstances through a victim mentality that is too often portrayed in broader societal commentary about Native peoples, they looked beyond themselves and their current situation and thought of ways to resurge (rise up) because they centered love for others and self. They remind us that we are love. And they reminded me how powerful living in love is. It's a weapon passed down from generations back. We are love.

Looking beyond themselves is a Diné teaching centered on a decolonial love and the survival of peoples within a place. "Indigenous communities have long been aware of the ways that they know, come to know, and produce knowledges, because in many instances knowledge is essential for cultural survival and well-being" (Brayboy & Maughan, 2009, p. 3). Native peoples continue to encountered oppressive actions that they have endured from settler colonization. The act of survival is therefore not simply an individual choice but a collective one, predicated on the continuance of a people that has been passed down from generation to generation. It is freedom. A freedom that is wrapped in blankets of love and wisdom that cannot be taken away by settler colonialism. A freedom of love that cannot be taken away by the financial hardship monster. A freedom to love.

Resurgence.

Part II

CONTINUANCE: KEEP GOING

Deficit (Not Enough) Monster

What if schooling were not riddled with hardship and despair? What if schooling affirmed the way you see the world, the attention that you give to more than human relatives, and a desire to motivate future generations? For Lauryn, aspects of relationality would be a cornerstone for her schooling. Lauryn called herself a "cattle girl." She found solace when she cleaned, fed, groomed, and worked her horses. She took note when the corral needed fixing and later returned to make repairs to the place where the animals slept, gathered, and played. Waking up before the sun rose to tend to the livestock was at first just a routine. Later, as she approached womanhood, looking after the animals and corral became a sustaining practice for Lauryn. It became a place for her to seek refuge and think through situations when life was frustrating, when something was not feeling right in the world. She would walk around the corral and sometimes talk to herself about how best to handle circumstances. The horses listened to and caressed her when Lauryn needed it the most. She was grateful for the corral and her more than human relatives who heard and saw her for who she was: a cattle girl growing into a woman and trying her best to be a good person.

Lauryn was attentive to her appearance, as her natural shades of makeup were usually flawless. Most mornings, she took time to curl her thick, long, dark-auburn hair. Often wearing casual teenager attire, such as denim shorts, stylish sandals, and a fitted T-shirt, she accessorized her look with polished nails, a delicate gold cross necklace, and half-dollar-sized, gold hoop earrings. She described herself as shy, intelligent, and a teacher's pet in school. She was easy to talk to, and I quickly saw a lot of myself in her when I was her age. Lauryn spent the majority of her life at Folded Canyon (pseudonym), with a population of roughly 300 people. A small, rural reservation town, Folded Canyon was near a busy Indian Health Service clinic and a well-stocked trading post with an array of goodies and supplies.

Her immediate family (mom, dad, and younger siblings) moved from place to place on the reservation when she was young. They had to move to take care of family hardships and seek employment opportunities. Lauryn then attended four different reservation elementary schools and attributed the frequent moves as a reason for her shyness because with every move, she had to make new friends. Lauryn was the elder sister to her two younger siblings. She felt a responsibility to be a "good mentor" and a "good sister" to her siblings and younger cousins. She wanted to form "footsteps that they can follow." Her father instilled in Lauryn a solid work ethic focused on performing well in academics and sports. Lauryn told me with a smile that during high school, her dad punished her if she did not score more than 15 points in a basketball game. Punishment meant being restricted from using her cell phone—a big deal for a teenager. Her dad could have increased the point goal on Lauryn, but he knew that others on the team were just as important and talented as she was. Teachings that Lauryn learned from her father included teamwork, self-discipline, and thinking of others.

Lauryn's mom did not drill Lauryn on her schoolwork or sports, but what she did do was reinforce the importance of keeping up the homestead and the power of practicing prayer and attending ceremonies. Her mother reinforced that Lauryn get in the habit of caring for the home and the corral, teaching her discipline that reinforced a responsibility to others. Often Lauryn had to watch after and care for her younger siblings as her mother tended to work and family obligations. Responsibility was something that she learned at an early age. And when the stress load intensified, especially during state playoffs in sports and exam time, Lauryn's mom would gently remind her to pray for strength, clarity, and endurance. Lauryn credits many of her achievements to her parents. They both instilled teachings that carried her through the often difficult and frustrating times in school.

During her sophomore year, Lauryn's oldest cousin tragically died. He was a senior and highly regarded in the community and school for his athletic leadership. The sudden death devastated Lauryn and her extended family. Lauryn had looked up to him. They were in high school together, and she saw him in the halls, full of hope and determination. Colleges were already recruiting him to join their athletic team. He would have been the first in their extended family to go to college. So, with the passing of her beloved cousin, Lauryn quickly became the oldest grandchild in her extended family, and potentially the first to go to college. She was even more determined to be a role model, a possibility, for her younger siblings and cousins. She used the same energy on the basketball court in the classroom. Teachings from her family helped Lauryn to stay up late into the night, after returning home from a long day of school and basketball practice, to finish up her schoolwork. Her efforts paid off. Lauryn graduated as covaledictorian of her class.

With sorrowful tears, she told me about the day of her graduation. She explained that there were many emotions among her classmates and families. They had completed high school, a milestone for many. In the midst of the joy, fear, and wonder that thickened the atmosphere of the gymnasium, Lauryn also felt a deep sense of connection, of love and loss, to her cousin, who had gone too soon. She felt his presence: "I was in tears. He was just watching over me. I just wanted to show him I'm trying to make grandma and grandpa proud."

Lauryn and the other Navajo teenagers in this book graduated with honors. But what I learned, and what you will read later, is that she (and the other Navajo teenagers) also told me how they often felt that high school in many ways failed them, which later hindered them during their first year in college. The second monster, the *deficit (not enough) monster,* emerged. I define the deficit (not enough) monster as having its roots in assimilation to Whiteness, which functions to occupy and maintain control of Indigenous minds, behaviors, and ways of life, which in turn disrupts belonging to home(lands), college possibilities, and self-worth. Recall that Whiteness is the normalization of White supremacy and is embedded in everyday normative constructions, practices, and activities. Assimilation is the apparatus to wipe out distinctions and variance. Assimilation is to manifest homogeneity's destiny. We have been fighting the deficit (not enough) monster—rooted in assimilation and Whiteness—for centuries. And a battle that we must keep fighting.

I am a descendent of the fierce matriarch Asdzáá Tł'ógí (Weaver Woman), also known as Juanita, and Hastiin Ch'ilhaajinii (Man of the Blank Plants Place), also known as Chief Manuelito. Sha'áłchíní (my children), you are descendants of them too. We all come from a lineage of leaders who in some way have fought for us, the land, and the ability to live and learn in our own terms and ways. Juanita and Chief Manuelito are examples of fighting against the odds, especially when the odds were stacked against them. During the period of the Long Walk, when our relatives walked over 300+ miles to the prison camp at Hwéeldih, Hastiin Ch'ilhaajinii (Man of the Blank Plants Place) was one out of twenty-nine who signed the 1868 treaty that ended the period of imprisonment at Bosque Redondo and returned our people home to Diné Bikéyah (Navajo Land). And like many of our mothers, grandmothers, aunties, and sisters, I like to dream that Asdzą́ą́ Tl'ógí (Weaver Woman) was nearby, probably giving words of encouragement and thoughtful instructions to Hastiin Ch'ilhaajinii (Man of the Blank Plants Place) on how best to proceed. She was a weaver. I have heard that while at the prison camp, many weavers resisted the colonial forces by unraveling the Germantown blankets that were given to them. I imagine them gathering together, threading out each blanket, and then coiling the wool into balls of different shapes and colors. Then the weavers would take the wool and re-create their own textiles. With the wool in their fingers, they would pull renewed strands through the warp, embedding Diné philosophies and stories into their designs for clothing, protection, and continuance. I learned that the biil (dress) was often woven in deep black so that the women wearing those dresses would not be seen by soldiers at night (Pete & Ornelas, 2018). Weaving for freedom and futures. We must all take part in our own ways of weaving, like Asdzą́ą́ Tl'ógí.

While our Navajo people were finding ways to survive, political negotiations were taking place between tribal leaders (such as Chief Manuelito) and the federal government. Settler colonial tactics were growing more oppressive. Policymakers believed that civilizing Native people was imperative, especially given that many of them had damaging, racist mindsets that viewed us as "hopelessly primitive and unsophisticated" (Carney, 1999, p. 16). These framings were producing conceptions of deficiency, of Native people not being enough, thereby legitimizing efforts to civilize the Natives. Civilization meant assimilation. Civilization justified the White gaze. The settlers' White gaze formed "Indianness" from a place of anger, greed, and longing for what they could not fully possess: land. The Lakota scholar Vine Deloria Jr. (1970) noted, "To the non-Indian world, it does not appear that Indians are capable of anything. The flexibility of the tribal viewpoint enables Indians to meet devastating situations and survive. But this flexibility is seen by non-Indians as incompetency, so that as the non-Indian struggles in solitude and despair he curses the Indian for not coveting the same disaster" (p. 13). Therefore, civilization as assimilation would be done through education.

The first school building for Navajo people was established in 1870 at Ft. Defiance, Arizona (Iverson, 2002). Not surprisingly, school officials had a difficult time getting Navajo students to attend school—our ancestors were getting their flex on. Stories of abuse, overcrowding, and lack of health care spread throughout the Navajo community. These stories were on top of the lived experiences of relatives who had just returned from Hwéeldih and faced imprisonment, starvation, abuse, rape, and death. To then consider sending children to White, settler-led schools was not on the forefronts of Navajo people's minds. We are not dumb people.

There were four mission schools that opened during this period: The Navajo Methodist Mission School, located at Hogback, had 13 students in 1899; St. Michael's Indian School had 21 students in 1902; Rehoboth Mission had 6 children in 1903; and Ganado Mission School began in 1906. Shimá sání (my maternal grandmother), your great-grandma, eventually attended the Mission School. The buildings are still there. I've walked around those buildings and imagined what life was like when our relatives attended. Grandma told me that the dorm maids were mean. She once got in trouble and had to drink castor oil as punishment for insufficiently acting in ways deemed inappropriate (deficit) in the eyes of the dorm maids. Her face pinched together as she relived the memory. Pictures of former students are hung up in the Presbyterian Church. The last time I was in the church, I looked at each face, saw my uncle and aunties in their crisp shirts and carefully styled hair staring at the camera. Their young faces looking at me. It's difficult to hear the stories of how much the church influenced and hurt our people for not assimilating to White standards—not being enough.

Chief Manuelito, our grandfather, was an advocate for schooling. He is known for stating, "Go my child, go and get an education," which is often requoted in our Navajo community to motivate our people to do well in school. Chief Manuelito sent his two sons and a nephew to Carlisle Indian School, located in Pennsylvania, which was considered by policymakers as a modeled boarding school and consequently over time was replicated across the nation. Richard H. Pratt was the founder and longtime superintendent of Carlisle Indian School. At an 1892 convention, Pratt began his remarks with the following, which sheds light on his views on Native people and on how to educate them: "A great general has said that the only good Indian is a dead one, and that high sanction of his destruction has been an enormous factor in promoting Indian massacres. In a sense, I agree with the sentiment, but only in this: that all the Indian there is in the race should be dead. Kill the Indian in him, and save the man" (Pratt, 1892).

Pratt's words of destroying the Indian and saving the man describe the roots of assimilating Native people to not be Native. Chief Manuelito's three boys died of tuberculosis while at Carlisle (Iverson, 2002). Many other children died at Carlisle as well. Later, I learned that Chief Manuelito was devastated about the death of his children. His attitude about boarding schools changed, and he demanded that all Navajo children be returned to their home(lands) (King, 2018). Pause. Remember. *Resurgence.*

During the 1930s, educational funding for "Native-centered" education emerged; however, embedded assimilation ideologies remained, which maintained the vitality of the deficit (not enough) monster. Community day schools were formed that opened opportunities for Native children to attend schools, but they were still predominantly managed and taught by non-Natives. Many of these schools emphasized that they were bilingual and bicultural and recognized a culturally relevant curriculum. Yet, closer examination of the curriculum revealed that assimilationist tactics remained to what Lomawaima and McCarty (2006) refer to as refined forms of colonization. For example, federally funded bilingual *Indian Life Readers* books such as the Navajo Little Herder Stories were gaining popularity in schools. These books connected with Navajo readers because the characters were Navajo children and the storyline described the children caring for sheep. These books appeared relatable. With the turn of each page, though, there were subtle messages that promoted assimilation values, such as the little herder stating, "Father says, that next year, He will try the white-man's way of breeding sheep" (Clark, 1940, p. 58).

Then, in 1946, there were an estimated 24,000 Navajo children between the ages of 6 and 18, and out of those children, 6,000 (or 25%) of them attended school (Roessel, 1979). While most White children in the nation had been attending school for centuries, only a quarter of Navajo children were attending school. For many Navajo children, the boarding school era had not ended. A majority of Navajo youth from 12 to 18 years of age attended off-reservation boarding schools. Once again, the U.S. Bureau of Indian Affairs developed assimilation programs such as the Special Navajo Education Program in 1946, where 12- to 18-year-olds were enrolled in urban-living boarding schools in California, Oklahoma, Nevada, New Mexico, Utah, Kansas, and Arizona. Miles and states away from Diné Bikéyah (Navajo land), during a period where few Navajos had the means to travel long distances, Navajo youth and children were again separated from their families and home(lands). The aim of this program was articulated in a report by the U.S. Department of the Interior titled *Doorway Toward the Light* (Coombs, 1962), thereby perpetuating the damaging, deficit ideas that Navajo children were "groping in the darkness of illiteracy" and that education away from home reinforced assimilation efforts with good/bad binary language such as "the light," in order to "live effectively in the non-Navajo culture" (Roessel, 1979, p. 19). Little did the government know that Diné people have always been able to see in the dark and in the light. These types of binary, dichotomous views (such as light and dark; Native culture and non-Native culture) are hauntings that create damaging, deficit perspectives of who belongs and who does not. The *deficit (not enough) monster*, rooted in assimilation and Whiteness, persisted to disrupt belonging and self-worth. An estimated 50,000 Navajos were enrolled in that program over a span of 12 years.

Another assimilation program was the federally funded Navajo Bordertown Dormitory Program, which provided bordertown reservation school districts with construction money and the full per capita costs of educating Navajo students that they enrolled. Designed as a program for youth ages 12 and older, from 1959 to 1960, over 50% of the 2,284 students in the program were less than 12 years of age—little ones yet again (Roessel, 1979). Given that many of the older Navajo youth were attending schools hundreds and thousands of miles away, bordertown schools wanted Navajo students because they received federal money for each body; therefore, young children were targeted. Because of the Special Navajo Education Program and the Bordertown Dormitory Program, an estimated 88% of

Navajo youth were in school by the 1960s. Those numbers also meant that Diné language and Diné ways of life were losing prominence in the daily lives of thousands and in the generations of our young people. The deficit (not enough) monster was attempting to prevail. The assimilation machine was in full effect, taking the minds and lives of children while also forming a generation of people who were beginning to second-guess their identity, their sense of self. The deficit (not enough) monster was sprouting a syndrome of "imposters." It was the system, the deficit (not enough) monster, that created the illness, not the Navajo people. This was the generation of my parents, your grandparents, not too far from us, from you.

With national attention focused on the civil rights movement, Native peoples and their social rights reached a powerful turning point. Navajo people asserted their sovereign rights and created the first Native community-controlled school, Diné Bi'ólta', also referred to as Rough Rock Demonstration School, in 1966. Located on the Navajo Nation, Diné Bi'ólta' provided instruction and curriculum in the Diné language and created bicultural and bilingual children's literature by and about Navajo people. In Teresa McCarty's (2002) book *A Place to Be Navajo*, she detailed the life history of the school and community, demonstrating Navajo people's resolute resurgence to claim education by Diné terms and to do so successfully. Then, in 1969, a Senate Subcommittee on Indian Education issued a report titled *Indian Education: A National Tragedy, A National Challenge,* which addressed the need for Native education to be facilitated by Native people. The report recommended that "Indian parental and community involvement be increased. . . . That state and local communities facilitate and encourage Indian community and parental involvement in the development and operation of public education programs for Indian students." In response, several milestone policies evolved, including the 1972 Indian Education Act, which appropriated funds to public schools to meet culturally related academic needs of Native students. In 1975, the Indian Self-Determination and Educational Assistance Act responded to the outcry from Native communities and leaders who argued for the need for Native education to be governed by Native people. Because of the success of the Rough Rock Demonstration School, Navajo Community College (now Diné College, the first tribal college in the United States!) opened on the Navajo Reservation in 1968. The achievements of Navajo Community College propelled the Tribally Controlled Community College Assistance Act in 1978, which helped to ignite the tribal college movement across the nation (Tippeconnic, 1999). Our people were fighting for education on our terms. They were saying, we are more than enough! *Resurgence!*

History sets the foundational understandings of what our Native people have encountered over time in education. They faced and fought through ongoing assimilation, which helps us to see the source of the deficit (not enough) monster. I revisited Gloria Ladson-Billings's (2006) article "From the Achievement Gap to the Educational Debt: Understanding Achievement in U.S. Schools," where she explained that educational debt is the culmination of historical, economic, sociopolitical, and moral decisions and policies, previously incurred and continuously accumulated over time, that disenfranchise groups of people. Educational debt is a useful concept because it addresses the long-term underlying problems (history) rather than solely focusing on short-term solutions to achievement gaps.

Many people talk about the achievement gap in education. Basically, people who use the achievement gap measure us (racialized populations such as Blacks, Latinx, and Asians) against White people. The achievement gap is a normalized measurement that presents White people as the benchmark, the place to be, the goal to be achieved, the place of "light." But we are more than simply light and dark—we are beautifully nuanced. We are a racialized and politicized group because of our home(land), treaties, and sovereignty rights. The deficit (not enough) monster attempts to assimilate us to an arbitrary state of being. That is a marker of educational debt. Lands stolen: debt. Lives taken: debt. Cultural genocide: debt. Separation of families: debt. Broken treaty promises: debt, debt, and more debt. I think there is an educational treaty debt owed to Native peoples that accumulates every second of every day.

Hauntings

With the *deficit (not enough) monster* lurking nearby, how did they influence the current realities of Native students? Wesley had a narrow, fit physique. He scheduled most of his days by prioritizing time for weight training. With short, dark hair, and often wearing a black T-shirt that had a rock band emblem on it and dark-colored shorts, Wesley was a music enthusiast. He taught himself how to play the guitar. Learning on his own was something that he enjoyed doing, and he was good at it. He read works about history, scientific discoveries, and various other topics where he could escape and explore life beyond what he learned in the classroom. Wesley described himself as an inquisitive person with a lot of questions and admitted that it was hard for him to stay focused. Wesley spent much of his youth in Purple Hills. He also lived in several places within the western region of the United States because his single-parent mom moved around a lot in order to find employment to provide for her three sons.

He was the youngest in his family and explained that he was closest to one of his older brothers. They spent a lot of time together after school and on weekends, which made sense given that it was mainly the two brothers and his mother who lived together. When Wesley was 10 years old, he and his older brother took apart a 1998 Dell computer. They then installed a DVD player and upgraded the random access memory (RAM) to improve the performance of their computer. As they adeptly disassembled and then reassembled computers, they not only demonstrated their intellect and tenacity, they also showed brotherhood and companionship. And as in most sibling relationships, they also fought. Wesley had a slight smile when he told me how they fought over who got to watch their favorite show on television. I related to Wesley, as I remember arguing with my older brother over the smallest things, like washing dishes. Wesley and his brother would eventually make amends and forget about the grudges they may have had against each other. I learned that that was a gift of Wesley's: He could let tough situations that happened in his life go. That's not easy to do. I learned and gained much from listening to Wesley.

Wesley was analytical and serious. From a young age, he was told that he was smart, but he did not like that label because he thought everyone was smart in their own way, and "smart is too simple." As an elementary student, Wesley was a "naughty kid, but I did my work." He was suspended from school when he was in kindergarten. Wesley's kindergarten story reminds me of another Navajo kindergartener named Malachi Wilson, who was also ordered to leave school in 2018 because his hair was deemed too long (Moya-Smith, 2018). Moreover, the U.S. Department of Education's Office of Civil Rights (2014) compiled national data and found that second to Blacks, American Indian and Native-Alaskan students are disproportionately suspended and expelled, representing less than 1% of the student population but 2% of school suspensions and 3% of expulsions. I highlight this data and Malachi's and Wesley's kindergarten experiences to illustrate that exclusionary practices among Black and Native boys and girls in school are a pervasive challenge that often gets dismissed, while simultaneously constructing haunting notions of deficiency and belonging. Where is the restorative justice and support rather than exclusionary punishment?

Since he was young, Wesley always "hated school." He disliked getting up early and going to school for seven hours. He would have preferred teaching himself at home or attending a class with seven or eight students per teacher because he felt like he would have learned more in a smaller, intimate group setting. Wesley attended six different schools, both on the Navajo Reservation and outside it, from kindergarten to high school. Because he experienced different schools, he grew to appreciate schools that had a diverse racial, ethnic population. Also, ever since he was a young boy, he was often teased in reservation schools for having a lighter skin color than his Native peers. When he attended urban schools, though, he was not teased or even questioned about his identity. He felt more accepted because he did not have to explain himself, nor did he get picked on for his appearance. Although he "hated school," Wesley performed well academically, often receiving the highest grades in his class. Yet, like Lauryn, he felt that school was not challenging him enough, confirming thoughts that his school was possibly failing him.

Sarah, Wesley, Jessie, Joy, Lauryn, Amber, and Chris attended Arizona reservation high schools for most, if not all, of their high schooling. They admitted that they were not academically challenged. Wesley shared, "In high school, the work was simple, like very simple. I didn't have to think about it at all, really." And with some hesitation, Lauryn told me, "In high school, I don't know, high school isn't that hard." Joy shared similar views: "I wasn't able to get a challenge because everything felt so easy to me." And Amber went as far as to state, "I was getting bored in high school because it wasn't so rigorous, and I hate that because I could learn so much at a better school and I could have been more well-prepared." These students were academically high-achieving students who wanted to learn and who wanted to attend college for the betterment of their people, home(lands), and future. They enacted resurgence and took the most rigorous classes available at their schools; and yet, even in those upper-level courses, they felt that they were not challenged enough, revealing how another monster, the deficit (not enough) monster, was ever-present in schooling. Although the schools may have taken the brunt of the blame for the lack of rigor offered to students, we must stare hard at the interconnected structures that reinforce assimilative normative constructions of success and achievement while simultaneously producing deficit views of Native students and families.

The Navajo Nation's educational system is complex and demonstrates a myriad of pressures and issues compounding Navajo education. In the Navajo Nation, there are 17 school districts, with a total of 244 schools that serve 38,109 students. The Navajo Nation educational system is highly fragmented, with multiple demands to meet national academic standards as well as the academic requirements of three different states (Utah, New Mexico, and Arizona). The Division of Diné Education, an organization within the Navajo Nation tribal government, strives to provide educational support for the Navajo people. A core goal of its work is to assert and fold Diné cultural knowledge and Navajo language into the standardized curriculum and requirements of different types of schools (public, federal Bureau of Indian Education [BIE], and charter) in different states. While our tribe is striving to assert tribal sovereignty by educating Navajo people in Diné ways, normative constructions of what knowledge should be taught (or standardized curricula) remain, and they monopolize tribal efforts. For example, in 2004, Senate Bill 1365 was passed in Arizona to allow tribal history to be included in social studies curricula. The late Navajo Nation chairman Albert Hale was a strong advocate for the inclusion of tribal governance in what is taught in Arizona classrooms. Yet, the inclusion of tribal governance and sovereignty was stripped from the bill, though tribal history was maintained. This clever positioning reinforces what Calderon (2014) calls "discursive logics," which maintain settler ideologies in educational curriculum. Diné scholar Cynthia Benally (2014) indicated that discursive logics depict Native people as only from the past and erase the sovereignty status of tribal nations, while also safeguarding settler colonialism as it exists today. In this case, Arizona set the standardized curriculum, evoking questions that Alutiiq scholar Leilani Sabzalian (2019) firmly asks of schools: Whose knowledge counts, and whose concerns matter? When these questions and answers are critically examined, we learn that they reproduce settler knowledge. Assimilation is therefore disguised in standardized curricula and justified in educational outcomes.

What students do not discuss, but what I believe is crucial to point out, is the link between the embedded deficit ideologies (deficit [not enough] monster) with systematic assimilation and meritocracy. Meritocracy is defined by Alon and Tienda (2007) as "a social system where individual talent and effort, rather than ascriptive traits, determine individuals' placements in a social hierarchy" (p. 489). Justification for assimilation and meritocracy comes in the form of educational outcomes, or what I like to refer to as "deficit scoring" of Navajo schools/Native students when compared to the state, when compared to Whiteness, and then placed in a hierarchy. These scores have not changed much over time, further intensifying perceptions of Native students as less than, lower than, below average, and failing. Deficit language that dates back to when settlers first arrived describes us as "hopelessly primitive and unsophisticated" (Carney, 1999, p. 16). Deficit language that damages views that people have about us today.

Hauntings of the deficit (not enough) monster are the measurements, the achievement gaps, the outcomes based on non-Native views of success. Now, I may be losing you as a reader because I am bringing in test scores and state policies. I recognize that I am even changing my tone, as if I am lecturing you. My apologies, but know that this information is critical to better understand the inner workings of the deficit (not enough) monster and its hauntings in school and legislative settings. Also, this information is too often not told to you, but it's a crude reality that you should know.

The Arizona legislature passed a 2015 budget that decreased educational spending in all K–12 schools but increased some funding for "Arizona's best schools" or high-performing schools (Arizona Education Budget Summary, 2015). That is an example of meritocracy. Assimilation and meritocracy are related. Overall, Arizona is ranked as the lowest state in the nation in providing financial support for students. A report from the National Education Association (2014) stated that the U.S. average per-student expenditure for public elementary and secondary schools in 2012–2013 was $10,938, whereas Arizona was the lowest (#51), with $6,949 spent per student.

Notably, several Navajo reservation schools were in the highest need of replacement because of their dilapidated buildings and facilities (Leo, 2015). For example, Little Singer Community School has had water damage, mold, and asbestos problems since 2004. Former secretary of the interior Sally Jewell opined that poor facilities for Native students is a result of "decades of neglect" (Klein, 2015). However, funding school construction has been a slow process that then stopped with federal cuts in 2013. During that year, Congress implemented across-the-board budget cuts, known as "sequestration," that cut $60 million for Native schools across the country (Morales, 2013). Reservation schools were then forced to do "more with less." In an interview with a Navajo Reservation school bus driver, Morales (2013) rode a school bus near Tuba City to get a sense of what it's like for students commuting to school. The bus driver shared how most of the bus drivers have back problems because of the daily driving on rugged terrain roads. A bus that should last 10 years normally only lasts 5 years due to the wear and tear of driving on rough roads. Superintendent Harold Begay of the Tuba City school district stated, "I'd like to take Congress on this bus ride because they don't see this. They have never been out here." Schools on the reservation that are situated in hauntings by the *financial hardship monster* are a target for reduced funding and lower standing on the meritocracy scale.

On May 21, 2014, Timothy Benally, the acting superintendent of schools for the Department of Diné Education, provided testimony before the U.S. Senate Committee on Indian Affairs. In his comments, he shared many concerns, including efforts to mitigate the fragmented educational system, research and statistical support, the value of higher education finances (scholarships), professional development for teachers including Navajo language and culture instruction, and a need for highly effective teachers, principals, and staff (Navajo Nation Office of Educational Research and Statistics Report, 2014). His concerns reminded me of a story that I came across in the *Navajo Times*. A new, non-Native teacher was on her way to a reservation school where she was going to teach. She interviewed for the position over the phone and accepted the position. On arrival at the school, she drove up to the school grounds, but she did not park her vehicle to greet people inside the school. Instead, she immediately turned around and began exiting the school grounds. The story described that the principal quickly stopped her and said, "Wait! You're in the right place." She stated, "I've made a mistake" and drove away, never to be heard from again (Yurth, 2010). For the Navajo Nation, the turnover rate for teachers is commonly at 30%. When 3 out of 10 teachers do not return the next year, long-term learning goals are more difficult to meet, and students' educational attainment and academic rigor is hindered.

One position that often is difficult to fill is for math teachers. I was a former 7th-grade math teacher on the Navajo reservation in my hometown. During my interview for the teaching position, I recall the search committee telling me how challenging it was to find math teachers, especially Native math teachers who came from the community and understood Navajo students. Being able to teach at home, alongside teachers who once taught me and with students who were younger siblings to some of my classmates, was priceless. Some of my fondest memories involve teaching and learning from those students. Looking back, all of the math teachers in the school during the time I was teaching there were White men, new to living on the Navajo reservation and working with Native students. After hearing stories about how math teachers were difficult to obtain, I was not surprised to learn from students that lack of math courses was most problematic in stifling their mastery of advanced math. They reached a ceiling in education because upper-level math courses were not available.

At the high schools that Sarah, Wesley, and Jessie attended, calculus 1 was the highest math course offered. An aspiring science college major, Sarah took calculus 1 two times because she had no other options to meet her 4 years of math requirements. She shared, "I took the same class, calculus, twice because I needed 4 years of math, so I was like, I will just take another year of calculus." For Amber, an aspiring medical student, the highest math course at her school was precalculus. If students at her school wanted to take calculus 1 or higher, their option was to take an online course. For Amber, that was not an option that she was willing to take: "I don't want to be taught by a computer because they don't have teachers who could teach a higher math class than precalculus. What if I didn't get it? There's no one around me to help. I like personal help." Sarah and Amber attended larger reservation schools that typically had more academic and extracurricular opportunities than the smaller schools on the reservation. Yet those larger schools still did not offer upper-level math courses, or if they did, the course was facilitated by an online source, making it difficult for high-achieving students to receive teacher guidance and instruction. The Arizona Board of Regents implemented core curriculum requirements for students who aim to attend one of the state's three public universities. Of the 16 core course requirements, Native students scored the lowest in math, such that 30% of Native students did not complete 4 years of math with at least a grade of C (Milem et al., 2013). I wondered how many schools had teacher turnover in mathematics. I wondered what math courses were available to students. I wondered how many math classes taught Navajo rug weaving, basketry, and silversmithing as mathematical concepts. I wondered how and why the system continues to fail students. Answers to these questions would reveal hauntings brought forth from the deficit (not enough) monster, rooted in assimilation to Whiteness, which in turn disrupts Navajo students' college possibilities and self-worth.

Students also started telling me that they did not have consistent homework, and they viewed that with mixed feelings. On the one hand, they were relieved that they did not have to do extra work outside of school hours, especially Lauryn and Amber, who participated in extracurricular sports and clubs. Yet on the other hand, they were also frustrated because not having homework contributed to their feelings of not being challenged. Sarah explained why she thought teachers might not be assigning frequent homework. She considered that teachers were possibly choosing to deemphasize homework because they were making decisions based on the broader struggles occurring in the community: "I think the teachers, knowing our background, they just really didn't force that [homework] upon us." She shared these sentiments with an utmost respect for her teachers. She felt that they were looking out for the best interests of her and her classmates by

understanding that students may have complicated lives and outside obligations. Homework may not be feasible for some students. Sarah's views align
with a research study in which Native educators who worked at reservation
schools were interviewed and asked about their experiences teaching Native
students (Huffman, 2013). In that study, one principal stated:

> Challenges are everyday. Challenges are getting kids here. Challenges are trying
> to make sure these kids come in and we got breakfast bars here. A lot of times
> they don't come with breakfast. Challenges are the parents may be fighting or
> are the parents even there? Challenges are, where is the kid going to go at the
> end of the school day? Make sure he gets home. Is it safe there? . . . Challenges
> are every day. (Huffman, 2013, p. 53)

That study confirmed that supporting Native students' basic living needs often
took precedence over learning, as "challenges are everyday." In Arizona,
52.4% of Native students graduate from high school, compared to the overall
graduation rate of 73.4% (Faircloth & Tippeconnic, 2010). Those numbers
have not changed much over time. Educators working with Native students
may place more attention on getting students to graduate. This takes away priorities for guiding students for life after high school, such as college planning.

   While these realities are very real, I wondered about how much of the deficit
(not enough) monster was seeping into the minds of educators; meaning, were
views of not being capable (not enough intellect, not enough time, not enough
resources, not enough energy, etc.) overshadowing students' potential and possibility? I am not forging an opinion that dismisses caring for students. That is
not the argument at all. I am posing questions to examine the system, the *financial hardship monster* that fuels the fact that "challenges are everyday" and the
deficit (not enough) monster that functions to control Indigenous minds, behaviors, and ways of life. It's a delicate balance to address the concerns of students
and the conditions that they are going through, while also meeting the needs of
students who are driven and ready for academic challenges.

   Lauryn had high hopes of attending an Ivy League university. It was
her dream to attend the place that "presidents attended." Her grandfather
planted the seed in her to attend an Ivy League university. She told me that
one day, she was at her grandparents' house. It was too hot to play outside, so
she sat inside the house watching television with her grandpa. The Ivy League
university appeared on the screen. She didn't know about that institution, but
her grandpa did. He told her, "That is where the president goes to school; you
do something like that when you get older." After that subtle but powerful
moment, she knew she wanted to go there. She was determined to get accepted. Her grandpa had sparked aspirations for college. Lauryn had a near-
perfect grade point average, was involved in sports and her community, and
demonstrated strong leadership at home and in school. Yet, she struggled in
getting a decent score on the ACT and SAT exams. She explained, "I started
taking my ACTs and SATs to get into [the Ivy League university]. I couldn't
get a good score. I was getting frustrated. We only had an ACT test at my high

school once every year, and if we wanted to take it again, we had to go to [state's off-reservation town]. So, I would go there, and I would take it there with those high school students." She had to travel almost 2 hours one way to an off-reservation school to take additional tests. While walking in the halls at that high school, she saw flyers for after-school test prep workshops and wondered, "Why don't we have that?" She realized that her school did not provide college prep workshops that could potentially help her to increase her score to get into her dream school. While walking through the school hall-ways, she felt immensely alone in trying to get into her dream college.

Lauryn took the ACT 10 times. Even with her highest score (the 10th time), she was not admitted. After learning that she did not get accepted into her dream school, she went into a downward spiral of self-doubt. She stated, "I don't know, I was just really brought down, and all my dreams and everything just didn't matter anymore." Lauryn explained that she wished her school challenged her more. Instead, she stated that she "felt like we were just a school to get a high school diploma. That's about it."

Lauryn was not alone. At another reservation school miles away, Amber acknowledged that her school did not instill messages that college was at-tainable for students. She explained, "It feels like they don't have so much confidence that you're going to succeed in life. They feel like you are on your own way, but they feel like it's going to be a constant struggle for us because of where we're going to high school, where we're growing up." Amber be-lieved that there was an underlying opinion by school staff that students from reservation high schools were less likely to go to college. And if students did go to college, most would not be able to earn a degree. These opinions may be driven by the numbers. The high school graduation rates for Native students who attended public schools was at 68% in 2012, while Bureau of Indian Education schools fared worse, with a graduation rate of only 53% (Stetser & Stillwell, 2014). For Native students who matriculate to college, the num-bers are not encouraging either, with the total enrollment being 172,900 in 2012 (Musu-Gillette et al., 2017). While the overall Native American popu-lation increased by 39% from 2000 to 2010, the college enrollment and de-grees conferred stayed at 1% during the same period (Norris et al., 2012). This is a stagnation crisis and a sign of the hauntings. In the Navajo Nation, the second-largest tribal group in the United States, only 7.3% of its citizens hold a bachelor or graduate degree (Navajo Nation Roundtable on Remedial Education Summary Report, 2012). From those numbers, Natives, including Navajo students, are viewed from a disempowering perspective. Our people have been historically problematized and considered a deficit, not enough. I wondered how much measuring up against Whiteness has seeped into the school structures and the mindsets of teachers and administrators, demon-strating an influence of the deficit (not enough) monster that has its roots in assimilation. Yet, the schools are not the only ones at fault; the state and larger structural forces have a very heavy hand in restricting the ability to learn. Since their arrival, they have always had a heavy hand.

Monstrous Internalization

The story rug informs us that the time is right to weave in the internalization of the monsters. How does the *deficit (not enough) monster* in turn influence some of the Native students? Jessie was tall and slender. She often wore fashionable jeans and fitted tops that matched her delicate stud earrings—red top and red earrings, turquoise top and turquoise earrings, and so on. Her brown hair was thick and long, often styled nicely into big, loose curls. Some days she wore glasses, and other days she wore contact lenses. She described herself as "well rounded." She explained what this meant by telling me that she could dress really nice if she had to and then relax by putting on a pair of boots and hat: "I can fit into my surroundings." As a young girl, her cheii (maternal grandfather) taught her how to butcher sheep, brand cattle, and make bread—Navajo teachings that have been passed down for generations. She was proud to have those skills. Shoot, I was proud of her. There are not many teenagers who know how to butcher a sheep. She reminded me of the first time shinálí (paternal grandmother) told me to help butcher sheep. I think I was around 11 years old. My nálí gave me the job of cleaning out the intestines by pinching the fingers of one hand tightly around the long, slimy intestine. Then, with my other hand, I pulled the intestine to allow the brown substance to squeeze out of it and into a plastic bowl. We were outside near shinálí (my paternal grandmother) home. Even with the occasional breeze, the stench was inescapable. I tried to hold back the nausea that stirred in my body. But I couldn't resist the queasiness for long. My body reacted. I gagged and gagged. My nálí turned around and looked at me with a stern face. She scolded me for reacting that way. "Be strong," she said to me. "If you want to eat, you have to help." Butchering sheep is a life skill, survival skill.

Jessie was raised in a small community called Forbidden Springs (pseudonym; where her maternal grandparents were from) with a population of roughly 700 people. Nestled in the little town was a Navajo Housing Authority (NHA) complex with a handful of NHA homes, a school, and the chapter house (a tribal government office). Jessie's grandma worked as the secretary at the Forbidden Springs chapter house. This meant that Jessie grew up spending a lot of time with her family there. They volunteered and helped her grandma with food sales, "Just Move It" walks, parades, you name it—they were there to help. She also remembered attending chapter house meetings and being forced to sit still while the meetings took place. Diné teachings of disciplining yourself by being in stillness, in silence, respecting the people around you. Chapter house meetings are long, lasting several hours. Sitting on the aluminum chairs for hours was not fun, not easy. Yet, Jessie learned respect in stillness, and about local politics, about hay and wood distribution, and about the cattle and water needs in the community. She also learned about kinship, about the value of helping and being there for her grandma, for her mom. Diné teachings.

At an early age, her nálí asdzą́ą́ (paternal grandmother) and aunt took her on trips to California and other places away from Diné Bikéyah (Navajo land). She got a little taste of city life on those trips. One of her most memorable adventures was when she was 9 years old. Her nálí took her to a state college that she had graduated from. The campus was huge and pretty, with manicured lawns, big buildings, and so many people. They watched a college basketball game, and Jessie immediately loved the atmosphere. The school spirit during the game was on fire, with loud cheers and lively fans. Jessie felt like a lucky girl to be able to attend a college basketball game. Vibrant purple and black were the college's school colors, and the gym was filled with people wearing those colors everywhere—on their shirts, shorts, hair pins, jewelry, nails, and even drawn on their faces. After that game, purple and black were Jessie's new favorite colors.

Jessie was the only child in her family until she turned 9 years old. Then, her new little brother arrived. Soon after, a lot of changes happened in the family. With the new baby's arrival, her parents finalized their divorce. Transitions came quickly. Along with her mom and little brother, Jessie moved to Windy Sands (pseudonym; located on the Navajo Reservation). Jessie told me that during this time, she felt like she grew up fast. Every day after school, she got off the bus and walked to the babysitter's house to pick up her little brother. Gathering his belongings while also lugging her school bag, she walked back home, carrying her little brother tightly to her hip. She cared for her brother until their mom returned from work. A lot of responsibility for a young girl. As she was telling me about this time in her life, she glanced at me with an inquisitive look and asked, "Why would you have your daughter take care of your 6-month-old son? That's crazy." I did not have an answer for her, but I could relate. In the summer before my 6th-grade year, each morning at 7 A.M., my uncle and aunt dropped off my cousins at our house. The youngest was a toddler, and the oldest was 4 years old. I was hired to take care of them for the next 3 months. I learned a lot about responsibility, patience, and how to entertain little ones (reading with funny voices was the best!). For payment, I received brand new yellow and turquoise Nike running shoes. Those shoes made me run fast, fast into 6th grade. Jessie already had a reply to her question: She explained that there was a special, loving bond between her and her mom.

Jessie's mom had a gift for listening, and this gift meant the world to Jessie, especially as she shared personal struggles that she started facing in school and with her family. Jessie tasted the sting of disappointment and hurt many times over. And her mom was there with open ears and arms, ready to provide encouraging words.

Jessie moved around several times while she was in high school. The choice to move was her decision because she wanted to try new schools and escape heartbreak and feelings of unworthiness. She attended Hawk High School, located off the reservation, 60 miles away from Windy Sands, when she was in the 9th and 10th grades. The school provided housing for students who were not able to travel to and from school daily due to distance and cost. Jessie stayed in the dormitory and went home on the weekends. She enjoyed attending Hawk High School. She felt a strong sense of independence being away from home and the regular duties that she had as an older sister. The school also challenged her academically, something that she appreciated and welcomed. During her first year in high school, Jessie experienced her first relationship. She fell in love with her new boyfriend. He stayed in the dorm too, so they had opportunities to spend time with each other after school and develop their relationship. Everything seemed to be going well until Jessie admitted that she just couldn't balance family, friends, school, and the new relationship. Her grades suffered. And then during their 10th-grade year, they broke up. She didn't go into detail about the breakup. And I didn't ask.

When Jessie reached 11th grade, she returned to the reservation and attended Folded Canyon High School. She decided to attend Folded Canyon because her mom went to that school and she wanted to be in a new environment after breaking up with her boyfriend. While attending Folded

Canyon, she lived with her aunt. At first, the transition to a new school went well. But very quickly Jessie started facing difficulties. She felt like students at Folded Canyon did not like her. She was teased often and ridiculed. These experiences reawakened past experiences when she was little. Jessie told me about being teased by family and classmates because they questioned her Native identity. She explained:

> I'm full Navajo. I get mistaken for being Korean a lot of the time . . .
> A lot of people don't believe this, but when I was growing up, I used
> to be teased a lot. I was really thin, and everybody used to tell me,
> "Oh, you look Asian. You're not Navajo." I was always the one
> who was being teased. For me, I didn't like it. I was like, why am
> I different? I don't want to be different. Sometimes I would come
> home crying. Yeah, I cried about it. I was really upset about it. I was
> like, why am I so thin? Why can't I be normal like everybody else. . . .
> I didn't really feel accepted by others especially with the teasing and
> everything it just felt like why am I even here?

Those same questions were resurfacing during her junior year. While she was telling me this, I wondered what was normal. And what harm do we place on each other when we desperately try to be something that we are not? Normal is assimilating to society's standards on who is Native—standards that have damaged Native peoples for centuries. Jessie was illustrating how systemic monsters are internalized where we question our sense of self and belonging. The deficit (not enough) monster, having its roots in assimilation to Whiteness (normalness), functions to control Indigenous minds, which in turn disrupts self-worth and belonging.

And then there was the gossip. Ugly gossip spread about Jessie. It devastated her. The gossip was baseless, untrue, and callous. Jessie did not understand why people would want to hurt her, damage her. She spiraled into questions about whether she was good enough, whether she was Navajo enough, whether she was enough to live. The deficit (not enough) monster was oozing into her essence. Monsters can have that effect. They can get into our thoughts and being, where we begin to believe the lies that they tell of us. I call this monstrous internalization.

Overwhelming feelings of not being accepted, alone, unwanted, and unloved grew. After school, Jessie escaped to her room, closed the door, and listened to music. She didn't want to do anything in the outside world. To ease the pain that she was feeling inside, Jessie started cutting herself. She wore long-sleeved shirts and sweaters to hide the scars along her arms. While she was telling me all of this, I could sense an urgency from her, a need to share this part of her life, of her story. She was telling these truths because she wanted to help someone who may be going through what she had gone through. She wanted to tell her story so that other people experiencing similar hardships would not feel alone.

Jessie continued to pour her story out. And I sat near her, receiving it. She did not cry, but I could feel the somberness in the room, and my heart opened up to embrace Jessie and the many others who were and are hurting. With unwavering candidness, she elaborated on when she had the final straw:

> I didn't really feel accepted by others especially with the teasing and everything it just felt like why I'm I even here? I went through the whole phase, I don't deserve to be here, I don't deserve to be alive, no one wants me, and no one loves me. I just didn't want anything to do with the outside world. . . . I mean, there were suicidal thoughts, I wanted to leave.

The relentless teasing took a devastating toll on Jessie's sense of self-worth. She was in a battle with the hauntings brought forth from the deficit (not enough) monster. Hauntings of assimilation and conforming to ideas of how a Native person looks. She felt unaccepted and unloved. She thought that suicide was a way to relieve the scars left on her arms, her heart, her spirit. I learned that Jessie was not the only person questioning and wondering about life. Cecilia, Joy, and Sam also thought about suicide.

Cecilia attended a large, urban school and frequently felt ostracized because of the way she looked—having darker skin—and because of racist societal stereotypes of how Native people should look and act. She felt alone for being the only Native in most of her honors and Advanced Placement (AP) courses. She did not have a network of support where others could relate to what she was going through and even advocate on her behalf. Racist stereotypes that were birthed from assimilation efforts, that the deficit (not enough) monster heaved at her. She stated:

> It's really hard because when you are in school in the city, you are pretty much the only minority in class. You are the only Brown person. They have this idea that Natives or Indians are supposed to wear buckskin, feathers, or moccasins all the time. They knew that I was different because I was a darker skin color than most of my classmates. It was kind of hard growing up like that because they saw me as different. I used to get picked on a lot in school from probably like kindergarten and up, throughout my whole educational career I just got picked on.

At an early age, Cecilia learned that she was different. She was taught this difference by how her peers negatively treated her. Cecilia told me heart-wrenching stories about how she was mistreated in a predominantly White school:

> They used to pull my hair because I had really long hair past my waist. They used to dump sand in my hair. They used to call me very mean words, very derogatory names for Natives. They used

to harass me and my parents. I used to get in a lot of fights. Yeah, I was like the only one that was Native for a while until some moved into my neighborhood. . . . I went through some self-identity issues, and I went through self-esteem issues for a while. It was kind of hard because it affected me through high school too, the whole self-identity, self-esteem issues. It just built up in high school and it went hard from like sophomore to junior year, it was the toughest time. . . . I went through this sudden stage of depression where I was contemplating suicide.

Like Jessie, Cecilia battled with depression and suicidal thoughts during her sophomore year. She elucidated, "I don't know it just built up after a while, and it built up to the point that I was on my kitchen floor with a butcher knife to my neck." While sitting on the kitchen floor, she began questioning herself and thinking about her younger brother, who was also being ridiculed in school. She continued:

I was like, what am I doing? I have a younger brother. What if he sees this? He will think I'm a failure. I just pulled myself together because I knew I have to be strong, not just for myself but for my other little brother because he is going through the same thing too. I wasn't able to go through with it.

She placed the knife down and sobbed. Hot tears rolled down her face. Thoughts that she was "lower than them [her peers]" were hard to let go of, but she knew she had to do her best to not believe in those lies from the deficit (not enough) monster, rooted in assimilation to Whiteness. She stopped what she was attempting to do because of her younger brother. Love of family, k'é (kinship; relational based), and teachings of resurgence emerged and helped her close the door of the deficit (not enough) monster.

When I first began talking and learning from these 10 teenagers about going to college, I did not imagine that they would eventually tell me that they contemplated ending their lives. Most of us tend to ignore, or even push aside, conversations about suicide. For me, I was fearful of the idea, afraid of death, and scared to think that our young people were thinking about suicide. Yet, 4 out of the 10 students had at one time in their life considered—and almost acted—in taking their lives. As a nation, the U.S. suicide rate has increased by 33% since 1999, but for Native women and men, the rate increases are even more substantial: 139% and 71% (Dastagir, 2019). A Native Youth report published by the U.S. Executive Office of the President (2014) detailed that suicide is the leading cause of death for Native youth from 15–24 years of age.

With all the violence that Natives have faced across generations, the taking of lives and land, abuse, hurt, and so many more gruesome and heartbreaking experiences, historical trauma has become a reference to explain individual and community hardships. The Hunkpapa and Oglala Lakota scholar and practitioner Maria Yellow Horse Brave Heart (2003) defined historical trauma as "cumulative emotional and psychological wounding, over the lifespan and across generations, emanating from massive group trauma experiences" (p. 7). Historical trauma gave a name to what many felt and understood to be true but did not know how to explain it to ourselves, let alone to others. Our Native people have faced and continue to face multiple traumatic experiences. And what is particularly difficult to comprehend is that much of the trauma is unnoticed, especially by the general public. Historical trauma response (HTR) is the reaction to these types of trauma. HTR includes substance abuse, suicidal thoughts and actions, depression, anxiety, low self-esteem, anger, and difficulty recognizing and expressing emotions. An in-depth study was conducted in 2012 that investigated historical trauma among Navajo people, including 37 youth (Goodkind et al., 2012). Researchers found that most Navajo youth did not believe that historical traumatic events had any negative effects on their community or in their own lives. However, there were some youth who felt a sense of sadness and mistrust toward White people as a result of intergenerational trauma. Their research revealed the difficulty in disentangling intergenerational effects of historical trauma from the effects of poverty and current oppression, from settler colonialism and assimilation. Many Native youth do not see that the community's past experiences from settler arrival, forced removal during the Long Walk, and abuse and assimilation from the boarding schools are connected to the struggles that many Navajos face today. This makes sense, given that too often, our history from our perspectives is not taught in schools. Moreover, much research on suicide theorizes it as an individual problem; however, the First Nations scholar Emma Elliott-Groves (2017) asserts that among Native communities, suicide is also collective in nature and "embedded in specific and present experiences of colonization" (p. 337). Therefore, it is hard to make the connection to how our present situations are intricately linked to the past.

It is also hard for settlers and the general public to see that normalized, everyday practices, actions, common sense, and policies are reproducing harm and trauma today—the deficit (not enough) monster is sneaky, stays hidden, and destroys lives. What is needed is "structural competence," which means that when we talk or recognize historical trauma occurring in our lives or in our community, we must pay attention to how structural forces that are political and economic interact with our well-being (Kirmayer et al., 2014, p. 312). We must recognize that systemic monsters are generators of trauma, both in the past and now.

Jessie told me why she wanted to tell her story, and I want to share that with you. She said, "That is why I wanted to do this book because a lot of people throughout my life judged me based on looks or what they heard about me, and it kind of surprises me how people can quickly judge others. For me, it's always been about, it's not the cover, it's about the inside."

The deficit (not enough) monster leached into perceptions of who is and who is not Navajo, who has and has not assimilated based on appearance, based on skin color, based on normative measures. But the deficit (not enough) monster does not know what is inside all of us, what has been passed down from generation to generation, knowledge that equips us with much strength.

I am writing to you, sha'áłchíní (my children). And like a loving mother, I want to shield you from hurt and loss because I get scared too. But baby, I am here to tell you that you will be hurt, society will make you feel invisible, people and loved ones will hurt you. It's OK to hurt, to cry, but sha'áłchíní, don't stay in the hurt, don't stay there.[1] Sha'áłchíní, the lessons these accounts teach us is that the deficit (not enough) monster has its deep roots in assimilating us to Whiteness or the normalized ways of sameness. Yet, the measurement of sameness is not based on our views and ways of life, but on White supremacy. And when we look or act different or even bend away from assimilation, we will get hurt by society, and yes even by loved ones, and then question ourselves, our behaviors, and future possibilities. However, we have to remember that we have Indigenous weapons to help us fight the systemic monsters. We learned that resurgence, rooted in love, has given our people much strength and resoluteness. And what we will learn in the next chapter is the second Indigenous weapon of continuance, which will also help us to keep going.

Continuance as Life-Centered

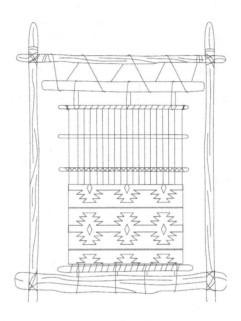

Death is heavy on the body and mind. After Jessie told me her story of contemplating suicide, we took a short break. I walked outside to take in the warm sun. I breathed in and out, big inhales and slow, steady exhales. And I began praying. I knew that the stories I was hearing from Jessie and the other Navajo students were hard to hear, but necessary. I asked the Creator for guidance, to be a conduit for the students. I also prayed for protection and blessings for the students and their families. I share this detail with you because I want you to understand that stories are complex, heavy, and sometimes difficult; and it is OK to pause and seek the strength needed to keep going. I wiped the tears from my eyes, gathered myself together, and re-entered. Jessie was sitting in the gray chair, scrolling through her cell phone. She had refilled her water bottle and draped her long hair on the right side of her shoulder. She looked at me when I entered the room. I smiled and asked her, "Are you OK?" She smiled back at me and said yes, and told me that she wanted to tell me a story of when she was a little girl.

Jessie began telling me that when she was 2 years old, she almost died. She contracted a severe case of pneumonia, a life-threatening condition for toddlers. She was immediately hospitalized, with a prognosis from the doctors that she might not make it. Through it all, day and night, her family stayed by her side. Her little body underwent surgery as the health concerns intensified. She shared, "A lot of doctors said that she is not going to make it. She is not going to live that long because kids that get sick that early, their immune systems can't take it. After that, I guess everybody, everybody was really scared." She was 2 years old and did not fully understand what was happening around her. One day, miraculously, as each hour passed, her body began to heal and restore itself. Fears of severe sickness and death were soon (but cautiously) released from the doctors' prognosis. Her family also let go of their worries and fears and rejoiced in the recovery of their little one.

Jessie's experience was considered a miracle. Her life was a miracle. That powerful truth was a healing reminder for Jessie when she battled through ideas of suicide as a teenager. And her great-grandmother reminded her that she was a miracle.

Jessie confided in her great-grandma about the struggles that she was facing. Her great-grandmother evoked the memory that Jessie's life was a miracle, which sparked the second weapon of continuance within Jessie:

> She told me, "You shouldn't question your life. You were put on this earth for a reason. You shouldn't take it for granted. You shouldn't take away the life that you were given." She continued and said, "When you were sick, you were given that second chance to live and you know the Creator thought this person is going to become somebody, so I'm going to give her the chance to live longer." And she said, "I feel you're taking it as a joke like you don't care, like you just want to kill yourself." And I was just like, "Oh." I mean she didn't yell at me, she was just talking to me. It made me cry, and I said, "No, I don't feel that way. You're not understanding me." But it was what I needed to hear at that time. It was that relief, it was just like OK, yeah, you're right, I'm not doing something right here, . . . Pretty much, she helped me. She said, "I'm here if you need to talk to anybody."

When Jessie felt alone and on the verge of despair, she confided her darkest secret to her great-grandmother. Her great-grandmother told Jessie that she had a purpose in life, a reason to live, and that was what Jessie needed to hear. Jessie's great-grandmother passed away later that December, soon after they had their talk. Jessie explained the significance of talking to her before she journeyed on: "I was really fortunate enough to have talked to her the way I did before she left and to have that intimate conversation with her." That intimate conversation was what Jessie needed. She was reminded of her life, her life as a miracle. All our lives are miracles.

Students such as Jessie activated the Indigenous weapon of *continuance*, the act of continuing or the ability to keep going, which is grounded in matrilineal teachings of birth and life. Continuance is life-centered, that reinforces k'é through Diné pedagogies of story sharing and listening as a process of healing. K'é is a belief system centered on a matrilineal society where the mother is the matriarch and giver of life, the core of the family and home, who carries much knowledge and stories (Yazzie & Speas, 2007). There is a deeply valued reverence for women, including mothers, aunties, and grandmothers. We recognize the influential responsibility that mothers have by producing life through childbirth. This is a strength of our people. *Continuance* is then tethered to *resurgence*. They are powerful when enacted together. *Resurgence* is to get up. Love gets us up. *Continuance* is to keep going. Life gets us going. All 10 students I talked to echoed these cultural values. They each identified how vital their mothers and grandmothers were in guiding them through various challenges, through the monsters. Mothers and grandmothers awakened vulnerability and resiliency, life lessons, and love, such that students were equipped to press on (continuance).

Continuance is to then go. K'é pushes us to go. K'é is what motivated Sarah to get a college degree. She wanted to continue; even though the *deficit (not enough) monster* was feeding her lies about being less than, Sarah pushed through. She continued for her grandparents. Sarah grew up learning to care for her ailing grandmother, who was battling diabetes. Her grandmother had several seizures, and it was Sarah who held and secured her grandmother when seizures struck her body. Eventually, her grandmother had to have both her legs amputated. In tears, Sarah shared:

> My grandma, she's like my best friend. It's hard because my grandma and grandpa, they both are in nursing homes now. When I was younger, I promised myself, they are not going to go in there. I'm going to always be here and take care of them. But as I grew older, you know, I can't take care of my grandparents without anything to fall back on. How am I supposed to get them places if I don't have a ride [vehicle] or gas money or anything? . . . And it just hurts so much. But that was my main influence. Once I get done, I will bring my grandparents home, and I don't care how much money it will take, I'm going to do it. I'm going to bring my grandparents home. . . .
> That's how much I love my grandma. That is one of my motivations, and you know, knowing that I could have some money, and the home to bring them home and care for them, where they would feel most comfortable, that's what gets me through, you know, day to day.

During Sarah's later years of high school, Sarah's grandparents resided in a nursing home. Knowing that her grandparents were no longer living at their homestead was distressing for Sarah. She looked past the deficit (not enough) monster. Sarah was determined to obtain a college degree and to one day have the resources to tend to her grandparents.

For Sam, Wesley, Jessie, and Cecilia, their mothers nobly sacrificed their time and resources to support their families, even when their own economic pressures were extreme. Sam desperately tried to maintain composure, but his openness surfaced as he expressed heartfelt words about his mother. With tears and a soft smile, Sam described his vision of his mom: "My mom, she's definitely a strong woman. I can definitely tell you that she's my hero, my inspirational figure in my life out of everyone else." Sam's mother worked extra hours to support their extended family, and, after witnessing her tenacity, he hoped to one day be like her. Sam knew that his mother wanted nothing more than for him to go to college. To reciprocate the care and support that his mother gave him, he wanted to honor her wishes. During the application process, he developed a personal awareness that attending college was not only for his mom, but also for him. Sam recalled:

> My mom's number one goal is to get me to college, so there was no choice if I was going to or not going to go. I was going to college, so thank God for that. I'm not sure if we can pay for it. She said, "We can do it. You got to put the work in. I will do what I can. It is you that has to do it." And so I kind of took it upon myself, I want to go to college. It ain't going to be, I'm going to have to. No, it's I want to, it's a personal thing. It ain't a responsibility, it's like a job. I took it as a personal self-fulfillment, to fulfill my purpose.

Money was tight, as Sam's single mother cared for his younger siblings and extended family members, but her words of financial assurance encouraged Sam.

Jessie, Sam, Joy, Amber, Cecilia, and Sarah explained that recalling and comparing their difficult experiences with their grandmothers' personal hardship stories instilled in them a determination to push through their own struggles. *Continuance.* Amber questioned whether she would be successful in college, but remembering her grandmothers' boarding school stories made her reassess the situation. Amber stated, "I don't know if I can do this, and they [grandmothers] would always tell me about their boarding school stories, and what they had to go through, and what a better place I am in now. My situation is for the better." Memories of her grandmothers' stories of boarding school life helped Amber to reassess her situation and then work through it.

Joy had a similar experience. She shared her thoughts about listening to her grandmother speak about the past. She explained, "It's just something about when they told me stories, like the way they endured all those difficult hardships and how much more they had to go through compared to what we go through today. A lot of the stories, you can really visualize all these things. . . . Nobody else can tell stories like that." Their grandmothers' personal stories of adversity imparted continuance in students as they worked through their own tough circumstances. Students believed that because their grandmothers had endured much suffering, they should be able to conquer their obstacles too.

Experiential teachings through storying from grandmothers had staying power for students, especially during times of conflict. Joy encountered heated battles with doubters and anxiety due to her younger siblings' alcohol and drug abuse. With negative tension surrounding her life, Joy could have easily fallen into patterns of abusing alcohol and drugs herself and neglecting school achievement. Instead, she became more determined to excel academically, reinforced by her grandmother's engrained teachings of continuance. Joy explained:

> I remember during my kinaaldá, I don't remember what I was doing, but I didn't do it right. My older grandma got after me about it, but not to like a crazy point like anger. She said, "Just try it again, you'll get it." I think we were making kneel down bread. She said, "Just try it again, you'll be okay, just try it again." . . . I guess it goes back to that. Basically, I'm just able to push myself further.

Joy participated in a kinaaldá ceremony that occurs when a Navajo girl is coming to the age of womanhood (Tapahonso, 2008). During a kinaaldá, Navajo teachings are emphasized throughout the ceremony as women caretakers, including mothers, aunties, and grandmothers, guide girls on how to be a Navajo woman. Sarah articulated the continuance of Navajo cultural teachings: "It's something I take into high consideration because I am Navajo. Growing up traditional, you have that engrained in your head. The way you were brought up is something that you just don't throw away."

Therefore, most lessons are not meant to be isolated for specific situations and applied one time; rather, they are interpreted as lifelong guides. Likewise, cultural knowledge is not shared only during ceremonial occasions, as Navajo values and teachings are a way of life that is shared every single day. That explains why, after many years, Joy continued to go back to her grandmother's wisdom throughout her life. These students did not simply dismiss what they learned from their grandmothers and mothers. When circumstances became difficult, they evoked their fundamental matrilineal message to not give up and be beaten down by the deficit (not enough) monster, but keep trying, keep living, and keep going.

Continuance.

Monstrous Internalization and Indigenous Weapons as Watchings

Monsters haunt all of us. The financial hardship and deficit (not enough) monsters lingered in the lives of Sarah, Wesley, Sam, Mike, Cecilia, Jessie, Lauryn, Joy, Amber, and Chris. This act of lingering is the haunting, the ongoing settler horror that reminds us of its often-opaque existence by not allowing truth to come through, and thereby covering up the blemishes, the death, the harm, the reductivity. Hauntings are deeper than fears, trauma, and hurt; they're occurrences, conditions, and concepts that render and remind us that oppression and disappearance are real and occurring *all the time*. What I learned is some of the monsters' playbooks, again in hopes that you, sha'álchíní (my children), will learn the plays that they will attempt to run on you, because they will try (over and over again). The key to maneuvering through is to be ready, watching. Spider Woman taught me that. She prepared the Twin Warriors by telling them what to expect from the monsters. In this chapter, I am going to do just that—tell you what to expect by first explaining a bit more about the systemic monsters and monstrous internalization. Then I will expand on ideas of watching for and cultivating Indigenous weapons of resurgence and continuance.

MONSTERS ARE RELATED AND ARE PROTÉGÉES OF WHITE SUPREMACY, HETEROPATRIARCHY, AND CAPITALISM

It should not be surprising to recognize that the *financial hardship monster* and *deficit (not enough) monster* are related. They grow in strength when they work together to disrupt and erase Navajo presence and belonging. They strategize with each other with the knowledge that when they work together, the impact is greater. This was evident when we learned in Part I how students became dispassionate about college when they lived through financial struggle, when they were denied a scholarship, and then in Part II, when they were told, over and over again, that they were not enough. Hauntings. As much as we may think that tough life situations are separate from larger socio-conditions, I am here to tell you that they are often related. You have to figure out the relations and lineages of the monsters.

Learn the history and the context that shapes and strengthens them. And then see the connections. Name them too. Name the monsters and their hauntings. Spider Woman told the twins to name the monsters; they like to hear their names, and then they become preoccupied with their own egos. In that moment of their amusement, the twins grew strong and were able to confront the monsters.

Why are there monsters? And why do they haunt us? Those are tough questions, but critical for you to explore. From my perspective and experiences, the monsters were created by White supremacy, heteropatriarchy, and capitalism. Power and privilege drive White supremacy, heteropatriarchy, and capitalism. When people are intoxicated with power and privilege, they don't want to lose it, and therefore produce ways to keep the power. This is accomplished through laws, policies, and everyday normative constructions. We saw this in Part I, when we learned about how difficult it is for the Navajo people to seek employment on the Navajo reservation, due in large part to policies that restrict their opportunities to afford college. Again, this occurred in educational settings, where Native people were forced to change themselves. Settler colonialism and assimilation are products of White supremacy, heteropatriarchy, and capitalism. And we are haunted by these monsters because we have a deep relationship to the land and our lifeways with each other, our more than human relatives, and the great divine. Monsters are working on us so that we can relinquish those deep relationships. The Nishnaabeg writer Leanne Betasamosake Simpson (2017) refers to these interlocking systems of power (White supremacy, heteropatriarchy, and capitalism) as "expansive dispossession," which she defines as the "gendered removal of our bodies and minds from our nation and place-based grounded normativities" (p. 43). Glen Coulthard (2014) names them as "constellation of power relations" that sustain colonial power and their inner and external functioning embedded in structures, behaviors, and relationships (p. 14). Sandy Grande names them as "intersecting systems of domination" (p. 118). I call them "systemic monsters." Systemic monsters are shape-shifting, morphing in different ways, but deep within, they remain to maintain power over the land and peoples. Learn to recognize the multiple faces of the monsters.

MONSTERS ARE OLD, BUT AHISTORICAL

Monsters are old. They have lived in what is now called the United States for centuries. Over hundreds of years, they have learned to become more clever, more strategic, and sneakier. The financial hardship monster, rooted in settler colonialism, and the deficit (not enough) monster, rooted in assimilation, were generated when White settlers arrived at these lands. But at face value, the financial hardship monster depicts Natives as poverty stricken and insufficient in securing economic progress. That is their hauntings. Conditions that pathologize the challenges to the people. In 2020, because of COVID-19, there was an increase of media attention to our Navajo people. In most non-Native reporting, the story of deprived and poor Navajos was displayed on television and posted over and over again on social media. Hauntings. The monsters were at play. I noticed. I saw the monsters, felt the hauntings. Missing from much of the coverage were the historical roots of settler colonialism tied to present conditions. Too often, the focus is on the hauntings (conditions), not on the monsters (root causes).

The hauntings from the deficit (not enough) monster also distort us by portraying Natives as least likely to do well in school and graduate with a high school degree, let alone a college degree. The hauntings create illusionary conceptions of Nativeness, with perceptions that there is a certain way to be Native. Erased from the deficit (not enough) monster are the historical roots of assimilation that are tied to ideas of who belongs and who does not.

These two monsters originated because of settlers' desires to take land, bodies, and habits of mind away from us. Strip us from sovereignty and belonging. Monsters take. Monsters attempt to dispossess us from our land, relatives, and sense of self. Monsters steal. Over time, they are getting more slick in their efforts.

When we realize (and see) how old they really are, we can better understand our relationship to them, ourselves, and belonging. Although monsters are old in age, they still disregard the history, the centuries-old educational patterns that used methods of appropriating, stealing, using, abusing, lying, extracting, erasing, and harming our children for the sake of assimilation. Some of those same methods are still utilized today but are disguised in political rhetoric of "academic achievement," "school choice," "no child left behind," "meritocracy," and the list goes on. Monsters are old, but they do not account for the wrongs of the past; instead they re-create those wrongs in the present: hauntings.

MONSTERS ARE ACONTEXTUAL

The financial hardship monster and the deficit (not enough) monster attempt to make individuals feel inadequate both financially and academically, making it difficult for them to attend college. They not only erase history, but they also neglect the context. Yet, as we learned, monsters are intimately connected to context.

Although the Navajo Nation is a sovereign nation, its members remain limited in the ways they are able to assert their rights. Almost every development on Native reservations is controlled at some level by the federal government, primarily because of the federal trust relationships that were established in past treaties and federal court cases (Regan, 2014). Most of the land on the Navajo Nation is held in trust by the federal government.

Therefore, financing businesses on Navajo land is difficult, bureaucratic, expensive, and time consuming. Tribal nations are "locked in a poverty trap" (Regan, 2014, p. 5). The lack of businesses equates to a lack of jobs, contributing to the onslaught of the poverty trap. The monsters are at work in creating structural violence. Settler colonialism.

Structural violence amounts to the injustices produced and sustained through structures and systems of power that perpetuate extreme poverty (Farmer, 2005). There are pedagogies of power that shape and influence poverty, such as housing, access to health care and education, and economic opportunity (Farmer, 2005). As we have learned, Navajo Reservation students talked about living in homes lacking basic life needs, with limited affordable and healthy food options, scarce availability of jobs, and paths to a college preparatory education that were few and far between. These examples all signal a system that was and is designed to maintain impoverished conditions for people. Hauntings. The United States is the most affluent nation in the world; yet, poverty remains, and it is disproportionately higher among Native peoples. The national poverty rate is 15.3%, but the Navajo poverty rate is drastically higher, at 56% (Macarney et al., 2013; Arizona Rural Policy Institute, 2010). When over half of the people in a society live in poverty, that is a systematic monster working. This reminds me of what Avery F. Gordon asserts: "What is at stake here is the functioning of political status and systemic hauntings," meaning that there is an investment in maintaining political and economic power (Gordon, 1997, p. 18). Context matters. History matters.

The haunting of these monsters is visible when all 10 students acknowledged concerns about how they would afford college. We were able to better understand why college affordability is crucial for these and many more students in similar situations. There was not an adequate distribution of wealth and scholarship money that drastically influenced whether students would be able to afford college, let alone consider going to college, or forming conceptions of belonging in college settings. I hope through these stories, my children, you have learned how much context and history matters. Shenandoah, as cited in Wilma Mankiller's (2004) book *Every Day Is a Good Day,* described the significance of context and how context relates to our way of life as Native people: "Context is everything. We are all connected. We don't describe the natural world as separate. We are part of the natural world, and the natural world is a part of us" (p. 43).

Context, as depicted by Shenandoah, is the notion that we are interconnected to the environment and society, demonstrating the influence that context and people have with each other. From this perspective, context includes the structural forces linked to systems of power. Although the monsters attempt to disassociate themselves from context, we must understand and see that structural and systematic forces are rooted in the formation of these monsters. Do not let the monsters fool you into believing that you are the problem. Let me explain that concept a little more by telling you about the ways monsters attempt to ghost us through what I refer to as "monstrous internalization."

MONSTROUS INTERNALIZATION

When we focus our attention on these students' stories, we get a picture of monstrous internalization. We see and possibly relate to how the monsters ghost us. Monsters are the structures that attack our sovereignty and belonging. Hauntings are the conditions that pathologize the challenges to the people. Shaped by monsters and their hauntings, monstrous internalization is the beliefs, behaviors, attitudes, and feelings that diminish our brilliance and sacredness. For example, the financial hardship monster, rooted in settler colonialism, confronted students on a daily basis. Structure attacking. A majority (seven) of the students grew up with a single mother for most of their lives, which impacted the financial standing of their family. In these examples, the monsters (rooted in settler colonialism and assimilation) remain steadfast when Native families do not reflect White patriarchal family structures. Hauntings. Sarah, Mike, and Joy knew that their mothers could not afford much and were doing their best to make ends meet, so they learned not to ask for things. They also internalized fears of college affordability and fears of not being able to care for their family. Monstrous internalization of fear.

What I had not anticipated but became apparent in our discussions was the teasing and racial tensions that occur. For the reservation students, they did not look Native enough and were tormented for that. After Jessie shared experiences of constantly being teased, she remarked, "It makes me feel bad about myself." And then Wesley formed strong views around disassociating himself from being identified as a Native American. Both Jessie and Wesley felt cynical about their Native community. Hauntings and monstrous internalization. Trust was broken as they both experienced hurtful treatment from their Navajo peers. This is an example of the complexity of personhood, such that "all people are 'beset by contradiction'; they recognize and misrecognize themselves and others" (Gordon, 1997, p. viii). Eve Tuck (2009) also explains this as desired research, in that "desire-based frameworks are concerned with understanding complexity, contradiction, and the self-determination of lived lives" (p. 416). These students speak back to the often narrow framing of Native peoples, as well as the hurt that we cause to ourselves and each other. We must remember that.

For the students who lived off the Navajo Reservation, they looked Native based on their non-Native peers' perceptions (the White gaze) and were therefore ridiculed and humiliated. Hauntings. Chris and Cecilia provided vivid stories of how they were confronted with racist remarks and actions. The detrimental effects of the deficit (not enough) monster are illustrated by the fact that students like Jessie and Cecilia contemplated suicide and most of these students questioned their identity and connection within their family, community, and society. Hauntings register the harm inflicted by the White gaze, which have for centuries created and manifested what is and is not a Native person—stereotypes largely based on skin color, dehumanizing behaviors, and historicized notions of savagery. Hauntings are hypervisible but remain unseen. Monstrous internalization is what we tell ourselves based on the hauntings from the systemic monsters.

The playbook that I want you to know about is that there is a pattern to monstrous internalization. Know the pattern so you can become aware of how the monsters operate in our lives. Also, by knowing the pattern, we can do our best *not* to get distracted by their game plan. I came across Toni Morrison's quote on distractions, which helped me begin to understand the pervasive ways that monstrous internalization operates. Morrison stated in a 1975 speech at Portland State University:

> The function, the very serious function of racism, is distraction.
> It keeps you from doing your work. It keeps you explaining, over
> and over again, your reason for being. Somebody says you have no
> language, and you spend twenty years proving that you do. Somebody
> says your head isn't shaped properly, so you have scientists working
> on the fact that it is. Somebody says you have no art, so you dredge
> that up. Somebody says you have no kingdoms, so you dredge that up.
> None of this is necessary. There will always be one more thing.

Brayboy and Chin (2020) offer another explanation by extending on Toni Morrison's work and connecting distractions to deficits. They write, "Deficit narratives distract in order to preserve racial hierarchies that put Black, Brown, and Red peoples in our 'proper place' set out by white supremacy and colonization. Deficit is linked to a hierarchy of domination. Violence maintains the racial status quo, defining belonging through the hierarchy that entitles whites, disinherits Indigeneity, and displaces Blackness" (Brayboy & Chin, 2020, p. 25).

Once I learned how monstrous internalizations were related to distractions and deficits, I wanted to scare the ghosts away. Isn't that a powerful thought—we can scare the ghosts too. Distractions are a violent function of racism. I would add that settler colonialism and assimilation also want us to be distracted. Because if we are distracted by the monsters and their hauntings, we can't fully fight for presence and the connection to the land and our lifeways. Do not let the monsters scare you, for if we learn to recognize and see monsters and the ways they are working together in us, our fear is not paralyzing; instead, we see clarity in our own power, in our sovereignty, and in our own sense of belonging.

Power is our sovereignty, our ability to live according to the ways that our ancestors lived, to follow in the ways of beauty and balance, and to know that we belong to this land. Like the Twin Warriors, we have Indigenous weapons that have been passed down from your grandmother, and your grandmothers' grandmother, and on and on—generations of intelligence and brilliance. Monsters haunt. But weapons protect, defend, shield, care for, and watch. Weapons watch.

WATCHINGS OF INDIGENOUS WEAPONS

Indigenous weapons watch, and watching is something else, simple and yet powerful, ready and steady to defend and protect and uphold Indigenous presence. Indigenous weapons are what Glen Coulthard calls grounded normativity, which is "the modalities of Indigenous land-connected practices and longstanding experiential knowledge that inform and structure our ethical engagements with the world and our relationships with human and nonhuman others over time" (2014, p. 13). Similarly, Indigenous weapons and grounded normativity are in community with Django Paris and H. Samy Alim's views on cultural sustaining pedagogies that ask of us the important question, "What knowledges must we sustain in order to overcome and survive when faced with a power that seeks to sustain itself above and beyond—and sometimes shot through—our bodies?" (Paris & Alim, 2017, p. 14). What weapons must we hold tightly, care for, and share lovingly with our future generations? Indigenous weapons are knowledges and ethical engagements that are rooted in Navajo ways of knowing of k'é (land and relational based) that support Navajo students' survivance and reawaken the power and sovereignty of Indigenous presence and belonging in college settings and society.

Indigenous weapons have a powerful way of getting to the core of life lessons, particularly on Native students' journeys toward college. To understand and employ these weapons means to reach a deeper level of motivation and thought. Resurgence is love-centered and instills the action to rise, to enact the Diné axiology of love for family, others, and the land. Love in this way gets us up. Continuance is to push forward when armed with life-centered, matrilineal teachings of birth and life that reinforce k'é (kinship; relation based) and story sharing. Life in this way gets us going. I caution that Indigenous weapons should not be misinterpreted as following the American illusionary dream rhetoric, where individuals achieve success if they "pull themselves up by their bootstraps." Rather, weapons of resurgence and continuance possess inherent axiology and pedagogical knowledges and engagements that are woven into community perseverance through love, hope, k'é, intelligence, stories, and expansive relations. When the weapons of resurgence and continuance are bundled together— as woven knowledges—we see, feel, act, and come to know our Indigenous presence. Now, let me tell you about the bundling, woven knowledges as watchful.

History as Relevancy—Older Than Monsters

While the monsters are centuries old, much older than you, me, and your grandparents, Indigenous weapons are much, much older and wiser. They have been passed from generation to generation since time immemorial. Since then, they have grown and developed into much beauty and brilliance. Retold, reimagined, repracticed, reexplained, and relived, reliving. Indigenous weapons are encoded in the songs that we sing, activated in the prayers that are sent, ignited in dancing and playing, and rebirthed on each rising sun. Indigenous weapons are not created by only humans—no, they are much more significant than our limited knowledge and understanding. They have been formed and informed by animal nations, plant nations, water nations, the universe, and holy beings. An abundance of knowledges and technologies are encrypted into Indigenous weapons.

Unlike the monsters, Indigenous weapons honor and respect history as timeless. They are wise to understand that there are as many teachings in historical, present, and future struggle as there are teachings embedded in sorrow and joy. That is why stories are told and retold. There is an investment in the retelling and restorying. You are the investment. With each generation, family members sharpen their weapons based on the relevancy and occurrences of and in the interval. Then, they show and tell the next generation about ways they approached the monsters, equipping them for their battle. Our people are ingenious; they know that history is connected to the present. And that the present is connected to the future. Clairvoyant geniuses.

Intelligence and Agency Flow Through Relationships

Higher education scholars and leaders often indicate that economic gain is a leading motivation for students to go to college. That may be the case for some Native students. Yet for most of these students, their driving purpose for attending college was largely for the good of others and to take care of their home(lands). Relationships matter. These intentions underscored the compelling prominence that interconnectedness (relationships) with community and family have on Native students' college attainment. Caring for others is the foundation for a collective sense of justice. The Santa Clara Pueblo scholar Gregory Cajete (2000) stated, "Ultimately, Indigenous leadership was about commitment to nurturing a healthy community. . . . Leaders were predisposed to care deeply and imagine richly with regard to their people" (p. 90). In essence, these students were aware of the difficult conditions that were plaguing them, their family, and their society. With that predisposed knowledge, they were motivated by leadership intentions for the advancement of their community. They looked beyond themselves and thought of ways to move forward for others.

Students also found strength in having trusting relationships with others, and within that connection, vulnerability and intelligence were shared. Simpson (2017) regards relationships as a place for intelligence to develop. Again, that is a powerful teaching to reflect on: the relationships that we share with others and the land provides us with a wealth of knowledge, and that knowledge is reciprocated. By disclosing hardships, sacrifices, fears, and doubts with trusted others, students felt connected, supported, and empowered—restored—to get up (resurgence) and keep going (continuance). Grandmothers shared historical hardship stories and experiential life lessons and served as confidantes as students dealt with private and traumatic experiences. Mothers unselfishly sacrificed time and resources for students, alleviating fearful thoughts of the future. Mothers and grandmothers shared stories about their past and present struggles and served as examples of what was possible. Trust was built between the student and the person who was sharing (grandmother, mother, or teacher). And then students felt safe to disclose their personal hardships with them. Stories served, as Bryan Brayboy articulated, as "roadmaps for our communities" (2005, p. 427). There is an investment in restorying. The investment is you.

Indigenous weapons allow us to make connections with others across waters. I am thinking about our Māori relatives in New Zealand. We are related to them and share intelligence and agency. I am also thinking about our relations with Blacks, Asians, Latinx, and queer/trans/two-spirit beings who are in battle too. In each part of this world, we have relations who are facing monsters and their hauntings generated by White supremacy, capitalism, and heteropatriarchy. We must cultivate those relationships, lock arms, and develop global weaponry.

Ancestral and Memory Knowledge

When I return to the Twin Warriors story, I deepen my understanding and learn something new. That is why repetition, remembering, and returning are critical to the way we do things, the way we learn, and the way we teach. Through my most recent reconnection with the Twin Warriors story, I became more aware that there were many ancestors who helped the twins defeat the monsters. We know the incredible role of Spider Woman. Father Sun, messengers, Wind, Sun's daughter, gopher, and many more elements and beings that guided the twins. They sent prayers, whispered tips, warned, and fooled the monsters. How amazing it is to gain ancestral knowledge from the wind? Take a moment to sit with that. What can we learn if we pay attention to our more than human relatives?

The writer and professor bell hooks emphasized learning through the senses that was taught to her by her grandmother. She (2009) wrote:

> I want to share the aesthetic inheritance handed down to me by my grandmother and generations of black ancestors, whose ways of thinking about the issue have been globally shaped in the African diaspora and informed by the

experience of exile and domination. I want to reiterate the message that "we must learn to see." (p. 132)

Seeing here is metaphysically, as heightened awareness and understanding, the intensification of one's capacity to experience, reality through the realm of the senses (hooks, 2009). Ancestral knowledges are beyond learning from text and orality that is too often emphasized in schooling. It's seeing the unseen, feeling the untouched, tasting the flavorless, hearing the silence, and believing the unbelievable. This type of learning is metaphysical, spiritual, and sometimes laughable, meaning what is learned seems so unreal to be true. But it is real and true, as bell hooks describes, its aesthetic inheritance, and hózhó (beauty and balance) taught to us by our ancestors and the Creator.

With that understanding, there is respect in knowing that ancestral knowledge carries much memory. Whereas monsters tend to dislodge from context and relationships, a way of turning away from remembrance, ancestral knowledge holds memory and weaves it throughout. Repetition helps to retain memory. Repetition is in our songs, prayers, the telling of stories during specific seasons, and in names and naming. Memories coexist with life and survival. Not only do human beings carry memories, but so do the land and water, so do the birds and butterflies. They all remember what was and what is occurring.

It is important, then, to remember and recognize that those ancestral knowledges are within us. And it is our responsibility to carry on the legacy into the present and into the next generations. Our ancestors have generously shared their wisdom, struggles, secrets, and stories with us if we pay attention. Some of us may lose our elders earlier than we anticipate, or we may have elders who may not share openly, but that does not mean that lessons are not being taught. Sometimes I think we can get caught up in thinking that our elders are not doing enough, but before we get distracted by the deficit (not enough) monster, we must keep our eye on the teachings that are everywhere and occurring all the time if we pay attention. Remember that we must learn to see, as hooks indicated earlier, by taking the responsibility to learn and teach the knowledge gained to the present and the next generation. Ancestral knowledges are then a way of becoming, a learning process that embodies a future space that honors history and opens a way to look forward.

Inherent Sovereignty

The 10 students I spoke with activated the weapons of resurgence and continuance many times. They were top academic students who played on competitive athletic teams, took advantage of college readiness opportunities, and applied to high-stakes scholarships. They revealed powerful gifts that they had within them. Before they were equipped with college readiness opportunities, these students already possessed sophisticated attributes of initiation, intelligence, and selflessness. Advanced Placement (AP) courses were more available at most off-reservation schools, and three of the four students were enrolled in those academically rigorous classes and earned high scores. At reservation schools that offered college access programs, these students participated in them, which exemplified their efforts to carve out time and seize opportunities to be stronger college contenders. And for students like Lauryn, who did not have college access programs at her school, she did not let that disadvantage stall her. She applied to an Ivy League university, a prestigious and very competitive university. Several other students also applied to top universities. Wesley applied to two Ivy League institutions. Amber applied to one Ivy League school. Six applied for the Gates Millennium Scholarship. Six students already have visions to receive a doctorate degree.

These students had the courage to challenge themselves, particularly when opportunities aligned with their future goals of college attainment. Native students are too often viewed as a "deficit," but in these students' experiences, they were poised to excel. They remind us that when we move beyond the status quo, we unveil the impressive gifts that we have within. They remind us to live accordingly as sovereigns and in our sovereignty. Sovereignty is not viewed as domination, ruling over others as how the bilagáana (White people) think and act. Sovereignty is what Lee (2017) states:

> To have the absolute freedom to think freely, to believe and practice the ways we choose, to fend for our family and people in our terms. Sovereignty is a matter of life and soul. It is a matter of attitude; it is what we make of it. Defined by the here and will of the people. (p. 163)

I have also learned that sovereignty is to be in true relationships with others, to share and proceed with an ethic of love. Some have said that from a Navajo perspective, the rainbow is a symbol of sovereignty. A rainbow is a meteorological phenomenon that is caused by the reflection, refraction, and dispersion of light in water droplets, resulting in a spectrum of light appearing in the sky. Rainbows provide an array of illuminated colors and richness, detailing the depth and vastness of our natural world. Rainbows symbolize acceptance and love among lesbian, gay, bisexual, transgender, and queer/questioning (LGBTQ) communities. Rainbows also symbolize presence, promises, and compassion. For the Twin Warriors, the rainbow was a pathway, a conduit toward the future, a transporter toward fighting against injustice. Sovereignty as a rainbow means presence and reflection, understanding our relationship with the natural world, a deep regard and acceptance for the multitude of being Navajo, a fullness in pursuing forward for freedom, justice, and love. We are born with sovereignty.

SURVIVING THE FIRST YEAR

REVERENCE: THE COURAGE TO FACE "FAILURE"

Failure Monster

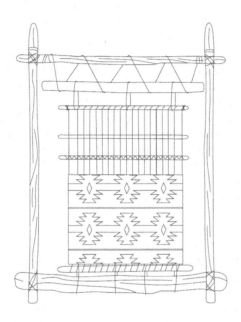

Sam would be considered another negative statistic by several educators, but he is more than a number. Sam stood over six feet tall, with broad shoulders and a medium-built frame. He regularly wore faded blue jeans, a basic one-color T-shirt (usually blue or white), and casual white athletic shoes. He grew up understanding the value of a dollar, hustling for cash when he was a middle schooler, so he did not pay much attention to purchasing and wearing name-brand attire. As he pulled on the tongue of one of his white sneakers, he looked up at me and said: "You can just get a decent pair of shoes and just keep them clean. You don't need Nikes. They're made of the same material, just different logos." He made sense, and I wondered where this perspective was coming from. It was not often that I heard a teenager, let alone a Navajo teenager, talk about not needing or wanting Nikes. Sam made me curious, and I was looking forward to learning more from him. With a sly smile, he sat back in his chair and brushed something off his jeans. I sensed that he took pride in his appearance. He maintained a clean-cut and easy look, with hair that was closely trimmed to an uncomplicated crew cut. Simple, convenient, and reasonable for a new college freshman who frequently worried about money.

Sam grew up in a large urban city. The "jewel" of the family, he was also the oldest, with two brothers and 16 cousins. He sensed the pressure of being the oldest son from his mother and his extended family. Pressure to do well, to succeed, to not mess up. Pressure that stems from the absence of a father in his own life and not wanting to manifest that pattern, of messing up, of being absent, of being like his dad. Sam was raised by a "strong" single mom, aunts and uncles who frequently stayed with his family when they were working on getting their life back on track, and a nearby Black church that he attended for nearly 12 years. Much of Sam's family depended on his mother. She was the person who helped loved ones get through tough times by regularly opening her home to her siblings when they struggled with finances and/or substance abuse. Sometimes their home contained up to 10 people (including Sam's uncles, aunts, and cousins) squeezed in a modest, two-bedroom apartment. At an early age, Sam learned a lot about hardship and love. He witnessed his uncles and aunts battle with alcohol and drug addictions. He still held them in the highest regard because he loved them.

And that love was reciprocated. Sam sat back in his chair comfortably and began telling me of the many times his uncles and aunts were present in his life. He looked up at the ceiling and reminisced about stories of when he embarrassed his aunt. I sat back too and listened. He shared two stories in vivid detail. One featured a time when his aunt was changing his diaper. As she was putting a fresh diaper on him, baby Sam looked at her with innocent eyes and peed in her mouth. He chuckled with a goofy grin on his face as he told that story, a playful story that must have been passed down to him. He roared with laughter in that remembrance. He considered that aunt his second mom.

Suddenly, while he was telling me stories of his aunt, he started crying. Teardrops and red blotches began to form around his eyes. I was caught off guard. It was rare for me to see a young Navajo man show vulnerability. I sat near him, gave him some Kleenex, and allowed his tears to flow while at the same time, I was trying my best to hold in my own tears. I said a silent prayer to myself: Be strong, Mandy, be strong. I understood how thinking about the past can sometimes open up emotions. That's love, and sometimes hurt, all mixed up, intertwined, and exposed. And I needed to be strong for Sam—that's the Navajo woman and mother in me.

I was beginning to see Sam. He exposed much depth and love. My heart was receptive. He continued to share story after story of how much his family shaped him. His aunts and uncles walked him to school on a regular basis, bought him goodies with their food stamps, and believed in him when he felt like others denied him. In tears, Sam shared, "Family is everything . . . all I need is my family. My family, they all want to see me shine. They believe in me, so family is basically my world." We all need family who want to see us shine. And we should all be the type of people to support the shine in others. That's what I learned from Sam.

Sam attended urban schools where there were very few other Native students. He was a smart and generous kid, so much so that classmates often asked for his help with their schoolwork. From elementary and into high school, Sam assisted others. He told me that he "helped some get through school" by the amount of assistance he provided. Then, in middle school, Sam became a bona fide entrepreneur. He started a business with only $5 start-up money that his mom gave him. He sold Mexican candy out of his backpack. In his first year of business, he made $750, and in his second year, he made over $1,000. Each morning, he stuffed a military backpack with sweet and sour lollipops and an array of treats. He estimated that he sold about 75% of his goodies on hand each day. He kept track of all the transactions in a little book, tallying how much money he earned and spent. With the money he made, he would buy more candy to sell, put a little bit of tidings in the offering plate on Sundays at church, and save some candy for himself to enjoy later. He described himself as a "successful nerd" because of the work he was doing academically and with his growing business. In high school, he tried to continue his business, but competition from other students (who had also started their personal candy stores) stalled his work. He could not compete with their more expensive candy options and decided to close his business.

Because of his entrepreneurial venture, Sam got to know many students at school, which expanded his friendship circle. During the lunch hour, Sam roamed the school grounds, talking with classmates near the cafeteria, and then ventured outside and stopped by to catch up with classmates sitting on the bench, then walked back inside to chill with others in the hallways. Sam knew many students, and they knew him. He was likable and good about emerging in and out of conversations. This was also the time when Sam began drinking and smoking weed. Meeting new people opened new doors to new drinks, new smokes, the newness of it all.

Sam was also getting frustrated at home with family moving in and out. It didn't help that at home, they were dealing with a bug infestation. Sam was squeezed out of his bedroom and sleeping under the kitchen table to get some relief and privacy. Then, during the fall semester of his senior year, he got into an argument with his mom. It was the night of homecoming, and Sam wanted to go to homecoming with a girl. He wanted to spend time with this girl because he liked her. But his mom told him no and that "it was dumb." She didn't want him to be out late and probably end up partying. Sam was irritated with his mom, but even more, he was hurt by her reaction. He walked out of the house, attended homecoming, and partied. The next day, he moved in with his uncle.

Later, he began working at a fast-food restaurant. Completing senior year while working late hours and continuing to party took a toll on Sam as he prepared to go to college. Although he was upset with his mom and the struggles that they were facing, Sam loved her immensely. His mother attended college for 2 years and then stopped to care for him. With a new baby, she did not have the means to return and finish college. She knew the value of a college degree and therefore impressed on Sam that he had to go to college. Sam internalized that one of his purposes in life was to obtain a college degree, in honor of his mom's wishes and to fulfill his own aspirations. As a junior in high school, he identified Big State University as his top choice because of its land-grant research status and distinguished aerospace program. A high school counselor guided him by questioning him, "What are your fields of interest?" and "What schools are you thinking about applying to?" Aside from basic questions like those, Sam applied and was accepted to Big State without further assistance from his counselor, or anyone else for that matter. He was confident that he would be admitted to Big State and knew that it was the only place he wanted to go. Therefore, he did not apply to any other colleges. Sam was invited to apply to the honors college, a privileged and prestigious college within Big State. But after learning that he would have to write a 500-word essay, he declined the offer.

During his last year in high school, Sam juggled a hectic schedule that included working late shifts at the restaurant. Consequently, devoting time to scholarship hunting was not a priority. He began to slip into a disruptive lifestyle and described that time as "working, going home, smoking, working, going home, smoking, same process, every day, try to party at least every Friday night. I did the bad life thing." Sam confessed that he was "lazy," which resulted in completing most of his college paperwork at the last minute and not sending out scholarship applications.

He was admitted to Big State University and was even invited to apply to the honors college. This means that Sam was brilliant. This makes sense, given that he had a strong high school record, took and passed several Advanced Placement (AP) courses, helped classmates get through school, and even created his own business when he was 12 years old. He lived in tough conditions, saw much love and strife with his family, and hustled his way through. Yet, he did not apply for scholarships, nor did he pursue the invitation to take part in the honors college.

Sam's story matters. Many would easily stamp his lack of effort in seeking opportunities, such as not applying to the honors college and scholarships, as problematic, potentially prone to failure, and even another individual negative statistic. These are the generations-old ideologies brought forth from the *deficit (not enough) monster,* as Natives have been historically framed as an impediment to progress, framed as savages with biological deficiencies that held the advancement of the White order of dominance, possession, and paternalism. Hauntings.

Too often, what is then erased from the narrative of Native peoples is the brilliance and intelligence that Native peoples offer. And too often, what is erased are the systemic faults. We can see the arrival of the third monster, which I refer to as the *failure monster,* which prominently appeared as the 10 students began their first year in college. But let me be clear—the failure monster began when the settlers stamped us as failures on their meritocratic and capitalist terms, and the system still applies that failure stamp with a heavy hand. The failure monster is also a close partner to the *financial hardship monster* and the *deficit (not enough) monster.* Monsters are related and therefore work together to question, disenfranchise, and oppress Native peoples.

When settlers came to these lands, many already believed that our Native people were inferior to them. "Indian life, it was argued, constituted a lower order of human society. In a word, Indians were savages because they lacked the very thing whites possessed—civilization" (Adams, 1995, p. 6). Recall that civilization to them meant assimilation (deficit [not enough] monster) and having possession of lands (settler colonialism; financial hardship monster). The settlers didn't realize that our thinking and being is not about possession, but rather about loving and caring for our relatives, and that includes the land, waterways, more than human relatives, and the divine. Civilization for us is having an advanced state of consciousness of love and relationality. For them, civilization meant that our ancestors were inferior according to their way of life, a failure by their meritocratic standards, "savages," and thereby merely resources to accelerate capitalist desires. In other words, they felt that the so-called savages did not deserve to thrive and prosper.

In the 16th century, Pierre d'Avity formulated a quasi-scientific research experiment to prove that Natives were indeed savages (Dickason, 1984). Unsurprisingly, the results did label Natives as "savages," which meant that our relatives were identified as uncivilized, untamed, and potentially barbaric. These measures were created and then analyzed by non-Natives, with a White consciousness that began formulating who does and who does not belong. There are foundational understandings of the "failure" of Native people to meet standards of Whiteness or to meet normative constructions, or the ability to meet those standards and yet still be deemed as failures.

Recall that meritocracy is a political system that privileges and advances individuals based on their talent, effort, and achievement, which is often determined and created by non-Native thought and perspectives. Therefore, meritocracy seems to act as a fair way to offer opportunity to individual citizens, but in many ways, meritocracy serves only the privileged.

The third monster, the failure monster, has its roots in meritocracy and capitalism and operates in two ways: (1) to create what I am calling *ideological convergence* of failure on Indigenous peoples. Ideological convergence is a body of ideas imposed on a group (example: the failure of Native peoples) that are false and harmful, but in actuality come from those who constructed those ideas (example: systems failed Native peoples). Thus, the failure monster is sneaky by flipping the script. (2) The failure monster also maintains heteropatriarchal paternalism that profits from Indigenous lifeways. By flipping the script, the financial monster abuses and uses Indigenous peoples while simultaneously benefiting from that destruction. Then, the financial monster in turn creates a culture of fear and a distorted view of belonging.

The failure monster was most prominent in college settings. Not many people know that one of the first forms of educating Native people was having them attend the early colleges that were emerging in the northeast coast of what is now the United States. However, settlers needed money to support these educational strategies, so what happened? Native peoples were used to get the money. And then those resources were supposed to educate them. In fact, the very first college to be built was alleged to be an Indian college referred to as Henrico College. From 1616–1617, Sir Thomas Dale, governor of the Virginia Colony, took several Native girls to England in hopes of garnering financial support to establish the college. Pocahontas, John Rolfe, their son, and 10–12 young Native women traveled with Sir Thomas Dale and were used to attract funding for the proposed school. Pocahontas has been romantically depicted in the eponymous Disney animated movie as struck by love for the White settler John Smith. In reality, as a young girl, she was kidnapped and kept in captivity, witnessed and withstood abuse and rape, lived in fear, and likely was forced to marry Rolfe (Custalow & Daniel, 2009). She was considered a "civilized savage" and made to travel to England to garner monies for new settlers' pleas and desires. Pocahontas was used for the benefit of Whites. With the exploitation of Native women, funding was generated to start the construction of Henrico College, an example of the financial hardship monster. Over 1,000 acres of land were seized from Native peoples. Yet, the college was never built. The capital received was misused and redirected elsewhere to support the Virginia Colony. Native women worked and sacrificed their lives for the advancement of a White male society. Let me be clear that during this era, only male students were allowed to attend college, distinguishing patriarchy and paternalism (fathers make the decision) as the prominent structure. Pocahontas and the other Native women were simply used to support male-dominated educational systems.

Harvard College, founded in 1636, rewrote its charter in 1650 to include Native students in "the education of the English and Indian youth of this country in knowledge and godliness" (Carney, 1999, p. 1). Donors such as the Boyle Fund gave Harvard 200 pounds and an additional 45 pounds yearly for Native education and missionary work. In addition, grants were awarded to Harvard in 1651 for the building of a hall to house an Indian college. The Indian college building was completed in 1656 to house 20 students; however, the first Native student did not arrive until 1660, and in the 40 years of its existence, only 4 Native students resided in the building. Instead, the Indian college building served White students and the campus printing press (Carney, 1999). Monies that were allocated for Native students were again misused. In all, Harvard continued to accrue funds for

Native education, but it enrolled only a total of 6 Native students prior to the revolutionary period (nearly a century after the 1650 charter!), with 4 of the 6 enrolled while the Indian college was established from 1656–1693. Similar histories also occurred at multiple colleges like William & Mary and Dartmouth (Carney, 1999; Wright & Tierney, 1991).

What is also not discussed enough is that, while early college leaders were harming and exploiting Native peoples, they were also enslaving thousands upon thousands of Black people. Monies generated from the purchasing and selling of Black bodies helped to build these colleges (Wilder, 2013). Indigenous land, Black labor, and lives lost were the building blocks of the higher education system in the United States. We must recognize the ways that the systemic monsters also harm and influence others.

Nearly 200 years passed, and only five Native students graduated with a college degree despite the significant amount of money allocated to the early elite institutions of higher education. The ongoing and prevailing view held by White settlers was that Native people were problematic, unable to succeed in college, expensive and wasteful of support dollars, and doomed to failure (Adams, 1995). Yet, the lack of Native peoples receiving a college degree was a success for Native people—especially given that those institutions were ill equipped to prepare them for life and designed by and for White settlers on the backs of Black and Brown peoples. Nevertheless, the failure monster worked to stamp Natives as failures, paying little attention to the ways that the higher education institutions failed and used them over and over for selfish desires—that is the ideological convergence in progress.

Across the lands on the western end, our Navajo people were not introduced to college until the mid-1900s. White settlers were growing in number and encroaching on our people and home(lands). This also meant that capitalist practices were invading Navajo livelihoods. Once a community that thrived on a subsistence economy that honored relationships and the land, our people were feeling pressure to change and adapt to a capitalist, wage-earned economic structure. Coal, uranium, and other mineral industries began targeting the rich minerals and waterways that were nestled on Diné Bikéyah (Navajo land). Diné geographer Andrew Curley describes the coal-energy-water nexus as "colonial beachheads—a temporal encroachment on Indigenous lands and livelihoods, over time, to augment material and political difference that eventually overwhelms Indigenous nations and curtails certain possibilities" (Curley, 2021, p. 2). These infrastructures and technologies exacerbate the structures of settler colonialism and capitalism. They are the hauntings of systemic monsters.

Large, extractive companies did not understand ways to work with our people, especially in negotiating for the precious resources of the earth. Rather than taking the time to learn Navajo ways, these companies couched White business views and principles as the only way to negotiate. This is a typical habit for the United States, asserting White dominance in thought and practices in business, education, law, policies, and lifeways; and this reinforces normative behaviors about "how things are always done," subjugating other forms of knowledge and practices as inferior, unacceptable. Since many of our people did not have an understanding of White peoples' style of negotiation, non-Natives were hired to help our people negotiate lease agreements, draft up legal documents, and execute transactions between the Navajo Nation and large corporations.

During the 1930s and 1940s, Navajo leaders experienced the need for Navajo people to be college educated so they could help safeguard the Navajo Nation from the growing capitalist interest of persistent companies and outside influencers. Education was not solely meant for individual Navajo people to be self-sufficient (meritocratic values) and gain in economic returns (capitalism), as the bilagáana (White people) often view the purpose for higher education. Rather, higher education was viewed largely as a tool to fight settler colonialism, to fight the financial hardship monster, and to fight capitalist desires that stripped land and people apart. Education could be used to maintain and strengthen Tribal sovereignty and community well-being, examples of Indigenous weapons of *resurgence* and *continuance*.

In 1946, the Navajo Tribal Council outlined major problems facing the Navajo people and shared these concerns with the federal government. Education was the most important priority: "Education is our greatest need. There are no schools for over 14,000 of our children. Our people are now very poor. Our children must have a good education if they are to learn to support themselves. . . . without education we cannot compete with the white man anywhere" (Iverson, 2002, p. 89). World War II had ended, and many of our people had served in the armed forces to protect not just the United States, but also Diné Bikéyah (Navajo land) and our people. Our Diné language also served as an unbreakable strategy during World War II, as Navajo men developed and utilized an encrypted code in Diné to transmit sensitive information. This effort helped the United States expedite the end of the war and saved thousands of lives (Tohe, 2021). Diné language—the savage language forbidden in boarding schools, colonial colleges, and non-Native society—saved thousands of lives and helped the United States prevail in the worldwide war against fascism.

Your great-great grandfather, my great-grandfather, Johnny R. Manuelito, was a code talker. A few years ago, your grandfather handed me a blue box. He did not say a word but motioned for me to open it. I opened the box carefully and saw the medal that your great-great grandfather received for his work. I looked at my dad and felt the emotions that he was holding in. He was proud of his dad, always has been, and always will be. Your cheii (maternal grandfather) even enrolled in the army to follow in his father's footsteps when he graduated from high school. He wanted to carry on the legacy of his father, the code talker.

Your older cousin, my sweet nephew, is now serving for our country, for Diné Bikéyah, for us. Many people do not realize that our language helped to save the country. Many people do not realize that our people, your family, continue to help and protect the country, the country that took much from our people. Your great-grandfather was not able to attend college, but he saved countless lives. I share this personal story to remind you that while systemic monsters have worked against us for hundreds of years, our relatives do what they can to care for many. That is love and life centered, evident in our Indigenous weapons.

With the end of the war, hundreds of Navajos returned home hoping for a good life. This was a time of transition for our people. Navajo leaders and our people were more affirmed to stop state and federal governments from taking advantage of our relatives—born of a legacy of appropriating, stealing, lying, converging, and mistreating our people (and others) in the guise of democracy and progress. Our people had just undergone years of turmoil over the killing of their livestock due to the federal government's livestock reduction policies, and they also had their young men give their time and lives to fight for the country. Not to mention that new forms of economic, capitalist developments were encroaching on Navajo life (Iverson, 2002). Twenty-three Navajo representatives traveled to Washington, D.C., to speak to congressional representatives about education matters for the Navajo people. The late Navajo leader Chee Dodge affirmed that the federal government had to honor the 1868 treaty by addressing education as "our gravest need" (Iverson, 2002, p. 191). Nearly a century had passed since the signing of the 1868 treaty, when our relatives returned from Hwéeldih, and the United States was not meeting its treaty obligations.

I am so proud of our Diné people because despite the frustrations, hurt, anger, and failures of the federal government, our people continue to find ways to keep going (continuance). That is Diné strength. In 1953, the Navajo leader Sam Ahkeah helped to lead the campaign for higher education. Navajo Nation leaders knew that they needed medical doctors, lawyers, engineers, and other professionals to care for the lands and people of Diné Bikéyah. Our Navajo people knew that advanced degrees were needed. Our Navajo people didn't see us as a deficit. Our Navajo elders knew that we were not failures. Therefore, the Navajo Tribal Council established a special fund of $30,000 to support Navajos who pursued higher education. The fund became the Navajo Tribal Scholarship Program, which provided 35 grants in its first year. Ahkeah stated that he looked forward to the time when "we would not have to depend on white people all the time" (Iverson, 2002, p. 197). The Navajo people were on their way to building a nation of college-educated Diné.

History tells us that the failure monster thrives by placing the blame on Native peoples—we are considered failures, so capitalism and heteropatriarchy remain. Rather than turning the mirror on itself, the failure monster continues to live on by turning the mirror toward us and allowing us to see ourselves as the failures. We must turn the mirror around or look away.

Hauntings

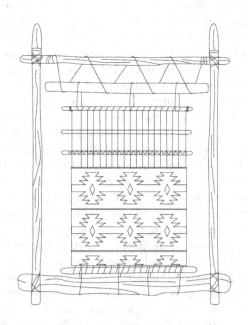

College is not free for Native students. Having formerly worked at a sports store during his senior year in high school, Mike had acquired an assortment of fashionable athletic attire. One day he wore the latest Michael Jordan basketball shoes, and then the next time I saw Mike, he wore old-school Allen Iverson blue and white kicks. Mike made a point to coordinate his shoes with his entire outfit, as if the shoes drove the corresponding attire. He often wore colored tank tops that matched a sports team cap and casual athletic shorts. And of course, the look was polished off by the shoes. The apparel connected with his commitment to be physically active. A competitive athlete, Mike took part in competitive sports (basketball and track and field) in high school, where he played in several state-level championship games. Mike described himself as a "keep-to-myself person" and "hard-headed." He explained that "hard-headed" meant being the type of person that when he wanted something, he would do "whatever I can to get it." A college degree was one such goal that he was driven to achieve.

Growing up with a single mom who struggled financially to support him and their homestead, he wanted to get a college degree and then one day care for his mom and future family. Mike grew up in a very small community on the Navajo reservation called Little Fields. Mike believed that his family valued caring for others. His late cheii (maternal grandfather) was respected in the community of Little Fields for serving the people. Occasionally, when Mike met elders in the community of Little Fields, they would ask him who his grandparents were as a way to get to know him. When Mike shared his grandfather's name, a warm smile would form on the elders' faces, followed by an acknowledgment that they knew his grandpa because he had once helped them or a relative in the past. Caring for others was also ingrained in his mom, as she often opened her home to relatives who needed a place to stay, sometimes for extended periods of time. Therefore, Mike, an only child, grew up with extended family members coming and going in their home. At the time of these interviews, Mike's mother moved in with his másání (maternal grandmother), who was battling Alzheimer's disease. Although as a family they struggled financially, they always had a warm meal and a home to care for.

In school, Mike described himself as a "teacher's pet." He explained to me that although some people would consider being teacher's pet as an "insult," he considered it a "compliment." I liked that because he was already deconstructing the commonly held views of a teacher's pet, making me more aware of how he sees the world. A hard-working student, he pushed himself to ask questions in class and study material "even when I didn't need to," and he enjoyed reading books. Mike attended Yellow Tree Elementary, which is located just a few miles from the Navajo Nation border, from kindergarten to 6th grade. He valued the fact that his mom placed him in private schools because he felt like he received a good education attending Yellow Tree. Mike attended two middle schools, one located on the reservation (in 7th grade) and then during 8th grade, he went off the reservation for school. During this time, Mike developed a temper, but he recognized that he was steering himself in the wrong direction; eventually, with guidance from his mom, he decided to transfer to an off-reservation high school.

He attended Hawk High School (located about 150 miles from his home) for 9th and 10th grades. During his freshman year, he lived with a friend, and then in 10th grade, he resided in a boarding facility provided by the school for students who lived far from home. Mike advanced academically at Hawk High School. For example, he was recognized for being the only student to pass more than six math exams without missing a single question. His work ethic was paying off, and it was something that he was proud of. Yet the cost of living away from home was too much for his mom. Mike was going to need to attend a school that was closer to home.

During 11th and 12th grade, he went to Fountain Springs High School, a different off-reservation high school approximately 60 miles from his home.

Still about an hour drive to and from school, Mike commuted daily to the neighboring city to attend school. He had heard stories and also experienced negative circumstances in 8th grade when he attended an on-reservation school, so he and his mom thought it was best if he made the daily commute to Fountain Springs.

Growing up, he did not have the luxury of buying items that he wanted. He heard stories that if people went to college, they got "paid," meaning that scholarship funds would be plentiful and he would not have to worry about money. These stories are pervasive among non-Natives and then sometimes also seep into the minds of Native people such as Mike. Hauntings. There is a myth that Natives go to college for free. What Mike did not know is that stories that "college is free" for Natives are constructed from history and racist attitudes toward Native people. You see, many think that Natives live off of the government—health care is free, education is free, homes are free, etc. Yet, these are fictions that at their root attempt to problematize Native peoples as insufficient, overreliant on the government, and incapable of self-sufficiency: failures. Simply put, in this telling Natives are lazy, wasteful, and a burden. These are examples of hauntings, the lingering lies that monsters create. Many of us Natives know that those ideas are false, and I see them as hauntings born out of systemic monsters. Yet, those hauntings are dismissed, unmentioned, and invisible. Systemic monsters cunningly slip away.

As a young kid, he daydreamed about one day having a fancy car and nice clothes. College would be a way for him to purchase nice things. As Mike matured, accumulating wealth was not the only reason why he wanted to go to college. He wanted to help his community and family. In particular, he wanted to help his mom. As a sophomore, he began picking up college pamphlets and then researched more about what those schools offered. Then, in his junior year, he grew more serious about the schools he would consider applying to. During his senior year, he eventually applied to 12 schools, a handful out of state and the rest in state. He was interested in becoming a graphic designer or an architect. Because of his interest in sports, he dreamed of one day creating his own athletic shoes. Mike was a dreamer, a visionary. I enjoyed listening to him talk about his thoughts on the future. As a young kid, he daydreamed and saw himself in the future. As a teenager, that visionary spirit remained. I silently hoped that he would not lose that imagination.

From the 12 colleges that he applied to, there were two schools that he had his eyes and heart set on. One school, Big State University, was his "superior" choice because it was not too close to home, but still near enough that he could be home in a day's drive if needed. Big State was known for its basketball team and, as a young kid, Mike often wore the purple-and-black jersey. While he was waiting to hear whether he was admitted into Big State, he confessed that he was "scared" because a part of him thought he might not get accepted and thus would be considered a failure.

Although he had stellar grades and a good reputation with his teachers, the *failure monster* still found its way into Mike. Mike, an 18-year-old, was battling a monster that has gained strength, strategic maneuvering, and prominence for 5 centuries. Compounded with the fear of failing to be accepted into Big State University, Mike was concerned with the overall cost of college. His mom had the resources to ensure that they had food and a place to live, but there was little room for anything more in the budget. Mike knew that she would not be able to help him pay for college, and he didn't want her to worry and feel that she had that responsibility. Mike felt that he had to figure out how to pay for college on his own. And he admitted that he still believed in those stories about Natives going to college for free. Hauntings. So he delayed applying for scholarships. At the same time, he was eagerly anticipating whether he would be admitted into his dream college.

Then, on one unforgettable day, Mike's mom told him to check the mail at the post office. Mike approached the mailbox, inserted and turned the key, and opened the small metal door. Inside, he saw an envelope addressed to him. He took the envelope and slowly opened it. The letter stated, "Congratulations, you have been admitted to the architectural program at Big State University." Mike stood there in shock. He quickly shut and locked the mailbox door and energetically walked out of the post office, carrying the envelope. He couldn't wait to tell his mom.

When he pulled up to their house, he quickly put the chidí (vehicle) into park and ran into the house. His mom was in the kitchen when Mike entered. As soon as he saw her, he spilled out the news that he had been admitted into Big State. Mike's mom walked toward him and wrapped her arms around him. She embraced him with a long hug. She was so proud of her son. And Mike was beyond excited and grateful. Thoughts were racing in Mike's mind about what he was getting himself into. Enthusiasm and a deep sense of embracing the news sunk in.

The very next day, Mike returned to the post office to check the mail. Sitting in the mailbox was another letter addressed to him. This time, the letter congratulated him on receiving a prestigious scholarship that would help pay for his college education, and even provide him with a laptop. He was glad that he was encouraged to apply for that scholarship. Even though he had applied at the last minute, he completed the application, and now he couldn't believe that he was a recipient. Since he was a young kid, he was deliberate about schooling and demonstrated a strong work ethic. He was brilliant and deserved the scholarship. The worry of cost was slowly washing away. He couldn't wait to tell his mom the incredible news.

During the first semester of college, Mike was shocked to learn that even with the scholarship, he still owed $1,000 to Big State University. He also received four other scholarships that were based on financial need and merit. Yet, he still had a balance to pay. The $1,000 balance was a lot of money for Mike. He worried about how he was going to afford paying down that balance while also paying for food, school supplies, transportation, and living expenses. He was scared to take out a student loan. He didn't want to start creating debt, especially when he was desperately trying hard to defeat the *financial hardship monster*. Mike worked part-time to help offset living expenses. That helped a bit, but working was also a condition of two of his scholarships. I later learned that juggling school and work with the heavy weight of financial strife intensified the power of the failure monster.

Mike's situation was not unique. Of the 10 students, all but 2 (Jessie and Cecilia) were eligible for Pell Grants, meaning that they had families with a total annual income of no more than $50,000, meaning in turn that it was more difficult for them to pay off the total college cost. Moreover, when students complete their Free Application for Federal Student Aid (FAFSA) form, the Expected Family Contribution is calculated, which is the estimated amount of money that a family can contribute for college expenses. In 2015–2016, half (51%) of American Indians and Alaskan Natives who completed a FAFSA had a total of $0 Expected Family Contribution (Espinosa et al., 2019). This means that half of Native students could not afford any financial resources for college. They are most likely living paycheck to paycheck.

In 1972, a bill was passed resulting in the creation of the Pell Grant to help alleviate the burden of college costs for students who needed financial help. During the era of the 1970s, colleges had increasing enrollments and states invested resources into building and expanding public systems of higher education (Geiger, 2013). The last years of the 1970s saw the highest public investment in higher education and the highest point of access for low-income students. Today, there has been a steady decline in state investments, and in most states a sharp increase in college costs as well. Colleges are motivated by neoliberal paternalism, which is the change from supporting social services (such as Pell grants or affordable college) to leveraging individualized free markets, which see students as capital to sustain colleges. Neoliberalism "obscures the political dimensions of social problems by defining them as matters of personal choice," which also means that individuals bear the responsibility of their choice to succeed (persist in college) or fail (drop out) (Soss et al., 2011). Paternalism is connected with neoliberalism because it reinforces the belief that men (fatherlike) have the authority to make the decisions for the children (in this case, the poor, the disadvantaged). "The child, in this view, lacks the capacity to know what is in her or his best interest and has yet to develop the self-discipline needed to act effectively on such knowledge" (Soss et al., 2011, p. 23). The failure monster, rooted in capitalism and meritocracy, is in a community with neoliberal paternalism.

The Pell Grant is not nearly enough to create a strong foundation for college affordability and access—its original purpose. Every year, millions complete the FAFSA form in hopes of qualifying for Pell funding. For example, in the 2017–2018 year, 18,969,616 FAFSA applications were completed, with over half (10,719,440) determined Pell eligible. At the time of my interviews with these students, the maximum Pell funding that undergraduate students could receive was about $5,635 a year, or $2,817 a semester, which makes up roughly only about 20% of in-state college costs, leaving students with the burden of finding funds to pay the remaining 80%. For many students, every dollar counts as they try to eke out the means to pay for the rising cost of college.

Obtaining a college degree is becoming increasingly expensive for many students, especially in states where state funding cuts have soared, and especially for Native peoples, who have for centuries battled the financial hardship monster—a monster that prides itself on stealing Native land and lives (settler colonialism) while simultaneously making it difficult for many Native people to thrive financially. When states decrease higher education funding, tuition likely increases. And sometimes the tuition rises faster than the growth of the median income. For example, college tuition in Arizona nearly doubled in just 5 years after the Great Recession starting in 2008. In 2007, Arizona supported 72% of the college costs for an Arizona resident student. For the 2016–2017 academic year, the state covered 34% (Arizona Board of Regents, 2017). The burden of college was placed more heavily on students and their families, making it that much harder for students from low-income families to make ends meet in college. When nations, states, and institutions are financially struggling and finding ways to survive, they often resort in their efforts to disenfranchising the marginalized further. When the system fails, in the process, the system projects the failures unto us: ideological convergence from the failure monster.

Mike was not the only one who was concerned about resources. Most of the other students told me how difficult it was to get by. Wesley decided to live with extended family and commute daily to school as a way to save money. On top of being Pell Grant eligible, he received a university grant and the Chief Manuelito Scholarship, a prestigious scholarship funded by the Navajo Nation that paid up to $7,000 a year or $3,500 a semester. He also took out a small loan. Still, even with the various funding options offered to him, he confessed that he considered transferring because of the burden of the cost: "I mean this year so far, I am spending $20,000. I don't think I could manage $20,000 every year, $20,000 is a little out of my reach. I mean, if I transfer to a community college or something, then I'll probably be able to continue on. But for now, no doctor. It's too expensive." Wesley had aspirations of being a doctor, but those dreams were changing, and it was because of the extreme costs involved.

During the time of these interviews, the tuition and fees for attending Big State University was estimated at over $5,021 a semester, or $10,042 a year. This cost did not account for housing, food, school supplies, transportation, health insurance, personal supplies, and entertainment, which were estimated to cost another $10,000–$12,000 a year depending on each student's living needs. In total, an estimated $20,000–$22,000 a year was required for in-state students to attend Big State University.

When Sarah's mom found out the cost of attending college, she was shocked. Sarah said, "It's a lot. Oh my gosh, my mom didn't know it was $22,000 here. She was like 'What?' and she was just freaking out. . . . It's like getting a car every year." College was like getting a car every year and paying it off in that one year's time. When Sarah and I talked about that comparison, we both started laughing because the irony was too real. It was true. Attending Big State University was like buying a car every year! And since most of these students and their families made less than $50,000 a year, affording a new car, let alone paying for college each year, was nearly impossible, laughable. And that reality was reflected in the students' lives. During the first year of college, while many new freshmen are concerned about doing their schoolwork, building friendships, and acclimating to a new environment, these students felt those same concerns while also carrying the extreme weight of thinking about money, worrying about failing to make ends meet.

Cecilia had a $5,000 balance remaining on her student account. After her scholarships and loans processed, Cecilia owed the largest balance to Big State University compared to the other nine students. Although she graduated at the top of her class in a large urban high school while also earning high marks in several Accelerated Placement (AP) courses, she had a difficult time finding scholarships that she qualified for. She told me, "That was another obstacle, which is the money issue because we're not from people with money and it was hard to apply for student scholarships because I wasn't eligible for some. . . . It was that big shock like, oh my God, I can't go to college. I have that tuition to pay." Cecilia did not qualify for need-based scholarships because on paper, her father was making more money than in past years. Yet, what the papers do not explain is that her aging father was working overtime just to meet the daily needs of their family, to meet the increasing cost of living in an urban city. Therefore, Cecilia was stuck in a hard place. She did not qualify for many scholarships, but at the same time, she and her family did not have discretionary monies to pay for the growing cost of college.

Cecilia did her best to apply for two scholarships that she did qualify for. One scholarship was from the Navajo Nation, and the other was from Big State University. Both were merit-based, and Cecilia had the grades. One of the last tasks that she took care of before graduating was to ensure that her high school sent her official transcript to the Navajo Nation Scholarship Office and to Big State University, which was a requirement for both scholarships. During the summer months before her first year in college, Cecilia's high school underwent a schoolwide renovation, and much of the summer staff and administrators were relocated to work remotely or at the district office. Unfortunately, the transition and construction at the high school would impact Cecilia. She learned that the high school did not send her transcripts, and the scholarship deadlines passed. As a result, she was ineligible for the Navajo Nation Scholarship and the scholarship offered at

Big State University. The high school failed Cecilia. And Cecilia had to do the extra work to advocate and prove to scholarship offices that she made the effort to complete applications in a timely manner. Yet, she was still denied funding.

Joy was also unable to garner scholarships that she had hoped to receive. She was salutatorian in her class, with a 4.3 grade point average, and she was raised in a single-parent household with two younger siblings. Her mother was unemployed and doing her best to make ends meet. Their family was living month to month on food stamps. On top of all of that, their home lacked running water and electricity. So Joy and her family learned to live without—a display of strength. It's not shocking, then, to understand that scholarships were a big deal for Joy and her family. What was shocking is that the college system did not provide the financial support that Joy desperately needed. She was offered a need-based university grant and received federal Pell grant funding. Yet, she still had a remaining balance and had to take out a $2,000 loan, but even that was not enough. She explained:

> Within finances, there are so many things that you have to consider, tuition, housing, meal plans and books and supplies and things like that. Money. What one of my teachers used to say back in high school was scholarships are easy to get, but you know, that's not really true. It's a hard process. You can't always be so sure of the outcome either at the same time. For me, this year I was constantly worried about where I would get my finances. I really didn't want to take out loans but I had to. There's only so much of a limit that you can take out for student loans per academic school year. For me, I thought like $2,000 was going to be enough for my meal plan. I don't know why I thought that because I'm a person who likes to eat.

Joy also applied for the Navajo Nation Scholarship, but she did not receive it. She explained that many of her Navajo friends did not receive Navajo scholarship funding, or even when they got it, several of them received the money late, near the end of the spring semester. Letters from the Navajo Nation Scholarship Office were sent to students indicating that funding would be late. Many students were left to figure things out with their remaining balances, with food to purchase and daily expenses accumulating. Navajo students and their families were upset with the slow response to allocating the scholarships that the students earned.

I understood the frustrations that these students were feeling because I also received scholarship funding from the Navajo Nation, but some years, the funding arrived late. Some years, I had to appeal a denial letter. Many times, I had to resend a transcript, Certificate of Indian Blood, and even a Financial Needs Analysis because documents were lost, and my frustrations escalated. It was not until I started working as a college administrator that I learned more about the dedicated staff and the complicated funding stream of the Navajo Nation scholarships. What many do not know is that the Navajo Nation Scholarship funding comes through various streams, each with various mechanisms for disbursement. Let me take a moment to explain this to you so you understand what the scholarship office goes through each year.

During the 2018 calendar year, $24 million were available for scholarships to Navajo students enrolled in higher education. A majority of the funding (56%) was provided by federal funds through the P.L. 93–638 contract with the Navajo Region Bureau of Indian Affairs, 36% from Navajo Nation General Funds, 5% from Navajo Nation Trust Funds, and about 3% from corporate funds.[1] More than half of the funding is provided by the federal government, which means that much of the dollars are dispersed based on the federal budget calendar rather than on the college students' calendar. The federal budget calendar runs from October 1 to September 30 of the following year. The calendar is adjusted to make room for newly elected officials to participate in the budget process during their first year in office. For example, when a new U.S. president and congressional members are elected in November, they take office in January, giving new leaders time to outline budget priorities, submit a budget to Congress, work with budget committees, and seek a majority vote in the House and Senate. Typically, the president receives the final budget in September and has 10 days to approve or veto it. If all goes smoothly, the federal budget process takes up to a year to complete. Yet, in 2013, 2018, and then in 2019, a budget was not agreed upon, and a government shutdown happened as a result.

The Office of the Navajo Nation Scholarship and Financial Assistance (ONNSFA) is dependent on federal dollars not only to fund students, but also to pay 28 staff members. When the federal government shuts down, thousands of Navajo students and families feel the effects. During the most recent government shutdown from December 22, 2018, to January 25, 2019, the former Navajo Nation president Russel Begaye commented, "There's a new semester starting at the universities, and federal employees are having trouble finding tuition money for their kids. Those young people may have to miss school this semester" (Krol, 2019). Colleges were back in session for the spring semester, and many Navajo college students were in a bind because their funding was held up by the government shutdown. Many (including me when I was a student) are unaware of the tireless advocacy by ONNSFA staff and Navajo leaders to maintain funding for Navajo people today and for the future, during government shutdowns and at other times when funding is jeopardized.

In recent years, U.S. president Donald Trump threatened to cut the Higher Education Grant, which provides funds to the Navajo Nation through P.L. 93–638, dollars that are earmarked for scholarships. In response to Trump's budget proposal, Navajo Nation president Jonathan Nez remarked, "The Higher Education Grant is a huge benefit for thousands of

Navajo students each year and for the future of the Navajo Nation. It's very disappointing that these funds continue to come under threat by this administration. We will look to our leaders in the House and Senate to restore these funds during the budget process" (Department of Diné Education, Office of Navajo Nation Scholarship and Financial Assistance, 2019).

Let's be clear—these funds are connected to treaty obligations, connected to the lands stolen, connected to the lives lost, connected to the Long Walk, connected. They are tied to the history and make evident how history is connected to the present. Trump sidelined that obligation by attempting to eliminate the Higher Education Grant program in the third year of his administration. Many times, leaders have selective memory and choose when to remember and forget the whole historical story. Rose Graham, director of ONNSFA, emphatically stated, "The Trump administration has made it abundantly clear that it is not interested in providing support to Native Americans seeking a college education. It appears the Trump administration is doing its best to keep a college degree out of reach of Native Americans. Our students need every available financial aid resource to attain a college education, even if it's a fraction of the total cost of attendance" (Department of Diné Education, Office of Navajo Nation Scholarship and Financial Assistance, 2020).

Most of these students were from low-income families who for generations have been subjugated to oppressive injustices that maintain the conditions that perpetuate low-income livelihoods. Since settler colonialism impinged on Navajo lands and livelihoods, the financial hardship monster continues to do its work. While White settlers gain land, resources, and privileges, the system holds Navajo people as inferior by creating hurdles for them to build strong economies. Debt and loans are an example of retaining the status quo. Hauntings.

If these students are seeing the financial struggle in their homes, you can imagine why there is a sense of worry over whether to take out student loans. Many have been taught to not create debt, not re-create the financial struggle. Joy explained that she had a teacher who instilled in her to not take out loans: "In high school, some of the teachers made it sound like taking out student loans was really bad." Yet, Joy and her family did not have the means to pay the entire cost of college. Joy then started questioning whether to take out loans and begin the debt process: "It worried me to death. That's all I could say. Do I take out loans to pay for this stuff, or do I just leave it and go home?" Joy eventually decided to take out a loan. She had to decide whether to generate debt or forfeit college. She chose college:

> If you know that your scholarships didn't cover the entire fee for
> your one year of school, it bothers you, and you stress about that
> alongside your schoolwork and being able to finish everything all the
> time. It's frustrating and it just puts more stress on you. . . . It was like
> that for me because I was like, "What am I going to do now?" Am

I going to have to stop halfway through my year and just drop from these classes? Because I didn't know if I would be able to get loans or I didn't really want to but it's like, you know what, I'm going to do this. . . . I had to do something about it. . . . That's when I decided I had to take out a loan even to pay for the rest of what my scholarships didn't cover. . . . I didn't really want to but it's like, you know what, I'm going to do this. In the long run, it's going to work out. . . . I'm going to make this sacrifice.

Affording college by generating debt is a sacrifice for many. Mike was also concerned about taking out a loan because he had family members who took out loans and he saw them struggle: "I don't want to take a loan. That's one of the scary things. My mom always tells me not to because I've seen it happen with my cousins. I don't know the exact situation but I just knew he had to get a loan. . . . I remember he had to do that, and it's kind of hard for him because of the loan." Mike did not take out a loan during his first year in college, but he worried day to day on how he was going to make it. Mike was part of a small few who declined the option of taking out a loan. Many other Native students did resort to loans.

In 2015–2016, 31% of American Indians and Alaska Natives took out student loans, averaging $7,069 per borrower. These loans included direct subsidized and unsubsidized loans, Perkins loans, private loans, and Direct PLUS parent loans. For Native students who eventually graduated with a bachelor's degree, the average loan debt for those students was $26,380, and 76% of Native students borrowed some money to pay for their college degree. After Black students (86%; average borrowed $34,010), Native students borrowed the most money (Espinosa et al., 2019). Black and Native peoples are some of the most economically disadvantaged in society and at the onset of college degree dreams, we and our Black relatives are forced to reproduce a debt burden life, for ourselves and for the next generation, and that is hard to swallow. While college institutions benefit from Indigenous lands and from the enslaved labor of Black people, Indigenous and Black people continue to carry the college burden, a burden of debt. Connecting both the profit of lands and the exclusion of Native students is the notion of *land debt*, which is used to "describe the economic conditions of contemporary Native peoples, with the understanding that the immense levels of wealth that currently benefit the US was built upon the theft of Indigenous lands and the enslavement of Blacks" (Tachine & Cabrera, 2021, p. 4). History and present coexist and are reminiscent of the power of the failure monster.

When money is limited and tight, expenses that we often take for granted are real concerns for students. For instance, Chris worried over whether to invest money toward buying ink for a printer: "I think the most, the biggest thing that stresses me out right now is buying ink for my printer. I don't have enough money for that. I have enough money, but when I buy it, I'm like, 'Now I have no money.'" He calculated the cost of purchasing ink by figuring out how much he would spend on not just the ink, but also the transportation to get to a store that sells the ink at a reasonable price. Yet, he worried about whether that expense was worth it, especially considering that he didn't want to be broke after that purchase.

Speaking of transportation, Wesley, who lived off campus, was constantly running numbers in his mind over the cost of public transportation, a cost that he was not anticipating when he started college: "Traveling cost came up as a big one because whenever I needed a pass, I would need to get money, and then I would need to break the cash, and then that it went from $4 a day to $20 a week, $100 a month, when I first got here, just because I didn't know how it worked." After the fourth month of his first semester, Wesley learned that there was a discounted bus rate for students attending Big State University. This helped, but the reality remained that in his first semester of college, Wesley had already spent up to $400 on public transportation. College transcripts were another expense that burdened students' budgets. Typically, at the end of each semester, scholarships request that students submit an official transcript that demonstrates that they have good academic standing in order to be funded for the next semester or the following year. Yet, the end of the semester is often the hardest time for students, as their money has been nearly depleted. Students were then surprised to find out that Big State University charged students for a copy of their official transcript.

Sarah told me what this looks like as she was squeezing by on only a few dollars during the last month of college: "If you're applying for a scholarship as an example, you need your official transcripts, and that's like 20 bucks, just for one. Twenty bucks isn't a lot, but it is a lot. It is a lot of money when you're in college. . . . Oh my gosh, they're 20 bucks, you know, and just imagine how many scholarships we applied for. It's like only 5, that's 100 bucks. How do I get 100? . . . They think all of us are rich but no, we're not. We're college students." Sarah could not have said that any better. Transportation, printer ink, transcripts, architecture supplies, apartment leases and security deposits, professional clothes, and traveling home to be with family were all expenses that strained students when money was tight.

Food was another huge worry that students encountered. They were concerned about what they would eat the next day because much of the food on campus was expensive. Lauryn shared, "It's a lot. It's expensive to buy food here [on campus]. It's hard to go buy groceries too. I know buying groceries cost less money, but I never have time. I don't have time to cook or anything like that, so it's easy to eat over here, just get something to eat. But it's so expensive." Sam estimated that a meal on campus cost up to $10, which was "more money that I really spend. It seems more of a waste. By the time I'm done eating that food, I'm full for like 30 minutes to an hour, and then I'm hungry again." Sam, like many other students, tried to eat healthy and work out on a regular basis, but finding affordable, healthy options was hard to do: "I don't want to eat simple foods, but it's what I got to do. I just need to keep my vitamins up, that's what I'm really worried about. Keeping myself nutritious. Keep the nutrients and all that. When you're working out, I lose a lot there. If I don't really get much from food, I'm depleting myself. I start stressing out more, I start getting very sleepless. I just don't feel good them days. I need vitamins. I need to keep up my nutrition. It's difficult because shit costs so much here."

With limited money, students resorted to purchasing potatoes, ramen noodles, Spam, peanut butter, and rice—staple foods that helped them to get by. Sarah only had $20 as the end of the semester approached, and she did all she could to stretch out that money for food:

> I went to Safeway and I just got noodles and a bag of potatoes (*laughing*), and that's what I lived on for two weeks. It wasn't that much, but I had to limit myself to one ramen noodle a day and a potato, and that is how I got through. I was hungry and everything. I told myself if I want to make it through the whole two weeks, I could only eat once. It was hard, just being used to getting, when you're home, you don't ever starve. . . . Your parents, your siblings, everything they are far from you, and you know, knowing that money is scarce for them too, you don't want to put that burden on them and say I need money.

The last two weeks of the semester are finals weeks, an already stressful time for any college student. But to also be hungry during this time is unjust for these students. The Hope Center for College, Community, and Justice partnered with the American Indian College Fund in 2019 on a large-scale research study to investigate food and housing insecurity among Native students attending Tribal Colleges and Universities (TCUs). Food insecurity is "the limited or uncertain availability of nutritionally adequate and safe food, or the ability to acquire such food in a socially acceptable manner" (Hope Center, 2020, p. 7). The study found that 62% of Native students were food insecure (compared to 37% of national participants). More specifically, 67% of the respondents indicated that they worried whether their food would run out before they received more money to buy more, which speaks to Sarah's anxiety over negotiating studying for her final exams and stretching $20 for food. When neoliberal practices are premised on every person for themselves, this is evidence of a flawed capitalist system.

Returning to Sam's story, recall that he applied for college late and also delayed seeking out funding to pay for school. He ended up receiving the Pell Grant, a Big State University scholarship, the Navajo Nation Scholarship, and an engineering scholarship, so in total he received $1,000 that was disbursed to him after all scholarship monies posted to his student account. He learned quickly that $1,000 was not nearly enough to sustain him for the remainder of the semester, and that financial reality strangled him where he sometimes dreaded attending college, especially after being home with family:

> I wish I didn't have to come back. Like winter break, I didn't want to come back but I had to. I've got to continue my journey that I started. It sucks to come back but I have to. . . . There's so much burden here rather than being at home, I don't have to worry about much. I don't have to worry about paying for college. All these worries, they kind of just disappear at home. They float away and as soon as they get here, they slowly drop like rain back on me.

Worries slowly drop like rain on these students, with each drop making a mark on their experience, dampening and weighing down on them. Worries that were a by-product, a symptom of the failure monster, a monster that was intensifying students' fears of failing because they did not have the relief to release themselves from the strangling financial worry. Hauntings. A sense of belonging to be a part of the college experience is what many of us want for our students. Yet, what many of us do not realize is that not having money to enjoy college is a real thing. Joy said it best: "It just makes you feel left out from the crowd that seems like they have money all the time." These experiences are not the students' fault; it is the centuries-old failure monster prowling nearby.

Monstrous Internalization

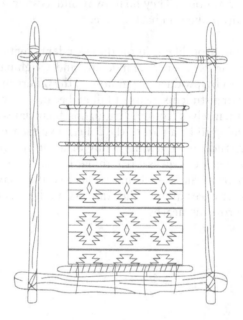

Who belongs (and who does not belong) in college? And who decides what belonging is? In the case of college, grades and money dictate who does (and who does not) belong in college. The failure monster prides itself on grades because that is a sure way of determining who passes and who fails. If students receive failing grades, they are in jeopardy of losing their scholarships. And if they can't afford college and they lose their scholarships, they cannot continue in college, and are deemed failures. The system works that way, privileging some but failing many. That is the game of the *failure monster.* Students are seen as pawns in the failure monster's game. Yet, what is not seen in all of this is the fear (monstrous internalization) that ensues when grades and money determine belonging.

Students told me how they feared failing. They illustrated how the failure monster creates a culture of fear. Rebecca D. Cox (2009) wrote a book titled *The College Fear Factory,* where she examined community college students' experiences and their tremendous anxiety about their educational trajectories and ability to succeed in college. In her work, she found that students had prior experiences in performing poorly academically, while some also believed that because they were attending community colleges, they were not quite ready for the university. Prior and present experience offered evidence to them that failing could happen, and they were fearful of it: the fear factory. Her work provided insight into the prevalence of fear among students in community college settings. However, the students whom I got to know attended a university and were high-achieving students (valedictorians, competitive athletes, leaders in their communities), and yet they exhibited a high degree of anxiety and fear of failing. I am not saying that these students had not experienced failing; they did. What I am saying is that these students were "top students" in an Americanized hierarchy of achievement, doing everything right to achieve meritocratic "success." Yet, I wondered why these students were still scared of failing?

Hauntings. When examining their situations with a monster framing, I am reminded how much history is a part of the present. I am reminded that the failure monster has gained strength for centuries. I am reminded that the failure monster is related to and built off of other monsters—namely, the *financial hardship* and *deficit (not enough) monsters*—that predate and dominate these students' experiences. They are not determined by an individualized student's choices, as the general public likes to believe—a belief premised on neoliberal paternalism. Their fears are not simply generated from perceived lack of self-confidence, such as the popular term "imposter syndrome" suggests. That is short-sighted and screams of Whiteness. Their fears are much deeper, generated from monsters that have been emitting failure (from savages to college dropouts) and gaining traction for hundreds of years.

Lauryn had a rough academic start during her freshman year in college. In high school, she had straight As and was the covaledictorian of her class, and therefore she was accustomed to performing well academically since elementary school. In the fall semester of her freshman year, she enrolled in 16 units of coursework that to her seemed "interesting," including chemistry, college algebra, European history, Eastern Asian studies, and Roman civilization. With Lauryn being an aspiring medical doctor, these courses met the requirements for physiology and prehealth, her major and minor. Yet, she did not fully realize the demand that these courses would entail. She explained, "I was taking subjects that I never, that I never knew. I should have taken classes that I was familiar with, but I didn't really know, and I was like, oh, this sounds interesting, so I'll take that. But then they were classes that were hard, and I didn't know." Lauryn tried to tell her major advisor that she didn't mind taking 12 units, which could delay her graduation an extra year, to ease the pace and demand of taking 16 units. But she was disappointed when her advisor commented, "Doctors don't take the easy way out." That advisor was sending messages of who belongs and does not belong in the medical field, implying that a decision to take one less course each semester was an easy way out—a failure route. Belonging was being shaped by a non-Native advisor who was not listening to Lauryn's needs and was imposing a standard of success rooted in meritocracy and paternalism. The advisor was acting in ways that jeopardized Lauryn's progress.

Lauryn stayed at 16 units and ended the semester receiving Cs in almost all her courses, putting her GPA at a 2.5, which placed her on academic probation for her scholarships. After just the first few months of college, she was already in fear of failing. She figured out that in the second semester, she would have to get straight As to keep her scholarships. That was tough, especially because she was struggling in another course, with the possibility of getting another C. Before the spring semester was over, Lauryn was already talking to me as if she knew that she was going to lose the scholarships: "That is kind of the situation I am in, right now, with me losing those scholarships. It is kind of like taking a big toll on me, and it just feels like I am not going to know what to do, now that I am going to lose those scholarships. . . . I just feel like I am just a failure here."

That feeling of being a failure "here" opened up discussions about how grades not only served as a gatekeeper for scholarships and college persistence, but for some students, grades also serve as a barometer of a sense of belonging in college, of feeling happy and your full, beautiful self in a particular place. Lauryn elaborated on this point: "Belonging is a place where you feel comfortable, where you can be yourself—where it makes you happy, I guess. You can be yourself, where you enjoy being, or where you like to be. It is like where you feel happy. . . . It's just if I were doing good in school and not in the situation I am in, right now, I think I would just be happy." Amber felt the same way about grades, which influenced her emotions and well-being. She told me, "Once my grades are good—if my grades are excellent, then my mood is so much better. The way I feel and the way I act, and the way I am—it like surrounds my grades—it reflects on my grades." Grades are a barometer for belonging, for mental and emotional well-being. Passing grades created an atmosphere of belonging, of being happy and whole. Failing grades create fear, a sense of unbelonging and anxiety.

Amber was a Gates Millennium Scholar, so the stakes were high for her to maintain good academic standing in college if she wanted to keep the coveted scholarship. As previously noted, the Gates Millennium Scholarship pays full funding for awardees throughout the duration of their academic trajectory. Students like Amber could receive a doctorate with the help of the Gates scholarship. When she received her first and then her second failing test score in chemistry, she panicked: "Lately I've been not doing well in tests. Even though I'm trying my best, I wasn't doing well, and I'm not used to failing, and with chemistry, I failed twice already. The first one was like a 51% class average and I got a 59, and I was just freaking out like the world's ending, and the second time, I said, 'Okay, I'm going to do better.' The class average is 49%, and I only got a 51, and I'm like, 'Why are they teaching us things that I cannot do?'" When I asked her how she felt when she saw the test, she looked at me with deep concern and said, "I feel like a failure. I feel like I'm just going to, 'Oh, I'm just going to drop out of college.' That's how I felt at first, and that's my first really bad grade in chemistry." The embers from the failure monster were spreading.

In the time of these interviews, half of the students aspired to work in the health field, either as a medical doctor or as a nurse. Their interest can be linked to longstanding health problems and efforts to address the health disparities facing Native peoples. We can see the health crisis amplified in the 2020–2021 pandemic. Lives are lost due to systemic reasons, which results in a community struggling to literally survive a virus that spreads fast due to the disadvantaged circumstances. These students already knew, by lived experience, the health inequities facing Native communities. It was not surprising that half of them wanted to do something about it, to protect and care for their relatives.

What was frustrating and surprising was that the failure monster was most evident in chemistry and math courses, which are foundational courses for health majors. Amber, Wesley, Lauryn, and Joy all shared hardships of feeling and fearing failure in those courses. Joy was an aspiring nurse and wanted to return home and serve the Navajo Nation one day. Yet, her college algebra course was making her second-guess herself:

> In high school, I was a straight A+ student the entire time, all four years of high school. And before that, I was a straight A student, ever since I can remember. I've always done really well in academics, and once I got to this level, I was like, what happened? Am I slacking off? Or, am I not doing something right? . . . And I just felt like, am I as smart as I thought I was? . . . That's been a struggle. I constantly try and study for it and push myself, but I don't know. I can do all the homework and everything, just not tests. I'd sit there and I'd take all the time that I can, all the time that's allowed, to think about all the questions and the problems that they give us, but no matter what I do to answer them, it's just not right.

Joy was frustrated because she did not understand why she was passing all her homework assignments, taking part in study groups, and attending tutoring, but she was still failing every test. She decided to speak to her math teacher about her failing grades. He responded to her by saying, "I don't know," which only infuriated Joy more. She and some of her classmates went all the way to the head of the math department to place a complaint that the math instructor was not teaching them well. But they were ignored. In the meantime, Joy continued to study for the final exam, losing sleep and worrying about the final grade that she would receive in that course.

In the end, Joy failed her math course. I asked her about what she thought about that. She stated, "I'm bummed out, but at the same time, it's too easy for me to give up." The experience in this course, combined with the high cost of attending the university, forced Joy to consider transferring to a different college, one that was more affordable and open to hearing students' concerns. She was not alone in making plans to transfer. Wesley considered transferring out as well, and he and Lauryn also contemplated changing their majors, leaving behind their dreams of helping address the health concerns of Native communities.

Sha'áłchíní (my children), I am thinking of the desperate call for essential health-care workers and researchers during Covid-19, especially Navajo health workers who understand Diné ways. I am irritated that the higher education system has created barriers for aspiring Navajo doctors to begin answering this call. The idea that people in higher education are not listening to students' concerns and/or are unaware of how they are reinforcing the systemic monsters in many ways is so hard to learn. I am sure that you are feeling that frustration too. Pause, if you need to. Put the book down and breathe in and out. But come back, because we need you.

Colleges are not the only educational institutions that create barriers for students. High schools do as well. Recall how the deficit (not enough) monster (rooted in assimilation) was present in rural reservation high schools, such that students were not academically challenged (in math courses, even!). Joy understood this more while struggling in college algebra. She described to me how she began to see how others in her class were more advantaged than she was because of their high school:

> I think the schools that they [non-Native classmates] come from, I
> feel that they were more ready. They were given all these different
> courses to prepare them. When I came for orientation, I remember
> there was a girl who said that she's already taking her Spanish and has
> already fulfilled her Spanish credits. There was another girl who took
> Calculus I and Calculus II. It's like, we didn't even have that at my
> school. The only class at my high school was precalculus. The teachers
> there weren't really effective in teaching it and wouldn't obtain really
> relevant information. That set us back a year 'cause we had to learn
> beginning algebra and intermediate algebra. . . . I'm already a year
> behind in my math. . . . 'Cause they're ready for things like that.
> They're already at Calculus I level.

Wesley was frustrated about the college math course too. An aspiring medical doctor, he was irritated that he was placed in remedial math in college. He was hoping to be placed in Calculus 1, a prerequisite to start his program, but instead was in Math 100, which meant that after Math 100, he would have to take geometry, trigonometry, precalculus, and then calculus. That is 4 semesters, or 2 years of remedial math, before he can even begin coursework in his major. He said, "I was a little disappointed that I wasn't able to take even Physics 1, Physics 101, I mean. I could have taken it if I enrolled earlier, but it's still the math you need to have calculus as a prelim. The math, my math score testing low for some reason. Holds me back from taking physics, so even if I was able to get into a physics class, I wouldn't be able to take a physics class." Wesley reminded me that he is paying about $20,000 a year for school, and that annoyed him. He questioned whether attending the university was worth it. I questioned that too, and I also wondered more about the relevancy of grades, placements, gatekeeping courses, and the high cost of college, which continue to keep students from receiving a degree so they could help our people, our society.

For some students, they felt alone struggling in their courses. Lauryn's dad encouraged her to go to tutoring for chemistry. The university provided free tutoring services in major core courses for students, like chemistry. Although Lauryn was desperately trying to stay afloat in that course, she could not get herself to take tutoring. She described that "I am kind of scared to go there." When I asked her to explain that a little more to me, she said, "I ask people, I say, "Do you go to tutoring? And they are like, 'No, I don't go there. I don't need it.' It makes me feel like no one goes there, you know?" She then began to explain that she goes to office hours instead. But she later revealed that the negative stigma of being a Native American discouraged her from going to tutoring.

I will return to this topic in detail in Part IV of this book. But for now, I want to recognize that there are much deeper reasons why some students do not take advantage of tutoring. Lauryn was not the only one who shared feelings of being alone in seeking help. Mike explained his frustrations over not seeking academic support in his math course, saying:

> It sucks because you feel stupid. I have a pride issue. I don't want to be the only person to raise my hand because I didn't understand it, so I always think I'll take the extra time to try and teach myself or I don't want to take the office hours. I don't want to go into office hours because I'm going to look stupid. It's kind of holding me back. . . . I noticed that I don't want to be the person to slow everybody down.

Mike mentioned that he had a pride issue, but I also wondered how much of the deficit (not enough) and failure monsters were seeping into students' sense of being (monstrous internalization) to the point that they did not want others (tutors, faculty, classmates) to view them as incapable, not smart enough, or holding their classmates back. There are systemic reasons for this that I will unpack in the next part of this book. For now, I wanted to acknowledge this, as it illustrates the powerful influences that monsters have on students' sense of self and belonging.

The weight of failure in courses impacted students' sleep patterns and overall well-being. Mike was so stressed about maintaining his scholarships and paying for college expenses that he sacrificed sleep on a regular basis. Mike worked part-time on campus as a condition of two of his scholarships, while also carrying a full and demanding academic load. He was averaging two hours of sleep a night, and sometimes he would squeeze in six hours on the weekend. I asked him what time he usually went to sleep. He explained, "Six in the morning and wake up at 8. I try to go to sleep before the sun comes up because that's when I am really tired, and I wake up when the sun's up. Just drag myself to wake up." He then described how he gets through the day and night:

> There's like nights when it's like physically, I can't move anymore. It's like I'll put my drawing board on something, set it high so I can stand and draw, drink coffee. It's like, 'Hey, it's your coffee. That's your coffee.' It's just really bad that I can't keep my eyes open anymore, my head hurts too much. I try to sleep for half an hour, and I'll get back up and just get back to it. This time, it's the first time that it's actually gotten really bad to where I'm stressing about it even in my dreams.

Not surprisingly, because of the lack of sleep, he admitted that he had difficulties in focusing in class and shared his strategies for working through that: "Sometimes, I get to my classes and it's really hard to concentrate. I buy Five-Hour Energy or there's this study buddy pill, and I'll take them when I study and draw, stuff like that. I'll take Tylenol when I have a headache, and then on Friday, I try to sleep maybe like six to seven hours. I don't want to sleep too much because I need that time to draw on weekends."

In college, almost everyone goes through high stress and lack of sleep, especially during midterms and finals week. But when lack of sleep is a constant reality, there is much concern over the overall health and well-being of a person. In the prior chapter (La'ts'áadah, Eleven), we learned how lack of resources impacted students' ability to eat healthy food on a regular basis, as well as their increased stress over paying for incidentals such as ink cartridges and academic transcripts. In all, students were not getting enough rest, neither eating well nor regularly, and grappling with anxiety over making good grades and paying for small but necessary items.

In one of my last interviews with Amber, she started to critique the utility of grades, questioning what grades really determine. Amber's right leg was resting on her skateboard, pushing and then pulling back the wheels as she spoke to me:

> I just think of the school like a robot, like it's controlling everyone else. Grades control everyone else. I feel like, well, grades show determination and how driven you are, but it determines so much. It defines a person, almost. No one cares like, 'Oh, you're really good with people. We won't know that until we look at your grades first or interview you.' 'Oh, you're a 3.25. You're not good enough.' Like, exams shouldn't determine our fate.

Amber again reminded me that grades do so much more beyond what we see in the classroom. Grades are like a barometer of belonging. They also determine the fate of a student's entire life.

I learned how much the failure monster was influencing students' lives during their first year in college. During our last interviews, which occurred during finals week of the spring semester, just a few weeks before they would wrap up their first year in college, fear of failing came up again. This time, a deeper understanding of that fear was addressed. Sam had a challenging first year; he was on academic probation, had an outstanding balance remaining on his student account, and had an unpaid police citation that he needed to take care of. The responsibilities of it all weighed on his mind:

> Failing is my deepest fear. In general, becoming a failure, just having this dream, just this whole monumental thing about myself and just seeing it all crumble before my eyes and for me to do nothing. . . . That's my deepest fear. Really just failing, becoming a failure to my peers, my mother, my family. I don't want to do that. I don't want to become a failure. Who does? Seeing the examples around and of people in general, more specifically my family. They failed. They live their life. That's how they live their life ever since they were kids. I've risen above it but the fear of failing and falling, falling on my knees and watching this crumble before and I can't do nothing. Helplessness. . . . Really seeing everything crash and just burn and I'm just watching and I can do nothing, it's my deepest fear.

Failure was Sam's deepest fear, and it was connected to his peers, mother, and family. He recognized that his family encountered difficulties in their life, having battled substance abuse addiction and financial hardships, and he wanted to show his family that college was a possibility. He told me that his family members "see me as having a great future," and he added, "I can't be a failure. I won't be a failure." The weight of failure is not an individual heaviness; it's collective. Sam did not want to let his family down, and from his perspective continue the legacy of hardships.

Legacies of disappointments were a common thread among students' reasons for not failing. Jessie also spoke of not wanting to let down her family, specifically her mother. She explained that because her mother had already gone through a lot of disappointments in her life, she did not want to carry on those disappointments: "The most painful thing ever is to see my mom cry. I think that's where it comes from is, I didn't want to disappoint anybody like my dad disappointed her. I didn't want her to think that, like, she's not worth it. I didn't want her to think highly of me and then for me just to disappoint her like that." These students were carrying legacies, generations of struggles and disappointments, on their shoulders. And failure for them meant continuing that legacy—they wanted to break free from that, for themselves and for their families.

Being tied to family was the community's influence on students' fear of failing. Some talked about not wanting to let the community down or giving the community something to talk about, especially those students who grew up in rural reservation towns. The community is small, and these teens were top students and most likely were mentioned in the local tribal newspapers, meaning that the community knew about them and the families that they come from. Lauryn disclosed, "Last semester, I started doing bad and the first thing I thought about is what the people are going to think of me at home, if I were to drop out and stuff, or not do well. . . . That's kind of, I kind of thought it was scary. I always think of it like 'What if I mess up?' All these people at home are going to be, 'Oh, it was all fake,' or something. It kind of has a big impact on me." Lauryn also explained that people were praying for her, and she did not want to let them down, which widens the depth of the metaphysical environments that come into play when students think about others. She said,

> There are people helping me and they are not giving up on me, and I can't give up on them. Every meeting I go to, I keep praying I am going to get that in school, and so I am not going to give up on that, I am not going to give up on them. That's going to make me feel so bad, like if I were to give up and go back in the meeting. I will probably feel really bad like . . . I just let them down.

The lessons that these accounts teach us is that the failure monster is the true failure, with its deep roots in capitalism and meritocracy. The failure monster teaches us that these influences have created legacies of ideological convergence that pathologize and stamp failure on our people by turning the mirror away from itself, toward us. There is capital investment in the ideological convergence and the retelling of Native peoples as failures. And the failure monster is clever, in that its glorified story of conquest, individualism, hierarchy, and paternalism has pervasively seeped into today's culture, university systems, and students. It is time for us to turn the mirror around. We know that *resurgence*, embedded in love, provides strength for our people to rise. *Continuance*, which is matrilineal and life-centered, encourages us to keep going. The third weapon of *reverence*, described in the next chapter, protects and sustains us as people.

Reverence as Sacred-Centered

There is sacredness in knowing the power of storying. Stories serves as "roadmaps" (Brayboy, 2005, p. 427). A close understanding of the Navajo Twin Warriors story reveals sacredness, respect, and beauty in the telling and teaching of the twins. The story is intertwined with Navajo creation stories. I recognized the sacredness and respect in the telling and teaching of the twins, their father, Sun, Spider Woman, Changing Woman, all the living entities, and the details of the story.

The twins were taught holy prayers and songs that protected them along their journey. Similarly, while students were confronted by the *failure monster,* they engaged the third Indigenous weapon of *reverence,* the act of believing, or an ability to get through that is grounded in a deep awareness of and connection to divineness, which is practiced through prayer. Reverence is sacredness-centered and protects and sustains k'é (kinship; relationship based) in the present and future. *Resurgence* helps us to rise. *Continuance* helps us to keep going. *Reverence* helps us to get through. The 10 students I spoke with talked about their belief systems in different and similar ways, including following each separately and sometimes intertwining them. They followed Navajo teachings, Christianity, and the Native American Church (NAC), revealing the complexities, contradictions, and beautiful multitudes of Indigenous personhood and belief systems. Diné scholar Lloyd Lee (2020) states, "Diné identity in the twenty-first century is distinctive and personal. It is a mixture of traditions, customs, values, behaviors, technologies, worldviews, language, and lifeways. Diné identity is analogous to Diné weaving, in that it interweaves all life's elements together" (p. 4).

I have been learning how to weave as our ancestors have woven for generations. And in that beautiful process, I am gaining a deeper understanding of the various elements that encompass weaving. Elements of earth, sky, holy beings, prayers, songs, spiders, permission, patterns, stories, and purpose. I am deeply grateful to my Navajo weaving mentors, including Velma Craig, Barbara Teller Ornelas, and Lynda Teller Pete. Their teachings, as well as being in a weaving community, have helped me (and my daughters) to learn the intricacies of weaving. Lynda Teller Pete and Barbara Teller Ornelas (2018) wrote a book titled *Spider Woman's Children: Navajo Weaving Today* to teach future weavers the expansive knowledge woven into each textile. Their work has also informed story rug methodology, as I see weaving as research.

Spider Woman taught us how to weave, and that the purpose of weaving is to bring hózhó (beauty and balance) to the Navajo people. I learned that Spider Woman gathered materials from the four sacred mountains. Spider Man constructed the loom, made of sky and earth. Plants were harvested to create an array of rich, natural colors in the textile. Spider Woman asked permission from the thunder gods to design patterns so we can use those same patterns today. Tension rods that hold the warp represent the female and male and were made of rock crystal and sheet lighting. And Spider Woman received prayers and songs to help her complete the weaving process and to carry those weaving knowledges to the next generation, and the next. Diné spirituality is also similar to weaving in that it interweaves from various teachings and knowledges. There is no one way that Diné weave; there are limitless ways of weaving and learning. And there is no one way that Diné practice reverence. We are beautifully expansive in our understanding of the Creator, Holy People, and the universe. We should do our best not to judge people based on what they practice and believe.

Lauryn, Cecilia, Amber, Sarah, Jessie, Joy, Sam, and Mike referred to their reverence in different ways. Yet, what they all shared was an understanding that their weapon of reverence included an acknowledgment that it was ever-present and sacred, protected their sense of being and purpose, and guided their future outlook. Jessie described how the NAC, an intertribal religion, held a sacred and foundational place in her life: "NAC has always been there for me. It's always been something I cherished. My family has taught me a lot of things through it, and I guess in a lot of ways, it built me as a person." Lauryn portrayed the way Navajo philosophy signified a universal aspect in her life: "I think it is pretty much everything that our life depends on and goes around; without it we wouldn't be here. Without it we wouldn't be alive and be the people we are. It's like being able to go to something if you are happy, if you are sad, if anything is bothering you. It's like our God and just someone there that we know won't ever leave us." And Amber felt that Christian teachings were "a good guide for life," meaning that biblical lessons taught her how to navigate her life's experiences. These students reminded me of what Lee (2020) posited, "Western ways, Christianity, and other worldviews have influenced the Navajo Nation, but these influences do not necessarily disrupt or eliminate Diné identity. In many respects, the influence adds to twenty-first-century Diné identity" (p. 9). All these students add to the multitude and beauty of what it means to be Diné. Many of us do.

Sarah, Jessie, and Sam believed that a higher power inspired their sense of purpose, which helped them confront the systemic monsters and work toward that purpose. Sarah remarked, "It gives me more than strength. It gives me a sense of to, you know, to wake up the next day and do the same thing, like a sense of purpose." Jessie felt the same way as Sarah. When Jessie was 2 years old, she fell very ill with pneumonia and almost died. She shared, "For me, I believe that God gave me a second chance to be able to help somebody, to fulfill my purpose." Purpose was driven by something greater than the students themselves. *Reverence.* Sam told me that he grew up attending a Black Christian church, a place where he learned about God and biblical teachings. As a young kid and a teenager, on Saturdays he frequently helped with cleaning the church, and then on Sundays he regularly attended services. As his spiritual faith grew, he explained that God made him feel less alone. He believed that God was always with him. Sam did not know his biological father, which took a toll on him. Although he was hurt due to not knowing his biological father, he told me the significance of having a sacred father to guide him. Sam took a deep breath, looked down at his hands folded on his lap, and sat for a few seconds in silence. I noticed tears dropping onto his hands. He looked up at me with pensiveness and explained:

I'm not in this fight alone. I'm not against the world by myself. You know, someone is making a way for me. Knowing that He is there, it's great. There are times when I'm just like awww, man, so much stuff is going wrong. You know, life sucks right now. I know He is still there. You know, it's great having Him there because at times when I don't have my dad [crying], I wish he [dad] was there. All these times, I wish he [dad] was there. He [God] still got me on the good path. You know, He showed me a lot. I just . . . I'm glad He is, He is the father. God is there, and I'm glad He is. He's the father that I never had. [crying] . . . I'm honestly happy God and Jesus are there, because honestly I don't know where I would be. I probably wouldn't be here.

At an early age, Sam was disconnected from his biological father, and that separation was painful for him both then and as he grew into a young man. That disconnection was not of Sam's choosing, but a choice that his father made. However, Sam conceptualized God as his father, and because of that relationship with God, Sam felt that he was not alone, especially during traumatic situations. One such hardship was when Sam had suicidal thoughts, and it was God who was with him:

> Like there have been so many close calls. There are so many times I could have died. Honestly I felt like killing myself so many times because life sucks. Not having a girlfriend, having everyone else being happy and stuff, while your family is in a struggle. I can't talk to no one. (*crying*) It's just, you know He is there. He's like don't worry. How can I not worry when all there is to do is worry? Worry about what I'm going to do with my life. Worrying about how I'm going to pay for stuff. Seems like everybody else, they get it paid for, I don't. (*crying*) I actually have to make something out of my life. . . . I'm glad He is there because there were so many close calls.

Sam's story illustrated the internal conflict that he was going through. He was worried about money stemming from the *financial hardship monster* and the failure monster. He also believed that he did not have anyone to confide in. Yet through those trials, and when he was in a state of overwhelming worry, Sam knew that God was there. And believing in a higher power helped him to move past the turmoil. *Reverence.*

Lauryn was worried about failing her classes and the impact that that would have on her scholarships. It seems like the failure monster was on her at every turn, haunting her. She told me that when she is able to go home and attend a Navajo ceremony, that strengthens her to not give up. She explained this perspective:

> I think because I go to meetings and I ask for help and I pray, it feels like it makes me want to do more, you know like, like it strengthens me to keep on doing it, to not give up, or to solve whatever problem that I'm having. It is just like, it keeps me going and doesn't break me down to like to a lower level. It makes me stand back up if I ever fall down.

Like all the students, Lauryn encountered many negative situations in her life. Despite those moments when she may have "fallen down," the weapon of reverence was what made her "stand back up."

The weapon of reverence gave students the courage to withstand a legacy of damaging perspectives of being stamped as a failure. In practicing reverence, students uncovered the sacredness and strength that prayer offered them. Prayer got them through. Jessie specified, "My mom has always taught me when things get rough or if you feel down, you know, you should pray.

She told me that even if things are good, that doesn't mean you shouldn't pray." Jessie explained that she practiced prayer during "rough" and "good" moments, indicating that prayer was an opening for supplication in various facets of life. Sarah described prayer as a precious stone: "Remember everything you say in your prayers, never forget, because if you forget, then you know it's just like you are forgetting a diamond somewhere."

This made me think of a treasured piece of turquoise jewelry that one may receive from a dear one. Often that jewelry can stay within a family for years because there is a deep relationship with the person who gifted the stone. The stone carries meaning. When Sarah described prayer as a prized stone, I understood the pain and regret one could carry if the stone is forgotten or lost. Prayers have meaning. The Potawatomi writer Kaitlin B. Curtice (2020) wrote about prayer as follows: "Prayer is a layered, complicated thing, and when we approach it that way, we enter into the mystery of what it is, of what it means to gather in community to choose sacredness around us" (p. 75).

Sarah indicated that prayers were a reflection of what was to come in life, and that was why prayer was special: "What you pray for is how you are going to live your life and how things are going to turn out for you." Prayers then offered a futurism space, a future worldview to aim for. Prayers offered visionary intentions of self-fulfillment. These teachings of future thought are aligned with Diné philosophy, such that "the people believe thought is sacred and has power. The world was created by thought. In thought, things are created, and life is nourished" (Lee, 2020, p. 96).

Connected to Sarah's idea of "how things are going to turn out," Lauryn elaborated that what you pray for should also be met halfway, meaning that she had to do her due diligence about what she was requesting. She explained:

You can pray and say like I want this, or like, I need help in this, but it's just not going to happen if you are not meeting it halfway. You have to have some kind of input on what you want, like it's not just going to happen in a day. . . . Some things might take a while. But you have to always meet it halfway, in whatever you do, whatever you pray for, whatever you believe, you have to always meet it halfway.

With that in mind, Lauryn internalized prayer as a tool that encouraged her to work toward what she hoped would occur in life. Imagining futures and meeting halfway through working toward those prayers are foundational Diné philosophies of nitsáhákees (thinking), nahatá (planning), iiná (living), and siihasin (reflection). These four teachings are woven into sa'ah naagháí bik'eh hózhóón, which informs us that "spiritual holisticism is good strong knowledge, it makes us understand that we are the center of learning" (Aronilth, 1980, p. 96). *Reverence.*

I asked the students what they prayed for while in college. Knowing that this was a personal question, I reassured them that they didn't have to tell me if they didn't want to. They shared. And my heart opened more to a deeper understanding of how they see the world, which was grounded in Diné teachings. They hoped and prayed for motivation to continue on their educational pathways, help with their families, and give them the overall strength to get through difficulties. Joy told me:

> I pray about my health and to be able to keep my mind clear from any negative feelings, and just to keep me on the right path, and to help me to continue down a more positive road of life. On my education, I pray about that all the time, continue to help me motivate myself to continue to just keep going with everything. . . . And then to be able to continue to respect my family, even though I face so many hard times with them, to somehow be able to help them realize that I am doing something to try to help them.

In Joy's experience, she dealt with family doubters, financial problems, and her younger siblings' abuse of alcohol and drugs. In the midst of all those challenges, prayer was a tool for her to withstand the difficulties. Throughout her prayers, she strived to live in hózhó (balance and beauty) by asking to "keep my mind clear," continue on a "positive road," to "respect my family," and to help them. Reverence for a clear and positive mind-set. Reverence for family. Hózhó. When Sarah started talking about prayer, tears welled in her eyes. She grabbed a tissue that I placed near us, and she explained the power of prayers that gave her strength:

> I prayed a lot (*laughing*) a lot. Just being in a quiet place . . . you know, I would pray. (*crying*) I would think back to my grandparents, you know, what they would tell me, and I would just keep that and not think of other things because your prayers can take you a long way. Even when you're like on your last string, and like you feel like you have nowhere to go, you know, you pray, and that's what I do. Even if I have a big paper due or I have to read and I can't find that, that, like uhm, like I can't find the, like, effort to push myself. I would just pray, strength to do this because I need to do it. And just having that mental thought of keep going, keep going, it just, it helped me a lot, and even with financially. . . . So, you know, trying to handle things like that when you are by yourself, no matter how small they are, it's really hard (*crying*) but you know, praying gets you through it.

Praying gets you through it. Financial burdens and thoughts of ailing grandparents overwhelmed Sarah. In those moments when Sarah felt like she had nowhere to go and there seemed to be a shortage of inspiration, prayer was her source of refuge and renewal. Prayer gets you through. Prayer helped the Twin Warriors defeat the monsters to save the Navajo people. Prayer helped Spider Woman weave for the people. Prayer helped our ancestors get through Hwéeldih. Prayer gave these students strength, purpose, and futures. Prayer. *Reverence.*

Part IV

REFUSAL: "SEEING SELF AS HOLY"

(In)visibility Monster

At the National Museum of the American Indian,
68 percent of the collection is from the United States.
I am doing my best to not become a museum
of myself. I am doing my best to breathe in and out.
I am begging: *Let me be lonely but not invisible.*

Natalie Diaz's poem, titled "American Arithmetic"[1]

We are here, and we are not going anywhere, even when people try to erase us. Chris smiled a lot. He had an infectious and welcoming smile. Often wearing a tank top, khaki shorts, and casual sandals, Chris dressed for the frequent hot temperatures. His hair was straight and cut to just above his ears. He often waved a hand to adjust the bangs that would lie sideways against his forehead. Chris was raised on the reservation in a place called Tall Corns (population 1,400) by both parents and his nearby maternal grandparents.

137

Having two older sisters and a younger brother, Chris was instructed on how to care for sheep and horses by his sisters, and then he had the responsibility of teaching his younger brother those same duties. Every morning before the sun rose, Chris and his siblings would gather the sheep and let them graze on their acres of land. His responsibility was to keep an eye on the sheep, ensuring that they did not get lost, hurt, or forgotten. Sheepherding would take up to 5 hours of the morning, so to occupy their time, they would play games in the vast lands by pushing boulders down hills or finding water wells where they could soak in natural, cool waters. Chris recalled those childhood sheepherding memories vividly and with that beaming smile.

Growing up, he had a close relationship with his grandpa. In the evening, Chris would walk to his grandfather's home and tell him that it was time for dinner, and his grandpa would walk over to Chris's home and eat with the family. Chris remembered listening to his grandpa share generational stories over dinner. When Chris was near adolescence, his grandpa passed away, which devastated him. He carried close these words that his grandpa shared with him: "I want you to be a good person, for the people." His grandpa's words were a constant reminder for Chris to help his people and to strive to be a good person. Teachings that I saw Chris carry with him as I got to know him more and more.

Chris attended high school away from his community, away from family, and away from his home(lands). He possessed an appetite for education, and yet he struggled within himself because he chose to be far from his loved ones for the sake of school. He questioned his future as he was stuck in the past, feeling guilty for leaving home. He told me a story that changed his outlook on the guilt that he was dealing with. It was a phone call with his mother that stirred his heart. He confessed to his mom that he was feeling awful for leaving home, and he missed being with them, and he felt guilty for choosing school over his family. Chris's mom replied, "What you do next, you know it's up to you. If you go to college, you go to college. If you don't . . . we are still going to be here for you." These words are similar to Navajo teachings of t'áá hwó' ají t'éego (it is up to your hard work). In the early morning, while his classmates were sound asleep in their twin beds, he stared at the ceiling, wide awake. He thought more about the conversation with his mom and had an awakening. He made a decision. He knew that education was central to him, his family, and their future, and being apart from them because of schooling did not take away the love he had for his family or home(lands). Chris sacrificed time away from home and family for the betterment of all their futures. That was love, kinship, the activation of Indigenous weapons of *reverence* and *continuance*.

Part of that sacrificial struggle that Chris dealt with, though, was connected to feeling invisible and encountering racism in a larger, White urban high school. These experiences were new to Chris since he had spent most of his schooling in rural reservation schools with predominantly Navajo students. While attending high school, Chris was often only one of two

Navajo students in Advanced Placement (AP) and honors courses. Most of the teachers and all of the administrators were White, with limited knowledge of Navajo experiences and ways of knowing, even though the Navajo Nation was nestled next to the school, the town, and the community. But for many Native peoples, that is our reality. Most people we encounter do not know about us as Native people. Many think that we do not exist at all. Chris was shocked when he encountered the sting of racism in his new school. As Chris began sharing this experience with me, he repositioned himself on the chair and then went into the details as if he had a sense of urgency to get this story out:

> I remember one time I was in math, my math class in high school, this is what changed my whole view on White people and how Natives are viewed in society. I was sitting there, I was talking to three of my other White friends. And this girl, she sits right beside me, she's White, and this was just after winter break. She's like, "What did you guys get for Christmas?" She's talking to her friends. I was talking to these people, and she's like, "Chris, what did you get for Christmas?" I said, "Oh just money from my parents, small things." She's like, "Oh you didn't get a piece of yarn?" I said, "What?" She said, "That is all you Natives deserve anyway, if you look back at the reservation, because I passed through there and it's just a piece of trash." I said, "If you look at it that way, I guess you can say it's a piece of trash, but that piece of trash is my home." She just froze, like she didn't expect me to say anything. Some people say things that trigger me off, then I will say something back to them. I was like, "That piece of trash is my home, at least I have somewhere to call home. Where is your home? Is this place your home, because this is Native American land"; and she didn't say anything after that. . . . I don't know, it was a really big awakening, everyone doesn't view you the same. You're not just human, you're who you are, you are your skin color and you need to stand and protect who, your skin color and your background and everything.

These types of remarks by other people can diminish a sense of self, re-creating the notion of (in)visibility and erasing Indigenous presence, brilliance, and intelligence. Erasure is the logic of elimination, which speaks to the structure of settler colonialism in maintaining territory by misrepresenting and erasing Native peoples (Wolfe, 2006). There is a strategic logic to the (in)visibility of Indigenous peoples. I sat there listening to Chris, and I understood where he was coming from. In my own life, I have dealt with racist and damaging remarks over and over again.

A deeper part of me understood that Chris's classmate were insinuating and maintaining the long history of Indigenous erasure. She was re-creating harm by erasing Indigenous presence, brilliance, and intelligence. As Native people, many of us understand this because Indigenous erasure is a part of our stories. The fourth monster, the *(in)visibility monster,* has roots in erasure and racism that work to dehumanize and erase our multitude of brilliance and intellect, which in turn sets us up to question who we are and our sense of belonging, and unsettle the connections we have to our home(lands). Parentheses are used with the word "(in)visibility" to mark that there are tensions (concurrently) in being invisible and visible. Brayboy (2004) indicates that there is a constant interplay between (in)visibility and visibility that "simultaneously create and are created by processes of marginalization, exclusion, assimilation, and oppression" (p. 128).

Yet, Chris answered the (in)visibility monster by stating his place, his location on the land: "This is my home. This is Native American land." We will learn more about the Indigenous weapon of refusal that he was employing. I am constantly learning from Chris, from these students, about ways to be.

Writing about this now brings forth a pain, deep and raw. I am holding in tears because it aches inside my bones, inside my soul. Sorry to have to tell you this, but I have to, so the aches inside your bones and souls are able to leave. We can't carry the hurt. It needs to transfer out. We must not let the (in)visibility monster win, the diminishment of possible selves, although it's everywhere and pervasive, benefiting others in really big ways. Remember that there is an investment in Indigenous erasure.

These are profound times. My friend Amanda Blackhorse and many others, including Suzan Harjo and Charlene Teters, fought for the removal of the racist mascots that depict Native peoples as their teams' logos, brands, and symbolic figures. For example, the National Football League (NFL) team the Washington *ed*kins profited immensely from the racist imagery of Native peoples. For Dan Snyder (coowner and co–chief executive officer of the Washington team), he claimed that the use of the mascot was based on honoring Native peoples. Historically, the r-word is rooted in the dehumanization of Native peoples as uncivilized "savages," language (the deficit [not enough] monster) weaponized to erase Indigenous presence. There was a time in history when Native people were hunted, and a bounty given for each scalp of a dead Native person, and this included women and children.[2] The term "red skins" was used in the announcements of bounty hunting. Offering bounties for Native scalps was a strategy to kill off our people, diminish our lives. In the 21st century, profits and hypervisibility of damaged Native peoples are strategies used to further eliminate Native peoples.

Research has found that mascots of Natives are harmful because they remind Native peoples (young people, like high school students) of the limited ways that others see them, which consequently influences how Native peoples see themselves (Fryberg et al., 2008). More research has circulated that asserts how mascots of Native people are associated with negative stereotypes of Natives by non-Natives, which impacts intergroup relations among Natives and non-Natives (Davis-Delano et al., 2020). Often these negative stereotypes reinforce the idea that Natives are primitive, aggressive savages.

Simply put, they dehumanize Native people and re-create Indigenous erasure; the (in)visibility monster is at play.

In an interview, Fryberg stated the following powerful words:

> Mascots are yet another way in which we systematically discriminate against Native people. And we give license to sports and schools for people to dress up, 'play Indian,' mock Native song and dance—there are so many layers. In many ways, that dehumanization of Native people on the playing field gets reflected in the high rates of death of Native people at the hands of police—among the highest in the country. It also—most people are not aware—in this country, every year, 500 to 600 Native women go murdered and missing, and yet the majority of those cases do not get investigated. This issue is not a small issue: It's about humanizing Natives; it's about allowing us to be seen for who we are (Stanton, 2020).

It's about allowing us be seen for who we are. In 2020, the Washington Football Team announced that it was discarding the *ed*kins name after mounting substantial financial stakes. For example, large corporations, such as Nike, pulled apparel that included the racist team name. Profits motivated that move, not Indigenous humanity. (In February 2022, the team announced that it was changing its name to the Washington Commanders.)

Erasure amounts to (in)visibility and nonpresence. Erasure is a killing off of people, lifeways, beingness. By now, you probably can guess that the reason for the erasure of Indigenous peoples is so others can acquire the land and not have to deal with the so-called problematic people (i.e., us) who are and will be different. Erase and replace. Erase and replace for the land. Replace for power. That is some bullshit, and yet the long history of this nation-state as (in)visibility is also about more than lack of representation; it's the continued reproduction of "an active 'writing out' of the story that both reflects and reinforces the status quo" (Fryberg & Townsend, 2008, p. 176). The invisibility of Indigenous peoples means the maintaining of Whiteness, the normalization of who belongs to the lands, in schools, in society.

The settlers did not stop their ferocious efforts and strategies to consume power and possession of the land and our lives. There are many federal policies that were enacted to remove us farther from our home(lands) and from the settlers' new settlements, their new homes, established on our home(lands). Many of them did not want Indigenous peoples near them. And the government was shrewd in obtaining the land. It still acts in clever ways. Settler colonialism.

In Part II, I told how early colonial colleges used Native and Black peoples to help start some of the most elitist and prestigious colleges, including Harvard, Dartmouth, and William & Mary College. Many more universities benefited (and still benefit) from manipulative behaviors in the stealing of Indigenous lands. I learned about the Morrill Act of 1862, which connects the ties between Indigenous lands, Indigenous lives, and universities. President Abraham Lincoln signed the Morrill Act into law on July 2, 1862. This act provided for public lands to be appropriated to states at a quantity of 30,000 acres per senator and their congressional representation. Bigger congressional representations received more acres—basically, more White people in a given area received more Indigenous lands. At the time, Indigenous and Black bodies were not counted—erasure. "Public"[3] lands were sold to states at $1.25 per acre, and the monies earned from the selling of Indigenous lands were invested in endowments that provided and continue to provide for capital earned in perpetuity.

Perpetuity means no maturity date. Perpetuity means ongoing predatory lending where the land has been unfairly handled through deceptive and exploitative practices. Interest from these monies is transferred to states to reinvest into endowments in support of universities. The Morrill Act allowed the taking of Indigenous lands, selling of those lands, and then using the monies gained from those sales to invest in the seedlings and growth of universities across this nation! When I read the Morrill Act, there was no mention that the lands were occupied by Indigenous peoples, that the settlers were new to the lands, or the reality that the lands were stripped from the Indigenous peoples who cared for, loved, and prayed with them. Indigenous existence was made invisible. Indigenous erasure and evidence of the (in)visibility monster.

High Country News, a news outlet, released a remarkable investigative account of the Morrill Act of 1862 that made us all aware of Indigenous presence in the retelling of this exploitation. The authors, Tristan Ahtone (from the Kiowa Tribe) and Robert Lee, researched more than 10.7 million acres (99% of Morrill Act acres) of Indigenous lands and found the original caretakers of 245 Tribal Nations to those lands and the principal raised from the land sales that supported 52 universities. Billions of dollars have been raised for higher education, and that total continues to grow. Indigenous lands are stolen, Indigenous and Blacks lives are lost, and universities benefit. In their reporting, they provided data that include geological mappings of the land parcels that were taken from Indigenous peoples and transferred to universities. I pored over those maps and found parcels of land connected to our people, the Diné.

The University of Arizona (UA), which is located in Tucson, Arizona, on the home(lands) of the Tohono O'odham and Pascua Yaqui Nations, benefited from the taking and selling of home(lands) of Tribal Nations, including Apache, Pima, Papago, Maricopa, Walapai, Cocopa, and Navajo.[4] In 1910, a total of 143,564 acres (521 land parcels) were sold at the price of $345 to benefit the UA. The Maricopa, Pima, and Papago had a total of 60,306 acres taken for $0 (20,102 acres per Tribe), which was the largest land acquisition for the UA (Lee & Ahtone, 2020). The Navajo Nation had a total of 3,720 acres sold for $354 through the Treaty of 1868. That is less than 10 cents per acre—less than one thin dime per acre. The Navajo

Nation was the only Tribe that received monies for land, but amounting to less than a dime per acre.

When I think about that time frame, 1862, I am drawn to recognizing that it was a time of profound fear and heartache as settlers invaded Navajo land and devised plans to imprison our relatives at Hwéeldih. Recall that the Long Walk occurred from 1864 to 1868. We can see here how policies and histories are intertwined. While President Lincoln used his pen to sign the Morrill Act, he was striking the pen many times over, to allow the enforcement of land acquisitions from Tribal Nations across these lands. Clever is an understatement to describe these actions. It was theft, manipulation, and violence.

The Navajo Treaty was signed in 1868 at Hwéeldih. Your great-great-great grandfather, Chief Manuelito, signed the treaty by marking it with an X. Even if I can go to that time frame in my mind, I can't begin to know the depth of fear, anger, and possibly some semblance of hope that our elders were facing. They wanted to go home. They wanted to return to Diné Bikéyah (Navajo land), to be reconnected to Nihimá Nahasdzáán (Mother Earth), to be embraced by the sacred mountains, and witness the sunrise greet them in the right relations and in rhythmic transcendence with the Creator (*reverence*). Those desires to return lay in those strokes of the pen that the 23 Diné leaders signed. Lands were taken, and our people were able to return to some portions of their home(lands). And probably not knowing or realizing that the UA would later benefit from 3,720 acres that once held the homes and livelihoods of our people. That is what I mean by saying that the transaction "was created through theft, manipulation and violence." Our people were in prison, hoping and praying that they could return home. They were in prison because they were Diné. No crimes were committed by the little children, the mothers and aunties, the fathers and uncles, and our grandparents, yet they were all deemed guilty of living and thriving as Diné. And to return to some aspect of sovereignty, they signed a treaty that gave land and power to the White settlers.

Last week, we traveled to one of the parcels of land that were earmarked as a Morrill Act grantee land that benefited the UA. There was a calling to be there, even when we were in a state of rest (or unrest) because of the COVID-19 pandemic. We were careful. Daddy packed our food and drinks. I packed our masks, sanitizing wipes, and hand sanitizers. You all packed your pillows, devices, and energies. I knew that this would be a long day to be in the vehicle. And I am very grateful that each of you was gracious and kind with Daddy and me. There is a part of me that wonders if the land was calling to you all too. I wanted to take all of you on that journey so you could return to, see, and feel the beauty of the lands of our ancestors.

As we approached the Morrill Act land parcel, I began to feel anxious. I remember telling your dad that I am feeling some way. I took a few deep breaths to calm my spirit. Your dad helped to find the exact location of a piece of land that was taken from our people through the Treaty of 1868 and then later sold to benefit the UA—my alma mater, the institution to which you all grew accustomed, the complexities all colliding in my mind and heart. We parked on the side of the road, and I drifted toward the land that was transferred from our people to the UA. I slipped my sandals off to feel Nihimá Nahasdzą́ą́n (Mother Earth) next to my skin. The air was warm as I wiggled my toes into the brown-red dirt.

The pandemic has taught me to be more appreciative of our relationships with the land and with each other. This does not mean that I did not have a relationship with you all or the land before; I did. Yet, we can all surrender to more depth and meaning of relationality. Do you remember how we talked about the land, about how the land was taken from our people, and how those monies benefited UA? Do you remember how we offered a prayer in gratitude to what the land offers us, to not carry the hurt that is felt when learning about our history, and to heal the peoples and lands that were in mourning and ill? I remember. I hope you do too, and that you will share that story with your future one day. Remembering is a powerful force, especially when remembrance is rooted in love, belonging, and relationality. We will never be erased because the land remembers. The land knows us.

Hauntings

Amber literally glided into our first interview, as she scooped up her longboard and took a seat. A natural athlete, she had a creative edge in her style of dress, often wearing shorts, Converse shoes, and a sweatshirt that declared, "GOD FIRST BRO." Her hair was usually pulled back into a casual ponytail and then polished with a headband. She wore black-framed glasses that often slipped slightly down her nose. By habit, Amber would frequently bend her pointer finger and adjust her glasses to a more comfortable position. She made me laugh in a good way because she was easy to talk to, and we connected with each other through jokes that you'd understand only if you were Native.

Growing up on the Navajo Reservation in the town of Red Sands, she relished running through the sand dunes and seeking out places to rock climb. Red Sands is one of the larger towns on the reservation, with a population of roughly 5,000 people. Because of its location near national landmarks, tourists frequent the town. A grocery store and a handful of fast

food restaurants are available. Amber grew up among a large extended family, with six of her maternal grandmothers living nearby and a "complicated"
immediate family. She elaborated on "complicated" by describing that her
mom and dad separated when she was in kindergarten. Amber was the oldest of six siblings, four of which were either stepsiblings or half-siblings.
Growing up, Amber's siblings lived off and on with her, her mom, and her
stepdad at different times during the year. Amber had affectionate memories
of her extended family. One time, her six grandmas and their family all came
together and organized a food sale to help raise money so that Amber could
attend a youth leadership program out of state. Through their combined efforts, Amber had enough spending money to pay for her food and lodging.
Amber smiled when she told me that story. I could tell that that memory
made her feel good.

Raised in a Christian home and having a devoted relationship with her
másání (maternal grandmother), Amber was instilled with teachings such
as believing in and connecting with God as an integral part of life. These
Christian teachings were a powerful force, but also a contradicting dilemma
that she later worked through while she was in college. I will return to that
tension soon, but for now, let's continue with Amber's views on college.

The first in her family to go to college, she wanted to "push myself
even more to show them [family] that anyone can do it." As a young child,
Amber was instilled with an ethic of competitiveness. In elementary school,
she worked hard to get better grades than anyone else in her class. She
told me that often she was the first person to get an assignment done and
recalled being told by her teachers to "slow down." Then, in 5th grade, she
received her first F on a paper. To make matters worse, she and her friends
had challenged each other to see who would get the better grade. Amber, as
competitive as she was, knew that she was going to beat her friends. When
she received an F, she was embarrassed and cried. Not only had she failed
the assignment, she had the lowest grade among her friends. That experience shaped her to always strive for excellence. It also made her realize that
she was influenced by how others viewed her. Competition was connected to
comparing herself with others, something that she faced over and over. She
wanted to be a role model for her younger family members. She also wanted
others in her community to see her positively as a student.

While in high school, she channeled her ambitious streak into the classroom and sports. A talented athlete, Amber participated in basketball, softball, and volleyball. Her team played in state championship games during
her senior year. This was also an important and difficult stage in her life.
Amber started feeling more frustrated with school, as she felt that Red
Sands was not challenging her academically. She was becoming accustomed
to being "bored" in her classes, and she "hated" that feeling—examples of
the *deficit (not enough) monster*. On top of her frustrations with academics, Amber underwent some challenges in her relationship with her mother.
During this time, she felt as though her mom was not supporting her in her

sports. What made this time even more difficult was that her grandmother, her confidant, the person she went to for advice and encouragement, was undergoing testing for cancer. This devastated Amber. She feared the worst. Amber described her senior year as "rough" and a time when she learned a lot about herself. What I gained from Amber is her ability to learn from life experiences, especially about herself. From the time Amber was in elementary school, she took notes about situations that were influencing her, aware of those experiences, and then worked on ways to do and be better.

Amber "just knew" that she was meant to go to college because it was an opportunity to gain skills so that she could help others (*continuance*). Whenever she was asked, "What do you want to be when you grow up?" she answered, "I always want to help people." She applied to five colleges, two out of state and three in state. She was encouraged to apply to highly competitive institutions, such as an Ivy League school, because of her strong academic and leadership abilities, as well as her tenacious work ethic. However, she was adamant about not applying to any Ivy League colleges. Although a smart and competitive person, Amber was "afraid" deep inside; she thought that she was only prepped for "a regular college" and thought that if she attended an Ivy League school, she could fail, reminding me how powerful the *failure monster* seeps into students' possible selves, even among star students.

Amber had her heart set on attending a college in California and enjoying life by the beach. But as the application process unfolded, she did not complete the California college application. It was too far from home, and being near home, near her grandmother, near cliffs to climb was important to Amber. She knew herself. She knew the powerful influence that home provided, sustaining her. We need to honor students' knowing. The Onondaga scholar Stephanie Waterman (2012) found in her research that Hondanoshonee college students' ability to go home on a regular basis helped them adjust and persist in college, referred to as "home-going as a strategy." Amber was already exploring home-going strategies even before entering college. She knew what would help her be successful. Home and family were key ingredients.

Of course, because Amber was a talented softball player, in-state community colleges wanted her. She was flattered to be thought of by those colleges. Yet as she embarked into college, she knew that her primary focus was going to be on academics. She made the decision to not play sports in college. Amber wanted to be a medical doctor, and she knew that pursuing medical school was not going to be easy. She also understood that college costs were going to be challenging and expensive. If you recall from Part II of this book, several students applied for the Gates Millennium Scholarship, and only one received it. That was Amber. She received Gates, which released the burdens of college affordability. Her family would not have to hold another food sale to help raise funds. Her grandmother was proud. And that made Amber feel good.

During her first year in college, she did not have to worry too much about paying for food, transportation, books, and/or living expenses, but what bothered Amber was feeling alone and wondering if she belonged at college.

The first semester was the roughest for Amber: "I felt like I was alone— I felt like I was alone and like I didn't feel like there were Natives here. . . . The first semester, I was depressed. . . . No one really cares about me." She then began to explain to me that if the university could talk, this is what she thought the university would say: "We don't care if you're Native. We just need you because we want to be a diverse college. Fail, go ahead, like most Natives do fail. You're just a number. If you fail, that's more money for us." The failure monster is related to the (in)visibility monster. Monsters are connected. They work together. Remember that.

If we were to examine the numbers, Amber is correct—Natives on college campuses represent a very small population. In 2015, Native students enrolled in U.S. higher education made up about 1% of the student population. Total enrollment numbers of American Indian and Alaska Native students has declined since 2000. In 2009, there were 205,900 Native students enrolled in degree-granting, 4-year, postsecondary institutions. However, by 2014, the enrollment had dropped to 152,900—the lowest it has been since the year 2000 (Musu-Gillette et al., 2017). Of Native students in 2016–2017, 4% graduated with an associate degree, and 5% graduated with a bachelor's degree or higher. Of the total number of Native students enrolled, 2% received a master's degree and 0.5% obtained a doctorate in 2016–2017.

When these numbers are juxtaposed against the larger Native population, the (in)visibility of Native college students is much starker. In the United States, there are 574 Native federally recognized Tribal Nations, in addition to 63 state-recognized Tribal Nations and more Tribal Nations who are fighting for recognition. According to the 2010 Census, 5.2 million people in the United States self-identified as American Indian and Alaska Native— one of the largest increases compared to other racial/ethnic populations. Yet, while the Native population continues to grow, college enrollment of Native peoples continues to remain stagnant, at 1%. We are in a stagnation deadlock, and the (in)visibility monster enjoys the lack of Indigenous presence.

In high school, Amber was a talented athlete and leader in her community. She was outspoken and competitive when it came to academics and the sports she played. Yet, during Amber's first semester at college, she recognized that she felt different, and that difference made her shy and transformed her into a person who questioned herself and the way people interact around and with her:

Once you're actually here and you know that you're stuck here.
That's how I felt, I felt like I was stuck here. I felt different. I felt like,
"Okay, I'm Native. I'm a huge minority." Back at home, everyone's
Native. Here, I was just like, seeing a bunch of White people, seeing a

bunch of perfect girls, sorority girls and frat guys. The dorm I was in, everyone was sorority and frat guys. I just felt like I was just so shy. I was really shy. I wasn't even talkative. I was just like, "Yeah, how are you?" You know, awkward. I was the most awkward person. I felt like I was being judged. I felt like I wasn't being liked. When people would talk to me, I would feel on the inside, like, "They're actually talking to me?" type of thing. I don't know why. I would just feel that way. "They're actually talking to me, like why? Do they feel sorry for me?" I would feel that way.

Amber's sense of worth was diminishing as she questioned why others would talk to her, sometimes thinking that they were simply feeling sorry for her. Listening to her tell me that reflection was so difficult. I wondered how many more Native students felt that way, thought in those same ways, such that the (in)visibility monster was erasing their possible selves. Lack of Native students, feeling different, not being included, and questioning of self all contributed to a weakened sense of belonging, a damaged sense of self. That is not the students' fault. Remember that it has been baked into systems of higher education for centuries, since the beginning of college formations.

The first weeks of college are a critical time for students. Many are hoping for a smooth transition, a time when they just want to fit in. It was during this time that Cecilia encountered the awkwardness of being different as a Diné:

I know the first week, I brought bitter medicine and I put it in a little plastic bag. I dropped it on the floor by accident. I didn't know I dropped it on the floor. The first couple nights, she [her roommate] freaked out and she called them [the Residence Assistant] and they were freaking out because they didn't know if that was weed or not. That's medicine. . . . It's like, "What's wrong with her?" That's medicine. She never gave it back to me. That was something. People thought I'm weird.

I asked Cecilia how that encounter influenced her first week of college. She further explained, "Sometimes the culture isolates yourself from society. . . . It's just like knowing that herbs have healing powers and people just look at you weird, and now they're like, that's weird, I don't know it's just, its kind of mainly sad because not many people will understand Native culture."

Cecilia framed incidents like this as isolating, even adding that culture isolates you from society. When your ways of being and doing are different from the majority culture, it makes a person feel alone, and in Cecilia's case, it created and reinforced schemas of weirdness. I noted that Cecilia used the word "sad" to describe how she felt. Feelings that are not something that most people want to experience, especially during their first week of college.

Sarah encountered difference during a Sustainability in Education course. The topic in class was food production and the inability of societies (like the United States) to conserve and the general public's lack of awareness on where food comes from. Many of her classmates raised their hands and discussed how grocery stores were the places they purchased food and goods. Many of them admitted that they had never planted, had not experienced cultivating the land. They did not learn how to grow food. Sarah sat in class and realized that her lifestyle of growing squash and corn, herding sheep, and hauling water was not something that her peers understood or practiced. Living by the land was normal and common for her family. She decided to explain this to her class because she wanted people to be aware that there were groups of people (Diné peoples) who grew up knowing and caring for the land. She shared, "That's how we live, that's who we are. He'll [professor] be like, 'wow, I didn't know that' or 'oh my gosh.' Just seeing that in his perspective of, like, nobody lives sustainable in the United States, we all take everything for granted, we all go to McDonald's. I'm like no, not at all. . . . That just makes me feel different because none of the other students have even done that."

Sarah admitted that this encounter gave her strength because she was more aware that she had teachings that were unique to her classmates, teachings that honored the relationship she had with the land. But she also recognized that her lifestyle was different and invisible to her classmates, and even her sustainability professor, and that recognition of (in)visibility and difference is an ongoing experience—sometimes it's a good feeling (as in this case) and then there are the many times when it's not.

For example, Sarah also told me of the frustrations she was feeling because of her roommate and other girls' insistence that Sarah change the way she dressed. Sarah explained, "I notice people always look at me because I'm always wearing jeans, T-shirt, and a sweater. It would be the hottest day outside and I'll be wearing my sweater, but you know I'm used to it. Girls are just, they have short shorts and see through shirts or T-tops, whatever they wear these days. Their mentality is different from mine. . . . like my roommate and my RA, my dorm roommate and some girls you know they dress like that, and they'd be like, you need to buy shorts, you need to buy skirts. I'm like, no." Sarah told me that for her, college is about getting an education, and that is where her focus is. She is not interested in clothing or changing the way she normally dresses. She is a rancher who works hard to train and exercise horses, and she understands that covering up can protect you from the sun. Not to mention that although it's hot outside, the minute you walk into a building, a blast of cold air-conditioning can shock you, and many might wish they had a sweater to put on.

Sarah confessed to me that these types of encounters made her feel like she did not fit in, that she did not belong. The (in)visibility monster works in ways that we often do not realize. Remember that the parentheses in "(in)visible" explain the tensions that exist, as there are times when you feel invisible and visible at the same time! Being visibly different in how one looks or dressed compared to others, while also being invisible because of the stark difference.

There are also teachings in Navajo families that young girls should cover up and avoid wearing clothing that shows too much of their bodies. Our history documents that settlers and Spaniards stole women and girls. Navajo people wove clothing in dark colors like black and deep blue, colors that were chosen for protection against settlers. Dark clothing allowed women to run at night without being seen, run to escape their captivity. As a mother of two daughters, I am coming to understand more of the protection we have of our womxn, protection even in guiding you on how to dress. Sadly, we still have to protect our womxn from violence and captives. In Canada and in the United States, Missing and Murdered Indigenous Women and Girls (MMIWG) is a scary reality that haunts our communities. Research by the National Institute of Justice found more than four out of five American Indian and Alaska Native women (more than 1.5 million women) have experienced violence (Rosay, 2016). More than 5,700 Native women and girls were reported missing in 2016, Native women are over 2½ times more likely to be sexually assaulted than women of other races, and one in three Native women has been raped. These numbers are reported figures, and likely are an undercount. They do not include the many unreported lives lost and abused, the invisible numbers. A majority of cases of missing and murdered Indigenous womxn do not get investigated.

This lack of attention is dehumanizing and speaks to the strength of the (in)visibility monster. I want to be clear that I am not stating that how a person dresses is directly correlated to how she or he will be treated. What I am attempting to say is that there is a real fear for our Indigenous womxn (historically and presently), that there are teachings (strategies) to protect them, and many are unaware of MMIWG and possible teachings utilized to safeguard our precious womxn. This is a reminder of how societal violence vis-à-vis lack of awareness affects the sense of personhood of Indigenous peoples. The (in)visibility monster is everywhere. There are long histories that connect to the present.

Returning to Amber's story, recall that she was raised as a Christian, and although she respected and practiced those teachings, her feelings of fear and confusion were magnified because she was coming to grips with her sexual identity—another intersection of difference. Amber enrolled in a gender class, which enlightened her views on gender and sexuality. She began confronting herself and exploring the newness of dating a woman. She did not tell many people about what she was going through, such as her roommate, family, or friends from home, until she met a new friend whom she instantly clicked with. This friend, Laura, was the first person with whom Amber could be "out" about her identity.

As Amber started telling me about finding her new friend, she spoke fast with excitement and happiness. She laughed with joy as she described the freedom of knowing someone who was nonjudgmental and fun. I could sense her relief in having a friend around whom she could be herself. Amber and Laura lived in the same residence hall, which made it easier for them to hang out with each other. But they soon learned that rumors were spreading in the residence hall about their relationship. Amber's roommate even went on Twitter and told the world about their "awkward" friendship. Amber explained, "My roommate was on Twitter, and whatever. Everyone looks at the stuff. She's like, 'an awkward moment walking into your room and the door is unlocked.' I'm like, beware, the door's unlocked. I'm not hiding anything. And then she's like, 'and your roommate's in another bed with another girl.'" Amber confronted her roommate because she wanted to clear the air and dispel the rumors:

> I confronted her. I was like, "Well, I heard there are rumors being spread around that me and Laura are together." I was like, "No we're not. Even if we are, why is that a big deal?" She was like, "Oh yeah, I knew that." So I said again, "There are rumors going around. I just want to clear things up." And then she said, "Okay." After that she was totally quiet.

For Amber, she was not only feeling isolated as a Native person, but also experienced ridicule because of her sexual identity. She told me that she felt that the residential environment was hostile—a place where people spoke in judgment, behind her back.

Although she was able to go home to Red Sands to replenish quality time with family and the lands and to not feel alone as a Diné, she learned that her home church was a place where she had to deal with homophobia. The church her grandmother labored over and loved; the church where Amber also learned to pray, to sing, and to love others. During spring break, she went home and was excited to attend church, but was shook upon hearing a homophobic message. She told me:

> We went to church on Sunday, and ugh it was horrible because I was so excited to go, and, you know how like the Christianity they bash out on gay people, and they started doing that. They started talking in Navajo so fast. I was like, "Mom, what are they saying?" I wasn't making it like it was bothering me. My mom doesn't know. And then my mom, she's like, "We're going to go after the offerings, and then we're going to get a doughnut, and then we are going to go." I wanted to be there for the last big prayer, where you just leave everything on the altar and everything. I wanted to be there for that, and then I was like, "Okay." I walked out, I was freaking out like oh shit. . . . I was feeling like crap because they're my elders who I grew up with, go to church, they still go to church, I respect them so much. And they were, just the little comments they make, even in Navajo. I was sitting there, like crap and

remembering I am in a sticky situation here. And that is when I started questioning myself. I started questioning my sexuality again.

Amber explained that after that incident, she was eager to return to college. She began recognizing that she started to dread going home to Red Sands because she was unable to be her true self, and she "hated" that feeling. Amber was caught in constantly trying to find the place where she belonged. While she felt like she did not fully belong at college because of her Navajo identity, she was able to be more open about her sexuality there. Yet, her home church at Red Sands, a place where she could be Navajo, was a space where she was fearful of expressing her sexuality. Race and sexual difference to White normative ways—rooted in heteropatriarchy and erasure—made her question herself in different places. She was embarking on contested ground which reminded me of the Black intellectual Audre Lorde (2020), who wrote:

Those of us who stand outside the circle of this society's definition of acceptable women; those of who have been forged in the crucibles of difference—those of us who are poor, who are lesbians, who are Black, who are older—*know that survival is not an academic skill*. It is learning how to stand alone, unpopular and sometimes reviled, and how to make common cause with those others identified as outside the structures in order to define and seek a world in which we can all flourish. It is learning how to take our differences and make them strengths. *For the master's tools will never dismantle the master's house*. (p. 41)

Amber provided a deeper and expansive perspective to belonging that encompassed multiple lived realities of who determines belonging. She opened up space for us to understand the power that the (in)visibility monster has on generating monstrous internalization. She also demonstrated that there is doubleweaving that occurs, which shifts conceptions of belonging, and that systemic monsters of heteropatriarchy and homophobia are very present, even in sacred places within home(lands). The Cherokee and queer scholar Qwo-Li Driskill (2010) described doubleweaving as "intertwined walls of a doublewoven basket, enable us to see the numerous splints—including Native politics, postmodern scholarship, grassroots activism, queer and trans resistance movements, queer studies, and tribally specific contexts—from which these critiques are (and can be) woven. . . . the weaving process also creates something else; a story much more complex and durable than its original and isolated splints, a story both unique and rooted in an ancient enduring form" (p. 74). Doubleweaving in many ways is related to the story rug, the interconnectedness of theoretical splints and threads in baskets and rugs draw on and intersect numerous stories and histories to create a stronger whole.

Monstrous Internalization

I am devoting an entire chapter to the fucked-up ways the *(in)visibility monster,* rooted in racism, further intensifies Indigenous erasure. When you can, I recommend that you pause and take breaks when reading this chapter, possibly take a walk or drink some water, maybe even pray, or scream. Do what you can to keep from allowing these stories to seep into your sense of self. Don't let the (in)visibility monster consume you. This is a warning before you continue to read.

As a society, as a world, Indigenous peoples are deemed inhuman. By now, you have read about how being labeled as "savages" has worked against us. Well, there are more labels. Students shared that there are many, many, many more damaging ways that society views Natives, reinforcing the (in)visibility monster's powers. When I asked Amber to tell me how society viewed Native peoples, she looked at me, paused, and then quickly offered a list: "Alcoholic, failures, dirty, lack of judgment, alcohol, alcohol, alcohol, quiet, shy, insecure, yeah." Chris had a similar list: "There's so many stereotypes from the general public. Natives drink a lot, Natives fail, and all of this stuff." And Jessie reflected on how society at large primarily viewed Natives in undesirable ways: "I feel like society's message for me is a lot of negativity, only because everybody's always saying like, 'Oh, you're no different, you're just going to go to school in a year and drop out.'"

These societal views physically and mentally troubled students. Joy explained that it was draining: "It's really tiring to know that a lot of people think of Native American as drunk people who just receive checks and rely on the government. In reality, it's not like that for everybody. And nobody is really there to express to the community that it's not like that for everybody. There's a really good percentage of people who are not Native American who are alcoholics, who do drugs, who drop out of high school, and things like that." She was right. In 2016, a research study stated, "In contrast to the 'Native American elevated alcohol consumption' belief, Native Americans compared to whites had lower or comparable rates across the range of alcohol measures examined" (Cunningham et al., 2016, p. 73). These research findings echo what Joy experienced. She continued to explain the contradictions that are at play in society and questioned why Natives are considered drunks, whereas White people are not: "Because I don't know why people think it's okay for, like, White people and stuff to drink and not be seen as, 'Oh, White people are nothing but drunks,' and things like that. They're not stereotyped like that. I don't understand why Native Americans are stereotyped like that. It's no different." Joy continued to express her frustrations with society's inability to open their awareness to ongoing destruction that they were contributing to: "They really focus on stereotypes. If they think one way it's kind of hard to help them think in a different way and to be able to open their horizons and for them to be able to understand that at a different level, and to just look past those negative things that they know or that they think of us." Joy brought up a good point. Why do stereotypes continue to exist, especially among Native peoples and other populations that are "minoritized"? Some researchers think it's because stereotypes allow dominant groups to remain dominant, meaning that Whiteness prevails by continuing to normalize inhuman perspectives of oppressed groups (Merskin, 2001). These are examples of the harmful ways in which the (in)visibility monster makes Natives visible.

Amber told me that sometimes you end up living up to those stereotypes, which speaks to the concept of stereotype threat, which is defined by Claude Steele (1997) as "the event of a negative stereotype about a group which one belongs becoming self-relevant, usually as a plausible interpretation for something one is doing, for an experience one is having, or for a situation one is in, that has relevance to one's self-definition" (p. 616). Amber explained:

Because we hear all the time, growing up, we hear like, "Oh, alcoholic, blah, blah, blah . . . trashy, dirty, going on and on." You just hear that growing up, and it's just like engrained in your mind and that's just all, you can't get it out. You know how people look at you. You know you're stereotyped and some of it's true. I can be quiet. I get scared talking in front of everyone, just because I don't want to be wrong. I don't want everyone to think I'm stupid. I don't want to be found wrong, so sometimes I'm quiet. I'm really quiet in class. I don't know why. I hate it. Hopefully I grow out of that and be confident in myself. That's what it is. I didn't have confidence. We could be super smart. We could do so much with our lives, but it's just the stereotypes that we know that we're judged upon. Someone puts stereotypes on me. I will eventually fulfill those stereotypes because I've been told that so many times. You think so less of yourself. You just believe that's you.

When hearing Amber share with me how stereotypes become reality, this made me think about how societal views play tricks on us, how the (in)visibility monster plays with us, such that monstrous internalization powerfully works to make us think less of ourselves.

As we continued to talk about stereotypes, students began giving examples that occurred in college. Remember that these are all freshman students, excited to embark on their first year away from home to attend college. During that pivotal time, story after story erupted of the fucked-up ways that they encountered damaging perspectives. Jessie stated, "It's funny because my White friends are like, 'Do you smoke a lot of those big pipes? Do you guys still live in teepees? My great, great grandma was a Cherokee princess.' A lot of the times, I'm just amazed how people's perception of Native Americans are. We're just right there. We're six hours away. How do you not know, you know what I mean?" I want to point out Jessie's distinction when she said, "we are just six hours away." What she meant by that is that the Navajo Nation was a short drive from the college campus, suggesting that people are unaware of what is right next door to them. Although Jessie recognized that Navajo lands were 6 hours away, what she did not state was that Native peoples are everywhere and that the university resides on Native land. All colleges reside on the home(lands) of Indigenous peoples. The irony of that fact, juxtaposed with the reality that many college students are unaware about Indigenous presence is a marker of the pervasiveness of the (in)visibility monster.

Joy also experienced a tough moment when she was walking to class and experienced discrimination and racism. She was walking behind non-Native girls and overheard them talking about Native college students. They were talking about students like Joy. Joy explained:

They were like, "These Native Americans here, they're so in pointless direction. They don't know what they're doing here. They should just go back to their moccasin worlds and live back in their dirt homes.

It makes no sense for them to be here. They're just getting everything for free." That's not true. Everything that we get, we have to work, I think, twice as hard than you do. "They're just drunk Indians," and stuff like that. It's horrible.

After Joy heard these girls speak poorly of her and her people, she went back to her residence hall and cried. She didn't want to cry in front of them; she wanted to cry alone. She then further told me that she was upset with Native people for drinking and getting drunk, basically living up to the negative stereotypes. She said that Natives should "really think about where they're coming from and who they're representing. It could be your whole tribe." I understand what Joy was expressing with regard to getting frustrated at those who do abuse alcohol; but hearing her last statement about the "whole tribe" made me sad. Joy, and many other Native people, carry the weight of representation heavily on their shoulders. For centuries, society has illustrated Native peoples as less than human, and our young people are desperately trying to erase those illustrations that have been baked into the framework of what is now the United States. (In)visibility is a double-edged sword chiseled on both sides by racism; to be visible in the United States as a Native is to be seen as damaged, but to be invisible in the United States as a Native is to be erased. The (in)visibility monster attempts to steal the uniqueness and beauty of Native presence, yesterday and today.

Sometimes it's not just a direct statement that causes offense; there are plenty of questions that these students experience while in college. Questions that many would consider as private and personal. Questions that you would not ask another person, especially when you do not know them. Lauryn told me of off-putting questions that she received from her classmates: "It feels like every time I see someone that's not Native, they think of us, they're asking questions like where we live and what we wear, and what we eat, like we're not. . . . It's just like they think of us as being how it was 100 years ago or something." Lauryn brought up a good point, as she clarified that her classmates' questioning demonstrated that their views about Native livelihoods were historicized. They could see the types of clothes that Lauryn wore, probably similar to many of the other students in their class. But were they really seeing her for who she is? They could not see that Lauryn, in many ways, lived the same way and ate the same food as many people in college. These types of questions often reveal how invisible people can be when they are staring the asker in the face. In school, I used to hear there are no bad questions. But in these students' opinions, there are some really bad questions that you don't have to answer. I am giving you permission to not answer questions that make you feel uncomfortable.

Chris encountered an incident in his political science course. This time, the experience occurred between him and the professor. In a class of about 250 students, the professor was discussing societies that preserve their cultures and are environmentally conservative. The professor asked the class if there are people who live and see the world in this way. Chris was hesitant to raise his hand because of how large the class was, but he found the courage to do it. The professor called on him, and Chris responded with, "Well, I'm Navajo and I'm Native American and we see the world that way." Chris explained that the professor questioned him further about Navajo governance and planting. And then the professor asked Chris, "Do you see yourself as a Navajo?" This question shocked Chris, and he responded with, "Excuse me, what did you say?" And then the professor began to question Chris's Navajo identity. Here is the story from Chris:

> Then he was like, "You're standing here in a tank top, you're standing here in a much modern outfit. You have a Mac laptop." Then I was so caught off guard, and then he said, "Well, does the color of your skin verify that you're Navajo?" . . . I was so mad at him. "I was influenced by you that I'm standing here. Your ancestors influenced me to go to school and my ancestors basically told me to stay home, but I can't because like I said, we're politically and geographically misrepresented that we cannot live the lifestyle that we should be living."

The professor continued to ask him questions for another 10 minutes, questions about living on the reservation and about whether he can still live as a Navajo in other regions of the world. Chris became more frustrated and finally told him that his ideas were "discombobulated." The professor got upset and told Chris to talk to him after class, where the professor continued to question Chris about his Navajo identity.

I asked Chris how he felt after that incident, and he told me, "I walked out of there feeling less of a Navajo." A professor who has political power in the classroom questioned Chris about his identity as a Navajo, making Chris feel as though he was not Navajo. Chris was not the image that the professor projected in his mind of what a Navajo or Native American should look like. Images that were distorted and limited. Images based on Whiteness, the White gaze. And the harmful part of all of this is that Chris began to second-guess his identity as a Navajo person. Monstrous internalizations of the (in)visibility monster.

Much of the experiences that students encountered occurred face to face, either in the classroom, residence hall, or in passing, such as while walking on campus. Yet, students also revealed that damaging perspectives of Native students spread on social media as well. I was surprised to learn that almost all 10 students I interviewed talked about an online Facebook University Confessions page on which people could anonymously post comments. If a person wanted to post a confession, they would submit it on an online webpage. Then, those comments were shared on the Facebook University Confessions page. Comments ranged from having a crush on a classmate, complaining about campus food, and venting other concerns. The Facebook page was also a place for students to spew racist comments. When Cecilia mentioned reading these items on the Facebook University Confession page, she got upset and saw how statements were connected to maintaining the inferiority of Native peoples:

> I feel like a lot of them think that Native students go to college for free, and that really drives me insane. That really gets to me, you know. . . . I'm like, "Do you know what you're talking about?" . . . They talk down, they're like, "They're just Natives, they're stupid." . . . it's just like they're being arrogant and ignorant, and it's like they really think you're inferior to them. That's something I've dealt with, but it's like bigger here.

In her first year of college, Cecilia felt that the injustices were more bitter and bigger at college. I was beginning to understand that the superiority syndrome complex is the real danger, not the imposter syndrome. I define the term "superiority syndrome complex" as the belief that power structures (systemic monsters) are always deemed successful, despite their patterns of consistent failures. I will discuss more about the superiority syndrome complex in Chapter tseebíítsʼáadah (eighteen).

After reading the Facebook page, Lauryn thought about the financial struggle that she and other Native students were facing, knowing that college was not free for her as a Navajo. She looked at me and quietly told me:

> It just made my motivation go down, even more, because that is what people think of me. . . . It made my motivation go down. Like it was worse enough, it was bad enough, for me to not want to go out there and tell people I'm Native, but it made it even worse when I saw that, knowing there is someone out there, that made me even more scared to go out there. What if someone thinks of me like how he did? We are just greedy. We are just taking stuff, or we are just here, spending and whatnot.

Recall that Lauryn struggled in academics and was not attending tutoring because she was concerned about what others would think of her because she was Native. Posts such as those on Facebook "scared" her even more (*failure monster*) from being her true self as a Navajo woman and taking advantage of the opportunities available at college. Sometimes the (in)visibility monster penetrated so deeply into the students' minds and hearts that they second-guessed themselves. Lauryn elaborated a bit more about what it felt like to have people think negatively of who you are, the community you represent, being Native: "I think they think of me like they downgrade me. They don't think of me being smart. They just think of me being a wannabe successful Native here. They don't think I can do it. . . . it's always there." Her last words in that statement, "it's always there," were telling as a product of systemic monsters, which is deeply entrenched in a White supremacy that works to suppress Indigenous brilliance. Lauryn stated, "You can't be you. . . . It does affect me, being Native. I get scared. I think that I wonder what they think of me. It's sad. I don't want to say I am ashamed to be Native. I am happy, but it does make me think, like what people think of me." Keep in mind that there are very few Native students on college campuses; a majority of the students at school are White. Lauryn is sharing vulnerable thoughts that some Native students may encounter, especially if they make up less than 1% of the student population.

Lauryn continued that when she returns home, to the rural reservation, she has the freedom to be herself. She smiled and told me:

> When I go home, it's different than when I am here. When I go home, I want to be the Native that is going to—it makes my self-esteem go up. I want to be the first Native to do this, or I want to be one of the few Natives to finish college and be a doctor or something. But when I am here, it feels like it just goes down. I see no Natives here. It's like I can't really do it. I don't know. I think it does affect my motivation because it prevents me from doing this other stuff, because then I think of the way people are going to think of me.

When she is home, surrounded by other Native people, her self-esteem and motivation kick in. She is determined to acquire a college degree. Yet when she is on campus, the (in)visibility monster intensifies, and she questions herself. On campus, there are few Native students, faculty, or staff who can model possible selves for Native students to become. It's not the fault of Lauryn or other students who feel this way. It's the fault of a broken higher education system. The lack of Native presence on college campuses has been a problem for centuries. Joy stated it best when speaking about how universities see Natives: "I think what they [the university] would say is, 'I forgot they existed.'" Hauntings.

The (in)visibility monster moved into the mindset of Native students. It's cunning because of its power to make students feel less than, inferior, unmotivated, and not their true selves, while at the same time it reinscribes dehumanizing and historicized depictions of Native peoples. The (in)visibility monster works to take away Indigenous brilliance and beauty, Indigenous presence. However, Indigenous weapons of refusal are nearby, ready to deploy, and available to use against the (in)visibility monster.

Refusal as Sovereignty-Centered

There is profound strength in knowing who you are and where you come from. When I asked Cecilia to describe herself, she started laughing and commented, "That is really hard." After taking a few seconds to think about her response, she answered, "I would identify myself as a Navajo." Being raised off the Navajo reservation much of her life, she admitted that it was "hard to correlate as being Navajo." Through constant support from family and regular visits to her home on the reservation, she developed a stronger understanding of herself as a Navajo. As mentioned at the beginning of this book, Cecilia brought to my attention and reminded me of the monsters and weapons story. It is fitting, then, that we begin and then end with Cecilia's story.

Cecilia grew up in an urban city in Delarosa County. However, she did not call the city her home; rather, she considered Sunrise Valley, located on the Navajo Reservation, as her home. She had tender recollections of visiting her extended family at Sunrise Valley during the summer months and on weekends: "I noticed that I'm happier when I'm out there because it's so quiet, and it's so peaceful, and you finally feel like you are in balance." Cecilia grew up with Navajo teachings from her parents and from a Native American group that she met with once a week. Through those teachings, she formed the values of striving to live in balance, respecting others and the land, and practicing prayer. Those teachings were a source of strength for Cecilia as she navigated personal and family challenges.

As a prestigious high school student, she maintained a 4.0 grade point average starting in elementary school. Attending schools that had predominantly White students, Cecilia struggled with finding a "bond" with others and described herself as a "loner" much of the time at school. Since elementary school, she was teased for looking different. Her classmates would pull her long hair and call her derogatory names. In middle school, the harassment continued. She vividly shared an experience when boys in her class threw balls of paper at her. Frustrated, Cecilia threw the paper balls back at the boys. At the moment when she threw the balls back, the principal came into the classroom and saw her. Cecilia attempted to explain and justify her action, but the principal disregarded her comments. She thought that because she was a minority, administrators were quick to label her as a "delinquent." The principal scolded her and eventually left. As soon as he exited the classroom, the boys resumed throwing paper balls at her.

In high school, she continued to excel academically. She was the only Native student in her Advanced Placement (AP) courses and honors program. Yet the harassment did not stop. During her sophomore year, Cecilia began to struggle with depression and almost took her life. Increasing tension from her constant teasing at school compounded with personal and family challenges to weigh down on her.

Connecting with Diné teachings, Cecilia developed a stronger sense of self. She later got involved with the Native community and surrounded herself with friends who supported her educational aspirations. Cecilia flourished by the time she got to 12th grade, passing her AP exams with the highest scores possible and then graduating in the top 10% of her class, an accomplishment that she was very proud of. As a freshman in college, she kept going and excelled in academics, instilling Diné teachings that she learned from her family and the Native American group. Cecilia, like the other students I talked with, drew on the fourth Indigenous weapon of *refusal*, a deep understanding of knowing who we are and who we are not. Refusal is sovereignty-centered, asking us to turn away from damaging logics and take up onto-epistemological (practices of knowing and being are not isolated) understandings of k'é (kinship).

The Kahnawake Mohawk scholar Audra Simpson wrote about the everyday ways that Kahnawake people affirmed refusal at every turn against the state, which is critical for a community living within a nation-state that continuously attempts to dictate the terms of membership, authority, and rule over Indigenous peoples (Simpson, 2007). She further states, "There seemed rather to be tripleness, a quadrupleness, to consciousness and an endless play, and it went something like this: 'I am me, I am what you think I am and I am who this person to the right of me thinks I am and you are full of shit and then maybe I will tell you to your face'" (Simpson, 2007, p. 74). That is refusal, a turning away of the logics that others have formed about us, about you. And a deep recognition of claiming sovereignty of self, in knowing who we are and who is not who we are. *Refusal. Sovereignty.*

What motivated Cecilia was reflecting and then refusing those negative comments that were expressed to her in grade school and college. Cecilia stated:

> But you know, you can't subject to someone's stupid idea and ignorance. You just have to get over the fact that there's always going to be people that aren't pleased with people going to college and stuff like that, but you know you got to, I guess, tough it out. I don't know. I feel like I've been using tough it out a lot, but it's true. You can't just let them get to you. You just have to overcome it.

Cecilia recognized that you can't subject yourself to someone else's stupidity. This is true, and what Toni Morrison discusses as not limiting ourselves to the White gaze. Refusing the White gaze. Damaging perspectives are pervasive in the consciousness of a White society that upholds power over communities by controlling how their stories are constructed in media, schooling, and public opinion. What Cecilia knows is that we write our own story, and we have the power to tell ourselves who we are. She also mentioned "tough it out," which is connected to the Navajo term "yéego." This is different from "grit," a popular term that at its roots is associated with the Americanized notion of independence and dominance. Yéego and toughness are about strength in mind, in body, and in spiritual facets of life, which is bringing yourself in alignment with hózhó (beauty and balance). Cecilia taught me to refuse living our lives based on their concepts of who we are, but to channel that negative energy into a catalyst in seeing our true self, seeing ourselves as our ancestors see us. *Refusal.*

What was unique in this weapon was that most students that I talked to recognized that the odds were not in their favor, which intensified within them the desire to be their true selves. During times when Jessie wanted to give up on college plans, she often would question herself: "Jessie, what are you doing? You're just proving to everybody that said bad things about you as right. Do you want that? Do you want them to be able to say that they were right about you? That for me is motivation." By asking those questions, she was able to pause and reassess who she was and what she wanted to accomplish. Those are teachings of Diné ways that connect to the foundational power of sa'ah naagháí bik'eh hózhóón to think about and question the self and then align those thoughts to purpose so that a person can proceed in actionable ways that cultivate harmony and happiness. Thinking and reflecting are critical aspects of Diné ways.

Amber also brought up a good point. She tapped into her competitive personality and basically told me that societal views of Natives are so low that she was going to take it on herself to crush them:

> I don't like people looking down on me, but I like it that they have so low expectations for me that I can easily crush them. . . . That's how I feel about how society and how the college set such low expectations for us just because of our history, just because of the stereotypes . . . It's mainly being competitive again. You're just like, "I want to show you that you're wrong."

Amber refused to allow the deficit narrative to dwell inside her. I imagined her staring down at the (in)visibility monster and telling it that it didn't know her at all, that it was wrong about her. *Refusal.*

As for Joy, she explained to me that she does her best not to let the (in)visibility monster get to her by honoring ways of being Diné. She explained:

> It's just stereotyping is a really, really hurtful thing, but for me, it's not something that I would let get to me. I'll wear turquoise and I'll talk my language out in public and things like that. It doesn't bother me at all. I'm proud to be able to portray who I am and to at the same time let others see that I am going to challenge myself with my education, that I am a smart person, that I am doing all the things that they're doing.

Listening to Joy describe how wearing turquoise and speaking in Navajo on campus made her proud put a smile on my face. Those markers of identity made her feel like herself, while also demonstrating that she, as a Diné woman, was just as smart as others at college. Joy then told me, "It's not them who I'm representing. It's my own tribe. . . . I'm not ashamed of who I am and where I come from. I make it obvious and let them know who I am and what tribe I come from, and where I stand as a Native American individual, Navajo." Those were strong words that I want to restate: *IT'S NOT THEM WHO I'M REPRESENTING.* Joy was correct. She was not representing herself based on White views of indigeneity. She was representing herself and the people that she came from. By being herself, she was simultaneously giving herself strength and also deconstructing how society often views Native peoples. She was demonstrating what it looks like to be Native and gifted, personifying Indigenous intelligence and brilliance.

Returning to using *refusal* as a weapon, students described that regardless of how society viewed them, deep down they knew who they were and where they came from. They had a deep knowing of their relationships through kinship (k'é) and the lands that they came from. Jessie said:

> Just to have your clan and your Navajo name that alone, I feel like, makes me who I am. It's just to have that sense of . . . to know exactly

who you are and to know exactly where you come from. I feel like it
makes everything more clearly for me. My White friends are always
like . . . I mean, even then, I feel like they always try to just figure out
who they are because they don't really know their past or anything.
For me, I'm glad I do because like our ancestors have been through a
lot with everything. I can say that I do have history and that I do have
culture and I do have traditions. . . . I mean, just being here makes me
feel like a lot better about myself and who I am. As long as I have that
sense of direction and as long as I have that sense of knowing who I
am and where I came from, it makes everything clearer and easier for
me. It makes my mindset a lot stronger.

That sense of knowing, onto-epistemological teachings of being a part of a
clan, knowing the history of the people that came before us, and respecting
what our ancestors went through are Diné teachings that ground us to each
other, the land, and the universe. When Jessie remembers those vital ways of
knowing and being, life is much easier and her mindset is stronger.

In one of my last interviews with Sarah, we were talking about what
had occurred in our lives since the last time we met. Our conversations
moved to how Sarah was committed to reengaging in Diné language, even
while she was far from fluent or frequent speakers. Although being away
from Diné Bikéyah (Navajo land) made it hard to hear and speak Navajo in
everyday circumstances, Sarah didn't want to lose the language. She didn't
want to lose a part of herself that she held close to her. I was fascinated
with her urgency to reawaken the Diné language, as that is something that I
am trying my best to do too. She explained her strategy: "You know when
I am listening to my iPhone or something, listening to music, and I know
all these songs. I could sing them, I know the lyrics, I know all of it, but I
was thinking, why do I know so many songs and I can't memorize Navajo
words? I can learn songs easily, but why can't I know Navajo easily?" After
Sarah questioned herself about why she can sing the latest popular country
song but is unable to remember Navajo terms, she went through her iPhone
and proceeded to add Navajo songs to her iPhone. She wanted to listen to
and learn Navajo. She wanted to remember the words that she was taught,
that were passed down for generations. She then told me, "I just listened to
it. . . . I just started articulating the dialect and more words and all of those
things like while I am studying, while I am just doing anything." In this example, Sarah refused to listen to certain music and instead accepted music
that would bring her closer to learning her first language, Diné.

There is a Navajo teaching that is often shared, t'áá hwó' ají t'éego, which
means that it is all up to you. This teaching is connected to the philosophy of
sa'ah naagháí bik'eh hózhóón through a person internalizing how he or she
wants to live life and what he or she must do to live accordingly. This teaching came up when Jessie was reflecting on what her grandma told her when
racism comes to haunt her: "There was also a point when she [grandmother]

told me, 'You're going to face at some point, racism. People aren't going to like you because you're a girl. People aren't going to like you because you're Native American.' She was like, 'That's when you decide what you're going to do about it and I'm not going to be there to help you.'" Her grandmother was instilling in Jessie that hardships, including the ugly sting of racism, will occur because she is Native American. Patriarchy and sexism would also come face to face with Jessie because she is a girl. Her grandmother understood, having lived in a time when schools were enforced to erase Indigenous presence, when the Navajo people struggled to find employment as federal policies exacerbated economic challenges, and during periods of racial and gender/sexuality conflict, often seen and unseen. Grandmothers know. And grandmothers have a good way of imparting wisdom that is grounded in Diné ways. It's up to you what you will refuse. It's up to you what you will welcome. It's up to you on how you will respond. T'áá hwó' ají t'éego!

While Cecilia worked through finding strength within herself, she reflected on teachings that her mother and grandmother shared with her. Teachings of healing and forgiveness. Teachings that restore harmony. Teachings of hózhó (balance and beauty). Cecilia remarked, "I learned from my mom and my grandma on my mom's side that you have to forgive someone in order to keep living. Because if you held that grudge, it's not going to get you anywhere. It's not going to benefit you in some way. But if you forgive, it's a healing portion to that pain that you felt, to let you know that you're a stronger person, to keep going." Forgiveness as an act of living is related to transforming ourselves into beauty. Hózhó. Navajo philosophy is about aspiring to live a long and happy life, or as the poet and former Navajo Nation vice president Rex Lee Jim (2000) affirmed, "May I be everlasting and beautiful living" (p. 232). To forgive others brings harmony to them, but also creates harmony in yourself. And that process cultivates beauty for the world. Cecilia was working on forgiving those students who pulled her hair in grade school, forgiving those who ridiculed her in high school, and forgiving those people who speak poorly of Native peoples. She was teaching me how much I need to forgive others.

What reinforced Native students' sense of self and belonging at college was having courses that centered on Indigenous topics and Indigenous knowledge systems. Often these courses were taught by Native instructors and included other Native classmates. Sarah stated, "We have doctors who are teaching at the university. It just makes you want to push yourself like, 'Yeah, they're Navajo.' They came from the reservation and they're here, they got their degrees. I can do it. . . . I think having them here guides us. They keep us in line, they keep us thinking where we want to be, what we want to accomplish, yeah." Seeing "possible selves" helped Sarah to enact weapons of *continuance* and *refusal* by reassuring her that she is capable of accomplishment despite the monsters that are nearby. Lauryn shared that when she saw other Natives in her class,

it makes me feel happy, to see another Native. It does. It does help. I find it really helpful. Because it feels like they understand you. It feels

like they know where you're coming from. I don't know, like they are
on the same page as you, as opposed to a non-Native. They don't know
what the rez is, or they don't know the struggles that you are going
through. But when you talk to a Native, they are on the same page.

Lauryn conveyed her joy at seeing other Natives in class. Representations do
matter. Natives understand the struggles.

Most people do not see or feel the ravages of systemic monsters that
affect their daily lives. But most Natives recognize the monsters. When you
have been living with and against monsters for a lifetime, there is a sense
of comfort in knowing that you are not alone, that others are dealing with
the same thing. But what is difficult is knowing that many do not recognize
your struggles, and whether they care to know or not, it's hard and tiring to
explain the struggle again and again.

Native college peers also served as what I refer to as "survival part-
ners." Joy expanded on Lauryn's thinking on the value of Native classmates.
In Joy's reflection, she described that Native peers understand the *financial
hardship monster* plaguing their lives, so they work together to help fight
that monster. Joy explained:

> We all know what it's like and we're all like financially unstable in
> some ways, so we all understand each other's problems with that and
> why we can't frequently go out all the time. . . . In a Native American
> community, it doesn't matter what tribe you come from, you all
> support each other one way or another. If you can't pay for your meals
> somehow or if you forgot your meal card or something, someone will
> always go, "I can spot you," and they won't make like any big deal
> about it. They're not like, you got to pay me back. . . . It's like our
> own network of a family and we're able to connect because of our
> lifestyles, because of our backgrounds.

This remarkable example of supporting each other is k'é. Native students need each other, particularly in places like college campuses where so
few Native representations can be found among students, staff, and faculty.
They need each other to help withstand the monsters, to refuse the harmful
rhetoric and societal perspectives that create (in)visibility.

Through their deepened consciousness of undesirable experiences
brought by systemic monsters, they resisted by "seeing self as holy," as Joy
stated through reclaiming Indigenous ways of knowing, such as remembering where they come from, finding place and belonging at college with
other Native students and faculty, and recalling coming from a people and
place of strength. Simply, these students activated weapons of resurgence
as love-centered, continuance as life-centered, reverence as sacredness-
centered, and refusal as sovereignty-centered.

Indigenous weapons.

Indigenous Presence and Relational-Sovereign Belonging

Once a weaver has completed a Navajo rug, he/she/they carefully takes the woven textile off the loom by using a sacking needle to unravel the tight strands that hold the rug to the loom. When the textile is off the loom, finishing touches are applied. Some Navajos get a damp rag and wipe the rug. In that process, the rug becomes more flexible and is therefore gently stretched into a square or rectangle. Some Navajos dig a hole in the ground, moisten the ground with water, and place the rug in the hole to rest. After a day, the weaver takes the rug out of the ground and stretches it in place. The purpose of the water is to nourish the rug, so it becomes more flexible and thereby stretched into form. For this chapter, I'm taking the story rug off the loom and adding finishing touches to ensure that it is properly cared for. I call this chapter the *stretching process,* a place where we can possibly stretch our thinking on the interwoven teachings of the monsters, hauntings, monstrous internalizations, and Indigenous weapons.

In the Navajo way, when there are stories shared with teachings embedded in the story and in the sharing, the storyteller often does not directly tell listeners the meaning of the story. The storyteller teaches us that it is our responsibility to make meaning from the story because we all come to the story with different roles, experiences, needs, concerns, and visions. It is our job to do the work in learning what was offered. With that teaching in mind, I am careful not to impose too much meaning from the stories shared by the 10 Navajo students. That is your responsibility. It is my hope that you will make meaning from them and their stories, for your own heart and well-being and for your own growth. Please note that the meaning-making that you create from the stories is methodology, is theory. Therefore, what I am offering in this stretching process are only a few *theoretical threads* to reflect on; monsters' sense of belonging, (un)belonging, and relational–sovereign belonging. I also wrote a brief note to your professors, administrators, and policy-makers. I then "leave a strand out," as a way to culturally care for this story rug and for future story rugs to come, because that is our way.

MONSTERS' SENSE OF BELONGING

In higher education, a sense of belonging is often referred to as an "individual's sense of belonging to a particular group and his or her feelings of morale, associate with membership in the group" (Bollen & Hoyle, 1990, p. 482). Not surprisingly, research has demonstrated that White students have the greatest sense of belonging compared to students of color (Johnson et al., 2007). This makes sense, given that college campuses are predominately White, with students, faculty, administrators, curricula, and programming that look like, speak to, and cater to them. This is called "ontological expansiveness," which means the privilege to have access to both physical and metaphorical space. Predominately White colleges are then sites of "White space," such that the proliferation of "Whiteness as property" is maintained. Monsters thrive in these environments, as they reinforce and reinscribe White supremacy, heteropatriarchy, and capitalism. The financial hardship monster, rooted in settler colonialism, maintained and reinforced impoverished conditions, which in turn threatened the dreams of attaining a college degree for the Navajo teenagers I spoke with. The second monster, the *deficit (not enough) monster,* emerged, spewing damaging perspectives about college possibilities and self-worth. Before students even entered college, these two monsters worked together to generate barriers, while constructing normative standards (Whiteness) of who belongs and who does not belong in college settings. For these students, who eventually did enter college, they faced the *failure monster,* a relative of the *financial hardship* and *deficit (not enough) monsters,* which asserts and maintains meritocracy and neoliberal standards of Whiteness. Standards of belonging that are cloaked in the language of "success." Then the *(in)visibility monster,* rooted in erasure, worked to diminish possible selves and further evoked questions of belonging. Native students were then put in positions that "presume they are in need of fixing instead of our institutions" (Quaye et al., 2018. p. 6).

Students shared the overwhelming experiences of not belonging and their attempts to belong to the "White spaces" of campus environments. Based on these students' stories, we must contend with how in many ways, campus environments are fertile ground for what I refer to as "monsters' sense of belonging," which is assimilating, diminishing, and harming those whose worldviews are not rooted in White supremacy, capitalism, heteropatriarchy, racism, and Indigenous erasure. Monsters' sense of belonging creates a culture that intensifies failure and (in)visibility. Concepts, naming, and perceptions are often formulated to further diminish our brilliance, sovereignty, and belonging. Concepts and ideas that we take up and tell each other without understanding the monster framing that those concepts are generated from, that cunningly keep portraying us as inferior and disconnected from each other and the land. When we better understand and come to see monsters' sense of belonging, the hauntings are more apparent. Let me explain further two examples of hauntings that reinforce monsters' sense of belonging.

The Hauntings of *Superiority Syndrome Complex*

As we have learned from the teenagers' stories in this book, we can see how our people (for centuries) have been pathologized, dehumanized, obfuscated (sometimes benignly), and maligned as savages, less than, drunks, lazy, and failures. *Hauntings*. These stamps, labels, markers, and namings are created by Whiteness, White superiority, the White settler colonial gaze to maintain their superiority over us, to unsettle our sense of belonging to our original home(lands), and to strengthen monsters' sense of belonging. As bell hooks (1989) stated, "Naming is a serious process. It has been of crucial concern for many individuals within oppressed groups, who struggle for self-recovery, for self-determination" (p. 166). Hauntings are then manifested as attempts to stamp us as inferior. Imposter syndrome is one such concept. I am taking up imposter syndrome because although the students I talked to did not use the term explicitly, they discussed how the monsters worked collectively to form a generation of people who second-guessed their identity and belonging. And there is a tendency for mentors, friends, and others to see their circumstances, listen to their struggles over belonging and ability, and take up the naming/ concept of imposter syndrome as their issue. I want to address the problematic ways that pathologizing through imposter syndrome dismisses systemic monsters that operate to confuse and reinforce monsters' sense of belonging.

We must examine the roots of the imposter syndrome to better understand our connection to it (or not). The White psychologists Pauline Rose Clance and Suzanne Imes (1978) coined and defined the term "imposter phenomenon (syndrome)" as "an internal experience of intellectual phonies, which appears to be particularly prevalent and intense among a select sample of high-achieving women" (p. 241). Clance and Imes (1978) claimed that in working among a large segment of women in individual psychotherapy and college classrooms, they began to see a pattern in women who did not have an "internal sense of success" (p. 241). To better understand this phenomenon, they took a sample of 178 highly successful women who had earned doctorate degrees, were professionals in their fields, or were students recognized for academic excellence. Participants were primarily White middle- to upper-class women between the ages of 20 and 45. White women studied other White women and set the foundational and pervasive discourse around the imposter phenomenon/syndrome. What was invisible in their analysis was their racial identity and the ways that White ways of knowing are entrenched and normalized in society. Whiteness, as a structure, was represented and simultaneously invisible as the participants and researchers are situated as the knowers for all women, including Indigenous women and other racialized bodies. Imposter phenomenon/syndrome has its roots in Whiteness. This analysis dismisses how bodies are enacted, treated, and experienced in different ways depending on their historical and cultural positions (Moreton-Robinson, 2015) in a dominant, White, heteropatriarchal society.

In these stories, Natives begin to see themselves as failures and question their sense of belonging, which we saw occurring more prominently in college settings. This is not surprising, given the efforts of the centuries-old deficit (not enough) and (in)visibility monsters to engineer a syndrome of "imposters" among Native peoples. Therefore, some would say that these students have imposter syndrome because they are internalizing that *they* are the phonies. Yet, I disagree. "Imposter" means a person practicing deception. "Syndrome" implies an illness. Sha'áłchíní (my children), we are not sick people practicing deception. We live in a world where systemic monsters rooted in White supremacy, capitalism, and heteropatriarchy have been haunting us since settlers arrived at our home(lands).

The real alarm is that Whiteness and White supremacy have a *superiority syndrome complex,* where there is a belief that power structures (systemic monsters) are successful despite patterns of consistent failure. Superiority syndrome complex is a denial of failure, a rejection of other ways of viewing success, and a preoccupation of maintaining superiority. Lies. We saw this many times when we examined Native peoples and education from history to the present. Superiority syndrome complex is the real danger.

Monsters lie. They know the truth. When they see their true selves reflected back at them, they cunningly rotate the mirror. They turn the mirror toward us. Like an abuser, superiority syndrome complex creates the conditions of failure and then manipulates them to create syndromes of imposters, while also maintaining their powers of success.

We must do better by recognizing the mirror's gaze. We must consider the naming that we place on ourselves (and onto others). Paris (2019) tells us, "Indeed, educational research often calls out our names, meaning that educational researchers often name people and communities not as they are but as the academy needs them to be along damaging logics of erasure and deficiency" (p. 217). Did you get that? I want to restate that: Names are not as they are, but as the academy needs them to be. Naming that erases and creates deficiency ideologies in what Eve Tuck (2009) referred to as "damage-centered research" (p. 409). Rather, Tuck (2009) calls for "re-visioning research in our communities not only to recognize the need to document the effects of oppression on our communities but also to consider the long-term repercussions of *thinking of ourselves as broken*" (p. 409). This means examining the hegemonic frameworks that are at play, the systemic monsters that are normalized and unseen that craft logics of brokenness, inadequacy, phoniness, insufficient, and so on. Superiority syndrome complex is working on us, if we let it.

The Hauntings of Living in Two Worlds

Here is where I want to return to the widely held views among Native people that we struggle over belonging because we are straddling between "two-worlds."

Two-worlds has been another popular concept, a "naming" that many of us have taken up in our lives and work. For example, I have attended many gatherings with Native people and listened to their college experiences, and several mention the challenges of living in two-worlds. Also, there are programs for Native youth that are framed around living in a two-world concept, where students learn to be proud of their Native identity and culture, while also striving to attend college and thereby live a successful life. These programs make sense and are appealing to many families, especially if schools are insufficient in providing support for Native students. Yet, often when "two-worlds" is referenced, if we listen closely, there is a diminishment of Native personhood and an uplift of Whiteness, as well as an awkward unsettling in grappling with the tensions and contradictions of framing in a binary sense.

In these stories, the (in)visibility monster affirmed the White gaze by reducing us to two-worlds, binary frames, a Native world and a White world. The (in)visibility monster operated in ways that diminish possible selves of Indigeneity through bullying, racist comments and actions, lack of Indigenous presence in college settings, and the hypervisibility of a damaged Native person in society. Chris mentioned being questioned about his Native identity by a White professor. Ashley was teased for not looking Native enough. Sarah was told that she did not dress appropriately. These students questioned their sense of belonging because of the way others viewed them. To help us move away from two-world framing, we must again examine the roots of this concept.

Lakota scholar Vine Deloria, Jr. (1988) wrote *Custer Died for Your Sins*, in which he discussed the harmful ways that early White anthropologists detailed assertions about us, such that we then have taken them up as our own. "Many Indians have come to parrot the ideas of anthologists because it appears that the anthropologists know everything about Indian communities. Thus many ideas that pass for Indian thinking are in reality theories originally advanced by anthropologists and echoed by Indian people in an attempt to communicate the real situation" (p. 82). White anthropologists, sociologists, professors, classmates, and many others compartmentalize our fluid and nuanced lifeways into basic understandings of difference. Binary framing manifests in other ways that we talk about ourselves: reservation Native and urban Native, traditional and nontraditional, full-blooded and nonfull (fraction) blooded, Native speaker and non-Native speaker, straight and gay, man and woman, and so on. There is no one way to be Native. When we take up terms not created by us, we diminish our multiplicity of worldviews and reinforce the deficit (not enough) and (in)visibility monsters' powers on us. And this is also true for how we think, talk, and refuse notions of belonging to institutions that are antithetical (in many ways) to our Indigenous ways. We can do our best to refuse a monsters' sense of belonging.

We can do this by examining the underlining frameworks, this reminds me of la paperson's notion of "theorize in the break," which means not only to engage and learn about the roots of frameworks, but then to disengage from the lineage of settler colonial theorizing and thinking, particularly when those theorizings re-create harm and erasure. As la paperson (2017) wrote, "Put plainly, to theorize in the break is to improvise theory in the rupture form the genealogy of the (often European) founding fathers. It is to think, sing, write, and embody theory in the elsewhere, in the sovereign, in the Black" (p. 19). This elsewhere is freeing, like a break-up. I am breaking up with the imposter phenomenon theory of phoniness. I am breaking up with living in the two-worlds concept. I hope you will too.

You must remember that we are not what others tell us who we are. Here is where I remember and return to Indigenous weapons of refusal. We must refuse the naming and hauntings of superiority syndrome and other concepts that reduce our sense of self and a belonging to a place that we emerged from. Audra Simpson (2014) asked of us, "What happens when we refuse what all (presumably) 'sensible' people perceive as good things? . . . When we add Indigenous peoples to this question, the assumption and histories that structures what is perceived to be 'good' (and utilitarian goods themselves) shift and stand in stark relief. . . . Indeed, from this perspective, we see that a good is not a good for everyone" (p. 1). From this perspective, imposter syndrome and living in two worlds may offer some benefit to many. But when imposter syndrome and two-worlds are examined through a monster framing, we can start to see that "good" is not always good. Therefore, I urgently write, knowing that sha'áłchíní (my children), you are better than us in "theorizing in the break," and you name yourselves with beauty and brilliance—for our future.

(UN)BELONGING

Recently, I listened to a webinar presented by the Quechua scholar Sandy Grande. The title of her talk was "The Endemics of Pandemics at the Settler University." She focused on ways that settler universities continue to uphold racial capitalist, neoliberal, settler colonial, and anti-Blackness aims, especially during pandemics like COVID. She stopped me in my tracks when she mentioned belonging. She stated:

> If you have any doubts, try refusing the gift of belonging and suffer the social isolation, the institutional marginalization, the ghosting, and sometimes even retribution. While we might rightfully fear the impact of exclusion, on self, on career, on family, on community, we need to consider the price of belonging. What are the costs of being invited to the table, of being included in the dialogue, of being the first, the only, to being singled out as the good ones? (Grande, 2020)

This is true. If we believe that having a sense of belonging means sharing a membership with systemic monsters, what are the cost to our sense of self and community?

Possibly, then, could there be a process of (un)belonging, a recognition of the politics of belonging, particularly from a monster's sense of belonging? Constructions of belonging are actively imagined and mutable over time through discourse and practice by those in power (systemic monsters). What if we peel ourselves from monsters' sense of belonging, a practice of (un)belonging, and a reconceptualizing of belonging from our ethical engagements and land-based sensibilities?

We must then look at belonging from our worldview. Along with Nolan Cabrera and Eliza Yellow Bird, I wrote about a *peoplehood sense of belonging*, which takes account of intertwined aspects of language, sacred history, ceremonial cycle, and land (Tachine et al., 2017). We adopted the peoplehood model that was formed by Tom Holm, a Cherokee-Muskogee Creek scholar. Peoplehood was deliberately utilized from the concept of "persistent peoples" to acknowledge that we are still here, despite centuries-old systemic monsters and their hauntings assaulting our livelihood. Language, sacred history, ceremonial cycle, and land speak to our complex and sophisticated experience, where belonging is rooted to a place/land and connected to our ancestors and relatives. From a peoplehood sense of belonging, we are not attempting to fit into Whiteness, White supremacy, and the other systemic monsters. We are reminded that the land is our relative and that campuses may sit on the land, but institutions are not in relation to the land as we are. The land can remind us that we belong here, everywhere, and elsewhere.

RELATIONAL-SOVEREIGN BELONGING

Yet, it may not be that simple to fully separate from systemic monsters. There is definitely power in knowing our peoplehood sense of belonging. But we have to constantly contend with living in a nation-state and a global world with and among systemic monsters. What I learned from these students is that they are constantly negotiating through multiple worlds (examples include home, college, church, and histories as Diné and gendered selves), such that belonging is shaped and redefined depending on context, time, experiences, and knowledges. From this perspective, they show us that they are forming *relational–sovereign belonging*, which is the moving through and honoring of self-determination while being intricately woven into relations (including ancestors, more than human relatives, land/place, and even monsters). It's living in complexity, nuance, paradox, and contradiction. Relational–sovereign belonging is recognizing that there is not one way of being Native in the 21st century. Relational–sovereign belonging is a knowing of the sacredness and multitudes of brilliance that we offer, while also reckoning with the reality that we are not separated from the monsters.

Reckoning with the understandings that we are in relations with monsters is not easy. But reckon we must. Early in this book, I asked (and attempted to answer) the question of why monsters exist. I mentioned that they were created by White supremacy, heteropatriarchy, and capitalism to strip us away from our deep relationship to each other and the land, to erase us. I want to revisit that question now and offer further insights after gaining a deeper understanding from the students' stories and also from the Twin Warriors story. This is what I learned.

Living and being Navajo in these times can feel like we are in constant battle, and many times those battles are unnoticed by you and others. These students I spoke with indicated weariness. Mike skipped sleep. Sam indicated feeling depleted. Joy lost sleep. They all worried about their finances, academics, family, sense of self, and belonging. Worry stole their joy and peace away. This is why it is important to listen to your body, spirit, and mind. When I returned to the Navajo Twin Warriors story, I learned that after the twin warriors destroyed the monsters, they rested.[1] You must rest too, because you are fighting monsters right now. I want to share with you what I learned from the Twin Warriors.

*   *   *

It is said that after the twins rested, they saw something like a red flare in the distance and wondered what was making that red flare? Possibly they had missed another monster? They walked a long distance toward the red flare and saw that smoke was coming out of the ground. As they approached the smoke, they realized that the smoke was from the hole. Curious, they looked through the hole and saw that there were old people inside. They went inside and found more monsters. One of the twins was about to attack a monster when the monster said, "Why would you kill me? I am Dichin Hastiih (Hunger). Would people eat just one meal forever because no one would desire to eat food or drink?" The twins decided that it would be important to keep the hunger monster alive so that people would know when it is time to eat and drink. The twins saw a different monster. This monster was lying down with its eyes closed. The twins made attempts to get rid of that monster. Then the monster said, "No, stop. Why would you kill me? I am Bił Hastiih (Sleep). What would people do when they are sick or need to rest?" The twins had just rested earlier and saw the value in sleep, so they decided that it was important to keep the sleep monster alive.

The twins saw another monster and thought that this monster was meant to be destroyed. Again, the monster said, "Why would you kill me" I am Yaa' Hastiih (Lice Man). What would people do if they did not clean themselves?" The twins understood that keeping oneself clean and healthy was important and so they decided to keep the lice monster alive. Two other monsters were left alive. Tę'é'í Hastiih (Suffering and Poverty) monster remained in order for people to produce necessities such as moccasins and clothing after they were worn. Sá (Old Age) monster continued to live as a way to maintain balance in life and death. It was told that monsters of hunger, sleep, lice, suffering/poverty, and old age exist to teach us to take care of ourselves and others and to respect old age and dying.

*   *   *

As I learned more about the monsters in our Navajo stories, it is said that monsters were created by us. Our people in worlds before helped to form the monsters that the Twin Warriors defeated. Long ago, the people were fighting with and against each other, living in disharmony, and acting in ways that were not aligned with hózhó (balance and beauty). Their acts then generated the monsters that then destroyed the people, reminding us how powerful our actions are in the creation of things/beings. When we return to these Navajo teachings, we can see that there is a cause-and-effect relationship between monsters and us. Causality manifested. Relationality. A recognition that despite not wanting to be near or a part of monsters, we are always connected to them. We even helped create them. What does that mean for systemic monsters that are rooted in White supremacy, settler colonialism, assimilation, capitalism, heteropatriarchy, and racism?

It is to recognize that those monsters were also created by people but reconstructed by us, meaning that we can reproduce those monsters too. It is a recognition that disharmony and discord among relations (people, land, and more than human relatives) generated those monsters. Teachings that remind us that we create monsters, we are constructing them now, and they can later attack us and our relatives if they are not already doing so. Just because you are Native, that does not mean that you do not operate and re-create Whiteness and White supremacy. Remember that Whiteness is the normalization in the everyday that we take for granted as simply how the world works, without examining why we do certain things and how those actions may harm or disenfranchise ourselves and others (including the land and our more than human relatives). Whiteness disregards systemic racism, avoids identifying with racial experience, and minimizes the fact that this country is built on racism (Cabrera et al., 2016).

But if we again return to the Navajo teachings of why monsters remain, we can also understand our relationship with systemic monsters. If hunger reminds us to eat, sleep reminds us to rest, lice to clean, poverty to restore, and old age to balance, then systemic monsters remind us of our Indigenous weapons. Settler colonialism may tell us to rise *(resurgence)*, to care for and protect the land and our loved ones. Assimilation asks us to keep going *(continuance)* and learn our Indigenous ways, centered on relationality and life. Meritocracy teaches us to practice *(reverence)* by acknowledging that we are sacred and brilliant in our own ways and on our own terms. Racism and erasure instill in us to look away *(refusal)* from the monsters' depictions of us and be in the knowing of our sovereignty and belonging, on our terms.

Recall that Indigenous weapons hold an interconnectedness, a bundling of woven knowledges of power. They are dynamic and interactive, exploding with energies of agency and intelligence. Indigenous weapons teach me that theory is active. When we think about theory, it seems so abstract and in many ways foreign, especially when we are taught about theory in college. Theory can be difficult to grasp; it can be confusing. This is true because we are often reading and learning about theories that were not created by us. And often, these non-Native theories are utilized on us to explain to others (mostly non-Natives) about why we do things, what may occur, and even who we are. That is troubling in many ways. There is fumbling in the explaining. Yet, for many the fumbling is profound, retaught, and repeated. Systemic monsters, monstrous internalization, hauntings, and Indigenous weapons are all theories. In these stories I have told, each student lived as theory. *Resurgence. Continuance. Reverence. Refusal.* Those are Indigenous knowledge systems activated as Indigenous weapons. Theory in action for futures.

In my lifetime, we may not be able to defeat the systemic monsters and the hauntings that are plaguing our people. But what we and you can do is sharpen our Indigenous weapons, and like the Twin Warriors, fight (and rest) as you negotiate through relational–sovereign belonging.

We are also reminded that the world that we are living in today is not a two-world dichotomy, but exists in multiple worlds such as the glittering world. That is our sacred Diné history and present. We are in the glittering world. Our ancestors emerged into the glittering world. That is in our creation stories. You see, glittering world is much more sophisticated than two-worlds. Glitter, like a rainbow as sovereign, is a reflection of an assemblage of brilliant, sparkling luster; many more than two colors. We recognize that there were worlds before us and there will be worlds after us. Brilliance. A span of phases tempered by the change in the patterns of the stars and moon, the awareness of transformation occurring within ourselves, other beings, and the universe. We have existed in worlds before us, in the glittering world, and in the worlds to come. And we survived and changed through world-making, and we will do the same moving forward. This is in our stories and teachings. We are in the glittering world.

A BRIEF NOTE TO TEACHERS, PROFESSORS, ADMINISTRATORS, AND POLICY-MAKERS

This book was written for Native peoples, as it should be, but I know that some of you who are reading are non-Native, possibly seeking ways to support Natives, possibly embarking on learning something new, possibly being required to read this, and/or possibly being given this book as a gift. For whatever reason that you came to enter this story rug, I thought it would be good to leave you with a note. Truth is that the decisions that you make affect my children and Native communities. Truth is, that is how life works and operates, in a cyclical nature, and sometimes I wonder if you realize that. That is why this note is for you.

I return to the question that I posed at the beginning of this story rug, and then again in this chapter. Repetition is necessary. *Who sets the terms of belonging?* There is a politics of belonging. And now you may also be more aware that there are monsters. Then with this knowing, what can you do to reckon through the unbelonging process and respectfully support relational–sovereign belonging? This is something that you will have to work through. I only have a few thoughts and a few more questions, but I hope that you will further engage in these questions and actively build meaningful relationships with others (and the land) to proceed with love and care.

Colleges and universities (as well as high schools) can do more with their approaches to build a systematic weaponry that students can use to be successful. Higher education institutions have a responsibility to all students, especially Indigenous students whose original home(lands) are places where colleges now sit and benefit from. Most Native people know that every stretch of land and the waterways spreading across what is now called the United States are Native land, cared for and protected by our ancestors. What this means is that *all* colleges and universities benefit from land dispossession, Indigenous and Black labor and lives, and the ongoing hauntings brought on by systemic monsters. I ask you: What does it mean (for you) to reside and benefit on Indigenous lands?

By examining systemic monsters that impede Navajo students' educational attainment, we have learned that education was seen as a means toward the betterment of not just individual students, but for their families, their Tribal nation, and society at large. With that understanding, college education should be available, not a fucking hurdle to get over. When state governments do not prioritize education, students are affected greatly, and Navajo students take the repercussions extremely hard. Therefore, state governments must stop cutting financial support for education. Policies must ensure that Navajo students (all Native students, in fact) have a challenging, rigorous K–12 education that honors their ways of knowing/being, asserts and affirms cultural-sustaining pedagogies, and equips them with Indigenous weaponry. Indigenous knowledges predate monsters, so we can learn a lot from the ongoing pedagogical power that they offer. Rather than reward schools and peoples that are fueling systemic monsters (meritocracy, assimilation, White supremacy, erasure, settler colonialism, and heteropatriarchy), recognition and financial support should be given to culturally sustaining schools. Specifically, as we learned from these students, upper-level mathematics courses (and other upper-level courses, for that matter) and college preparatory curricula should be offered to Native students. What can you do to support these efforts?

Rather than increase college tuition across the board for all students, Native students should attend college for free. President Barack Obama advocated for students to attend community colleges for free. I applaud Obama for advocating for college accessibility, but I recommend that national policy should do more than that. All colleges and universities should be free for all Native students, especially given the long history of land dispossession and genocide of the first peoples of this place/land. And "free" should mean free, meaning that monies should support the full cost of attendance for students, not just tuition. This is not reparations, but rematriations. Reparations are based on colonial, patriarchical concepts that view payback as profits and margins and/or a process of returning people to their country of origin of their forefathers. Yet, how can Indigenous peoples be paid back for death and lands lost? How can Native people return to a place that they have not left and view the land in relation to maternal lineages? Rematriation is a powerful process of regenerating the land and returning to ancestral knowledges. Rematriation is not payback—it's caring for and protecting the land for the present and futures. How are you practicing and asserting rematriation in your professional and personal life? And how can we offer affordable college to the first peoples of this land, as rematriation?

Rematriation also means cultivating lasting and respectful relationships with Tribal nations. This is more than a land acknowledgment. Tribes should be part of the decision-making process of creating policies, defining and measuring success, and envisioning possibilities for Native peoples and colleges. I ask you, dear non-Native, are you engaging and building relationships with local and national Tribal Nations/Native communities? It should not matter whether you have 10 or 2,000 Native students. You can help by pressuring federal and state governments to honor treaties, assert tribal sovereignty, and seek ways to achieve meaningful rematriation. Navajo and many other Native students have a right to a great education and should not be limited because of systematic monsters. You can help by advocating for these fundamental rights.

In 2019, I led the writing of an initiative supported by the American Indian College Fund titled *Declaration of Native Purpose in Higher Education: An Indigenous Higher Education Equity Initiative*. That document was based on convening a coalition of Native and non-Native advocates, students, and educators to discuss ways to increase visibility and promote college access and success for Native students. We outlined eight declarations for universities and colleges to take up as strategies to support Native students. Here, I am going to share the eight declarations and encourage you to read the full brief (American Indian College Fund, 2019):

1. We believe that Native American students have a right to a higher education and to attend any college or university of their choice.
2. We believe that colleges and universities have the duty to recognize and acknowledge that college campuses reside on the original homelands of Indigenous peoples.
3. We believe that colleges and universities have the duty to incorporate Indigenous knowledge for Native students to survive and thrive.
4. We believe in the inherent right of all Native students to have a place on college campuses that fosters their sense of belonging and importance in their campus community.

5. We believe that colleges and universities have a duty to make visible, to advocate for, and to empower Native students' degree attainment.
6. We believe that colleges and universities have a duty to cultivate an ethic of care in supporting Native peoples by listening, learning, and engaging with Native students, staff, and faculty.
7. We believe that senior leadership at higher education institutions must make a commitment to do system-level work that benefits Native students' college degree attainment.
8. We believe that colleges and universities have the responsibility to uphold tribal sovereignty by generating meaningful government-to-government relationships with tribal nations and tribal colleges and universities.

These eight declarations are starting points. Start there, if you have not already done so. They are simple. But you can make them difficult. I've been thinking about ways to have the eight declarations as outcomes. I know, I know, outcomes? Yes, outcomes. Often, outcomes are based on systemic monsters of meritocracy, assimilation, and Whiteness. What if institutions measured success based on how the Native communities measure success? What if institutions measured success based on how they are cultivating an ethic of care by listening, learning, and engaging with Native students (declaration 6)? What if institutions measured success based on upholding tribal sovereignty (declaration 8)? What if institutions measured success based on how they foster belonging on Native terms (declaration 4)? You can see where I am going with outcomes now. We must seek ways to create measures that are not rooted in normative ideologies of Whiteness. Institutions (and you) must theorize in the break.

You may have my children in your classroom, office, program, and university. They are beautifully intelligent and divinely brilliant. Take care of them. Don't harm them. Know that they carry with them those hardships brought by systemic monsters and their hauntings. Yet, they are not the problem; the monsters are. Name the monsters. See them. And stop blaming my children. They have magnificent Indigenous weapons that have generated beauty and power. It's not your job to teach them how to be; it's your job to let them be their truest, most radiant sacred selves.

And know that we will be watching.

THE STORY RUG: "LEAVE ONE STRAND OUT"

The story rug shows the interconnectedness of tension and beauty. The warp and the weft demonstrate the woven relationship among threads, a respect for the individual radiance and integrity of each strand, as well as the intention to tether strands with another, over and over again. When the threads are woven together, the firmness of the rug is strengthened and a complete, brilliant tapestry is formed, recognizing the connective power between individuality and collectivism. The story rug is created through stories that tell us the profound depth, divine expansiveness, and vitality that stories provide each of us. Stories bring the past, the present, and the future together; not separate, but tightly woven together. History and present coexist. Stories live beyond our time; they are timeless, and that is one of their strengths. We must help to keep them alive and ongoing. The story rug is one conduit for stories to travel.

When a rug is finished, Navajo weavers often say, "leave one strand out," meaning that you never close your rug. My mother-in-law, Alta Wauneka, is a beautiful weaver. She is patient and kind as she teaches me about Navajo weaving. While I was writing portions of this book, I shared with her what I was doing regarding weaving student stories as a metaphor for weaving a rug. She said, "Oh, OK, well in that case, let me tell you about the last strand." She told me that while weaving, all your thoughts go into the rug, the good thoughts and even the bad ones. Thus, when you are done with your rug, you should leave one strand out because you don't want those thoughts to be trapped. They need to escape, be free. That way, you are able to focus on your next rug. With that cultural teaching, for this story rug I leave a strand out.

My hope is that this story rug will travel toward the future, the present, the past, and back again to and through you. Ayóó ánóshní (I love you).

Postlude: Hopes for the Future

Sarah, Wesley, Jessie, Amber, Lauryn, Joy, Chris, Mike, Cecilia, and Sam were new college freshmen during the fall 2012 semester. I had the privilege to learn about and be a part of their lives during their crucial first year of college. With each interview, my heart opened as I listened to their stories of struggle as they battled with the mighty systemic monsters. And they motivated me with their stories of inspiration as they released the powerful forces of the Indigenous weapons. They are indeed Navajo warriors. I only wish the best for them. Before we departed from our last interview, they shared with me sentiments that they would like others to know. Their words could be interpreted as prayer requests or hopes for the future. Their words could also be understood as expressions of appreciation. I offer their words of hope and gratitude.

SARAH

Pray for us to be more humble and to remember who we are and where we come from. . . . Help us in that way so we can also help others. . . . Help us keep our minds right. Help us remember our main goals, help us be as leaders, and help us be thankful too and just look back, and this is what we've done and we need to pass it along. Bless us financially so it won't be a burden. Bless our academics. Bless our living situations while we are here. But most of all, like I said mentally, physically and emotionally, bless us in that way, to be strong, to keep strong.

WESLEY

Whoever helped me financially I'm grateful to them for that, just because it costs a lot to go to college.

JESSIE

Even if I feel weak, even if I don't want to keep going, even if I want to stop, even if I fall down or I sit down or if I start crying, that I'm always going to get back up. That I'm always going to have that will. That I'm always going to have that determination and strength to continue and to get back up. I think just that will to keep going is what I want.

AMBER

If I had one prayer to be answered, I would just say take care of everyone at home.

LAURYN

Creator, help me keep going, not give up, help me finish and protect me. Protect me when I'm away from home, and don't let me stop and give up, just finish. It will all be worth it at the end for other people. No matter what my mom always says, "Don't just always pray for yourself . . . include other people, like everyone here on Earth." Everyone be happy today and just keep on going.

JOY

I would just ask for Holy Ones to continue to keep me to be strong. . . . And to continue to introduce me to people that push the students that are Native American students. . . . I appreciate everything that I have been given and the education that I have been allowed to take part of and receive. Keep all the evil things away from me, and not to succumb to all the doubt that I've been put through and all the hardships that I've been put through. I just ask that they continue to keep me strong and to make me stronger as a person, so that I can go back to help my family.

CHRIS

I would ask for guidance on staying motivated. Help me with my decision-making because I feel like decision-making plays a really important role in what we do as humans.

MIKE

Balance and just strength to keep moving forward. . . . And keeping life lessons in mind, especially when it gets hard.

CECILIA

Just to keep my head on straight, to keep walking that path. . . . I was
going to say just to keep going and don't let me give up, just to know
that you're right there to help me and just stuff like that, positive
things.

SAM

Strength, energy, and clarity of mind to pursue my dreams and
continue on strong with my life. That my path will be cleared of any
obstructions and my vision is clear, that I will see what I need to do,
how I need to do it, just where the road leads. Really, the biggest
prayers, what do I need to do to become what I need to be.

In Gratitude...

Like a woven rug, this textile is complete because of the many (including more than human relatives such as the loom and weaving comb) and the home(lands) who influenced and shaped the development of this story rug. Knowledge is relational, ever-involving, that interweaves past, present, and future. Therefore, this story rug does not belong to only me. Much love to all who graciously held, prayed, and provided good energies for the weaving of this story rug because at the core of their care was the belief in the futures of our Diné peoples. Ahé'hee' (thank you)!

Ahé'hee' to the brilliant 10 Navajo students—Amber, Cecilia, Chris, Jessie, Joy, Lauryn, Mike, Sam, Sarah, and Wesley—for your stories and incredible knowledge and wisdom. It is my hope that your truths will inspire many more for years to come.

Ahé'hee' to the many Native students (from Mt. Elden Middle School, Ganado Middle School, Ha:san Preparatory and Leadership, University of Arizona (UA) Native American Student Affairs, UA Native SOAR, and Arizona State University *Turning Points Magazine*), who have been a big part of my life and the development of this work. In many ways, we weave for you.

Ahé'hee' to Django Paris, Emily Spangler, and the Teachers College Press (TCP) editorial team for inviting this work into the TCP family. Know that to write unapologetically for Diné peoples through a Diné lens is a tremendous gift, especially in this day and age. I do not take that for granted but am affirmed by your commitments.

Ahé'hee' to early readers of this story rug, including Terese Mailhot, Tiffany Lee, Jerome Clark, Eve Ewing, and Sandy Grande. Also much appreciation to Rae Tewa and Nicole Begay for your thorough edits of the final portions of this story rug. I hope to be as kind and generous as you all have shown me.

Ahé'hee' to the Diné artist Lynne Hardy (@ajoobaasani) for the beautiful cover design and story rug illustrations. I also want to thank my son Brien Tachine for conceptualizing the cover design alongside Lynne Hardy's illustrations.

Ahé'hee' to the organizations and generous people who saw and continue to see the value of this work and sparked inspiration for me to keep weaving: Rose Graham from the Office of Navajo Nation Scholarships and Financial Aid, Cheryl Crazy Bull and David Sanders from the American Indian College Fund; the Spencer Foundation and Spencer mentors, including Carol D. Lee, Sara Goldrick-Rab, Estella Bensimon, and Water Allen; the Auntie Way

Writing Retreat, organized by Michelle M. Jacob of Anahuy Mentoring; and the Storyknife Writing Residency, including Erin Coughlin Hollowell and Maura Brenin. I was restored from the beauty of the Nichiłt'ana lands, as well as the delicious foods of nourishment and healing.

Ahé'hee' to shi writing friends across lands and waters, who touched my heart in profound ways. Let's keep writing for love and futures: Adrienne Keene and Tim San Pedro—thanks for the weekly writing sessions during periods of highs and lows. Nolan Cabrera, much deep appreciation for the regular texts, advice, and contagious cheers. Kate Anderson, Meseret Hailu, Carlos Casanova, Chengan Yuan, and Shyla Dogan, for reading and providing comments on earlier drafts. Rudy Guevarra, Gina Garcia, Kari Kokka, and Alex Agloro, for laughter and delicious foods that reenergized our writing. My dear midnight sunset hearts, including Preeti Kaur, Amanda Galvan Huynh, and Heather Aruffo. I am grateful that our hearts aligned at Storyknife near the stratovolcano of St. Augustine. Much love to the Spencer "nonslacker" crew, including Claudia Cervantes-Soon, Nicole Panorkou, Deondra Rose, Niral Shah, Darris Means, and Ozan Jaquettte. Y'all are the realest! Mahalo to dear wahine, Kaiwipuni Punihei Lipe, for weekly Friday writing sessions that bridged desert lands to the Hawaiian islands as we wrote and wept for our peoples.

Ahé'hee' to the groups, institutions, and places that invited me to share portions of this book, to wonder and work through ideas: the Cultural Sustaining Pedagogies crew, for providing a beautiful space for us to gather and share portions of our sustaining work. Still in awe with the constellations of this deep and expansive work; the American College Personnel Association (ACPA) as part of the inaugural Presidential Speaker Series; the University of Arizona College of Education; Old Dominion University's Educational Foundations and Leadership department; Meskerem Glegziabher from Arizona State University's School of Human Evolution and Social Change; Christina Ore from Seven Directions; and the Northern Arizona University's American Indian/Indigenous Teacher Education conference.

Ahé'hee', acknowledging the compassionate and unyielding support of dear mentors, who in many ways and in different moments forged into joyful friendships: Jenny Lee, who was my dissertation advisor and the first to see the potential in me and this work and then pushed me to assert Indigenous methods and develop the story rug. Tsianina K. Lomawaima, my heart goes out to you for spending quality time with me and giving me permission to wrestle through writing and life. Regina Deil-Amen, thank you for helping me to be stronger in voice and for holding space for laughter, tears, and writing. The last major edits were completed in your sacred home, and I will not forget your generosity. Gary Rhoades, for your steadfast love and guidance over the years. I save and treasure your emails of encouragement. Bryan McKinley Jones Brayboy, I thank you for demonstrating the possibilities and imagination of Indigenous excellence for me and so many. You inspire me.

Ahé'hee' to cherished friends who held deep sorrow and joy through the life span of this story rug, which was woven through periods of a pandemic and the unfolding of racial terror and our reckonings: Karen Francis-Begay and Aleena Hernandez, thank you for your vulnerability and sisterhood, across waters and lands we held each other. Heather Shotton, Judy Kiyama, Susana Muñoz, and Leslie Gonzales (T&D Queens), many thanks for your daily texts of encouragement, giggles, stories, joy, and sadness. We needed each other—as mothers—during a time when only the Creator knew. Z Nicolazzo, thank you for Weaving an Otherwise with me, the turn-arounds of our threads healed our hearts and brought us closer. Saretta Morgan and Natalie Diaz—ahé'hee'for your beautiful and generous hearts. Being in your constellations is a blessing with a fullness of radiance. The sky is limitless, and you've both showed me how far-reaching possibilities and imaginations can and will be. Love you both. Eve Ewing—ah, dear one, thank you for inviting me to work alongside you on ways to cultivate Black and Native futures. Such joy in knowing the ever-expansiveness of your heart. You inspire me in profound ways. Let's keep going! Jameson Lopez, appreciate you so much and lucky to be your friend and coinstigator. Much gratitude extended to Leilani Sabzalian, Keon McGuire, Carrie Sampson, Leonie Pihama, Jamee Miller, Khalil Johnson, Charles Davis, Christine Nelson, Natalie Youngbull, Stephanie Waterman, Amalia Daché, Amanda Blackhorse, Marc Johnston, and Matthew Makomenaw for valuing this work and celebrating along the way.

Ahé'hee' to my beautiful family and friends of Ganado, Arizona. Once a Hornet, always a Hornet! Yéego!

With love and deep adoration, ahé'hee' to my beautiful family. To shimá sání and shicheii, who soared to heaven years ago, but in many ways continue to be close by, ever-present; through dreams, urges, and prayers, I felt your nudges to keep going and complete the story rug. Ayóó ánóshní. Much appreciation to my mom for reminding me to pray and encouraging that rest was needed, especially when my tank was empty. Thank you also for meticulously correcting the Diné terms throughout. Ahe'hee to my dad for your unwavering support and "fired up" attitude. Your positive energy is contagious, and I love you for that. Thank you to aunty Gloria for always making us feel special. I am lucky to have an aunty like you. Thank you to my brother Jay (and Sharon) and sister Hope (and Aaron). Pray that we live many years together, caring and being kind to one another. Thank you also for your beautiful babies. Know that I do this work for them. Thank you to my brilliant cousin Shelly and your dear children. I would not have known that a doctorate degree was possible if it were not for you. Thank you to the gorgeous Manuelito family, near and far, past and present. Our histories and legacies of Chief Manuelito and Juanita live in each of us and that gives us strength to keep going for our futures. Much appreciation to the ever-so-kind Wauneka family. Alta, Francis, Corey, and Vanisha, my love for you all is far and wide. Know that this work is also for Collin and Graysen, the future.

With all my heart, ahé'hee' to Coral Angel, Brien Lee, and Noelle Hózhó. Sha'áłchíní, this is for you. You each inspire me to love more, be kinder, and see the joy in life. Our world is better because of your presence and tenderness. I love you to infinity and beyond. Also, thank you to our li'l dog Layla, the little fluff ball that makes us smile with her abundant cuteness.

Ahé'hee' to my loving confidant and unyielding encourager, Brian L. Tachine. I love you, Brian, and I thank you for loving me. Prayers that we live a long and healthy life where we can dance into old age together.

Ahé'hee' Diyin God. Dóólá dó shiDiyin da! T'áadoo baa nishłíinii éidí shaa yiilééh.

Notes

Dedication

1. Many thanks go to Luci Tapahonso for her beautiful poetry and profound love. These words are from *A Radiant Curve* (2008), published by the University of Arizona Press.

Prelude

1. Navajo traditional stories, including the Twin Warriors story, are often told by males during the winter months. To honor the students in this study, I share the story in a respectful manner. In my attempt to abbreviate a version of the Twin Warriors story, I acknowledge that I sought guidance from various books meant for a range of audience members, from children to adults (Austin, 2009; Denetdale, 2007; Iverson, 2002; Locke, 1992; Mabery, 1991). Additionally, as a Navajo, I learned this story at various points in my life through oral storytelling at school settings, community meetings, and occasional social functions with family and friends. Through these multiple sources and experiences, I share the Twin Warriors story in an abbreviated format. Oral storytelling acknowledges that there are various ways to share a story and multiple ways to interpret the story; therefore, this version of the Twin Warriors story may be shared and interpreted differently based on the person telling it and the person listening to it. I encourage further reading and learning about the intricate teachings wrapped within Navajo stories such as the Twin Warriors, as these stories provide evolving life lessons.

Introduction

1. Lyrics from the Diné, Cheyenne, and European artist Lyla June's song, "All Nations Rising." Check out her beautiful work at lylajune.com. Ahé'hee', Lyla June, for your many gifts.

2. Shoutout to the Cherokee scholar Adrienne Keene, who is the writer for the blog Native Appropriations. She has written extensively on Native representations, stereotypes, cultural appropriation, activism, and more. Check out her work at http://nativeappropriations.com/.

3. Throughout the text, I use "systemic monster" and "monster(s)" interchangeably.

4. Adding an "x" here in "womxn" because Native two spirit, trans, queer, gay, lesbian, and non-binary folx also have been tormented.

5. There is irony in the phrase "latest available data," as much of the data on Native students are unavailable. Read *Beyond the Asterisk: Understanding Native Students in Higher Education* (Shotton et al., 2013).

Chapter 2

1. We will get to know Amber a bit more in Chapter 'ashdla'áadah (Fifteen). But I want to gently remind you that through the story rug method, I will begin weaving in students' experiences as they relate to particular threads of the overall design. See this notation as a subtle guide to help you move through the story rug. As you progress through it, the notations will not be needed as much. Remember that there is a pattern for a story rug. It's a bit confusing at first, but stick with it—you will soon understand the pattern.

2. Same notation as before. We will get to know Wesley more as the story rug develops. Have patience and keep going!

3. Referring to "bordertown" as one term that Nick Estes, Melanie K. Yazzie, Jennifer N. Denetdale, and David Correia utilize in their 2021 book *Red Nation Rising: From Bordertown Violence to Native Liberation* (PM Press).

Chapter 7

1. For help, WeRNative has great resources: https://www.wernative.org /resources.

Chapter 11

1. Visit the website of the Office of Navajo Nation Scholarship and Financial Assistance (ONNSFA): https://onnsfa.org/funding-sources, for more information.

Chapter 14

1. Diaz, N. (2020). *Postcolonial Love Poem*. Graywolf Press. Celebrations to Natalie for receiving the 2021 Pulitzer Prize for this collection of her poems.

2. Listen to Amanda Blackhorse's interview on Global Sport Matters titled "The Huddle: The R-Word, Racist Mascots, and Reporters' Roundtable" (https:// globalsportmatters.com/listen/podcasts/2020/07/03/the-huddle-the-r-word-racist -mascots-reporters-roundtable/).

3. Interesting how "public" is used as a catch-all concept, since in reality it does not include everyone. Similar to when All Lives Matter is weaponized against Black Lives Matter, the universality of the language use of "public" and "all" is not about everyone, but really about White lives and maintaining the social order. I was inspired by Candis Callison's attention to redefining language in an article titled "Who Tells the Story of the Present?" (https://thenarwhal.ca/candis-callison-on-redefining-journalism -in-canada/).

4. These Tribal names were written in the original documents, but they do not reflect the way the Tribes refer to themselves.

Chapter 18

1. The rendition of this story is retold during the winter months by family and community members. I thank Ethelou Yazzie's (1971) edited version through the Navajo Curriculum Center from the Rough Rock Demonstration School.

References

Abu El-Haj, T. (2015). *Unsettled belonging: Educating Palestinian American youth after 9/11*. University of Chicago Press.

Adams, D. W. (1995). *Education for extinction*. University Press of Kansas.

Alejandro, A. J., Fong, C. J., & De La Rose, Y. M. (2020). Indigenous graduate and professional students decolonizing, reconciling, and indigenizing belongingness in higher education. *Journal of College Student Development, 61*(6), 679–696.

Alon, S., & Tienda, M. (2007). Diversity, opportunity, and the shifting meritocracy in higher education. *American Sociological Review, 72*(4), 487–511. https://doi.org/10.1177/000312240707200401

American Indian College Fund. (2009). *Creating visibility and healthy learning environments for Native Americans in higher education*. Declaration of Native purpose in higher education: An Indigenous higher education equity initiative. https://collegefund.org/wp-content/uploads/2020/01/Creating-Visibility-and-Healthy-Learning-Environments-for-Natives-in-Higher-Education_web.pdf

Archibald, J. (2008). *Indigenous storywork: Educating the heart, mind, body, and spirit*. UBC Press.

Arizona Board of Regents. (2017, January 27). *Unnecessary tuition cap misses the point*. https://www.azregents.edu/insights/unnecessary-tuition-cap-misses-point

Arizona Education Budget Summary. (2015). State of Arizona. https://www.azospb.gov/documents/2015/Executive%20Budget%20Summary%20Book,%20FINAL,%20Online%20Version,%20with%20Links,%201-13-15.pdf

Arizona Rural Policy Institute. (2010). *Demographic analysis of the Navajo Nation using 2010 Census and 2010 American Community Survey estimates*. https://gotr.azgovernor.gov/sites/default/files/navajo_nation_0.pdf

Aronilth, W. J. (1980). *Diné bi bee óhoo'aah bá silá: An introduction to Navajo philosophy*. Center for Diné Studies, Navajo Community College.

Austin, R. D. (2009). *Navajo courts and Navajo common law: A tradition of tribal self-governance*. University of Minnesota Press.

Becenti, A. (2020, March 17). First Diné tests positive for coronavirus. *Navajo Times*. https://navajotimes.com/reznews/first-dine-tests-positive-for-coronavirus/

Benally, C. (2014). Creating and negotiating Native spaces in public school systems: An Arizona example. *Journal of American Indian Education, 53*(3), 11–24.

Bighorse, T. (1990). *Bighorse the warrior*. University of Arizona Press.

Bollen, K. A., & Hoyle, R. H. (1990). Perceived cohesion: A conceptual and empirical examination. *Social Forces, 69*(2), 479–504.

Brand, D. (2006). *Inventory*. McClelland & Stewart.

Brave Heart, M. Y. H. (2003). The historical trauma response among Natives and its relationship with substance abuse: A Lakota illustration. *Journal of Psychoactive Drugs, 35*(1), 7–13. https://doi.org/10.1080/02791072.2003.10399988

Brayboy, B. M. J. (2004). Hiding in the Ivy: American Indian students and visibility in elite educational settings. *Harvard Educational Review, 74*(2), 125–152.

Brayboy, B. M. J. (2005). Toward a tribal critical race theory in education. *Urban Review, 37*(5), 425–446.

Brayboy, B. M. J., & Chin, J. (2020). On the development of terrortory. *Contexts, 19*(3), 22–27.

Brayboy, B. M. J., & Maughan, E. (2009). Indigenous knowledges and the story of the bean. *Harvard Education Review, 79*(1), 1–21. https://doi.org/10.17763/haer.79.1.l0u6435086352229

Brayboy, B. M. J., & Tachine, A. R. (2021). The immoral triad of the Morrill Act. *Native American and Indigenous Studies, 8*(1), 139–144.

Brayboy, B., Fann, A., Castagno, A., & Solyom, J. (2012). *Postsecondary education for American Indian and Alaska Natives: Higher education for nation building and self-determination*. Jossey-Bass.

Brown, B. (2010). *The gifts of imperfection*. Hazeldon Publishing.

Brown, B. (2017, September 11). Finding our way to true belonging. Ideas.ted.com. https://ideas.ted.com/finding-our-way-to-true-belonging/#:~:text=So%20many%20of%20us%20long,True%20belonging.&text=%E2%80%9CBelonging%20is%20the%20innate%20human,of%20something%20larger%20than%20us

Butler, O. E. (1998). *Parable of the talents*. Grand Central Publishing.

Cabrera, N. L. (2019). *White guys on campus: Racism, white immunity, and the myth of "post-racial" higher education*. Rutgers University Press.

Cabrera, N. L., Franklin, J. D., & Watson, J. S. (2016). Whiteness in higher education: The invisible missing link in diversity and racial analysis. *ASHE Higher Education Report, 42*(6), 7–125.

Cajete, G. (2000). *Native science: Natural laws of interdependence*. Clear Light Publishers.

Calderon, D. (2014). Uncovering settler grammars in curriculum. *Educational Studies (Ames), 50*(4), 313–338. https://doi.org/10.1080/00131946.2014.926904

Canby, W. C. (1998). *American Indian law in a nutshell*. West Publishing Co.

Carney, C. M. (1999). *Native Americans in higher education in the United States*. New Transaction Publishers.

Clance, P. R., & Imes, S. A., (1978). The imposter phenomenon in high-achieving women: Dynamics and therapeutic intervention. *Psychotherapy: Theory, Research & Practice, 15*(3) 241–247.

Clark, A. N. (1940) *Little herder in spring* (English ed.). Education Division, U.S. Office of Indian Affairs.

Conover, C. (2013, April 26). *Running water: Not taken for granted*. Web Log Post, U.S. Office of Indian Affairs. http://support.devel.azpm.org/s/14545-looking-for-water/

Consortium for Student Retention Data Exchange (CSRDE). (2002). *Executive summary 2000–01 CSRDE report*. Center for Institutional Data Exchange and Analysis, University of Oklahoma.

Coombs, L. M. (1962). *Doorway toward the light: The story of the special Navajo education program*. U.S. Department of the Interior, Bureau of Indian Affairs, Branch of Education. https://files.eric.ed.gov/fulltext/ED024491.pdf

Coulthard, G. S. (2014). *Red skin, white mask: Rejecting the colonial politics of recognition*. University of Minnesota Press.

Cox, R. D. (2009). *The college fear factor: How students and professors misunderstand one another*. Harvard Education Press.

Cunningham, J. K., Solomon, T. A., & Muramoto, M. L. (2016). Alcohol use among Native Americans compared to whites: Examining the veracity of the "Native American elevated alcohol consumption" belief. *Drug and Alcohol Dependence, 160*(1), 65–75.

Curley, A. (2021). Infrastructures as colonial beachheads: The Central Arizona Project and the taking of Navajo resources. *Environment and Planning D: Society and Space, 39*(3), 387–404.

Curtice, K. B. (2020). *Native identity, belonging, and rediscovering God*. Brazos Press.

Custalow, L. L. B., & Daniel, A. L. (2009). *The true story of Pocahontas: The other side of history*. Fulcrum Publishing.

Dastagir, A. E. (2019, June 21). Suicide rate for Native American women is up 139%. *USA Today*. https://www.usatoday.com/story/news/nation/2019/06/21/suicide-rate-native-american-indian-women-men-since-1999/1524007001/?fbclid=IwAR1PFUav4z8QPMUqGcMgW-0QD5BYuVOIahAnsGr1WnQWQ_3rgZYu2XPUMTU

Davis-Delano, L. R., Gone, J. P., & Fryberg, S. A. (2020). The psychosocial effects of Native American mascots: A comprehensive review of empirical research findings. *Race Ethnicity and Education, 23*(5), 613–633.

Deloria, V. (1970). *We talk, you listen*. Macmillan.

Deloria, V. (1988). *Custer died for your sins: An Indian manifesto*. University of Oklahoma Press.

Denetdale, J. (2007). *Reclaiming Diné history: The legacies of Chief Manuelito and Juanita*. University of Arizona Press.

Denetdale, J. N. (2016). No explanation, no resolution, and no answers: Border town violence and Navajo resistance to settler colonialism. *Wicazo Sa Review, 31*(1), 111–131.

Denetdale, J. N. (2020). Refusing the gift of democracy and embracing Diné concepts of kinship: The Navajo nation, citizenship, and practices of gender. *Theory & Event, 23*(4), 1053–1065.

Department of Diné Education, Office of Navajo Nation Scholarship and Financial Assistance. (2019, March 25). "Navajo Nation issues request to restore higher education grant." https://onnsfa.org/stories/f/request-issued-to-restore-federal-funds-for-scholarships

Department of Diné Education, Office of Navajo Nation Scholarship and Financial Assistance. (2020, February 12). https://img1.wsimg.com/blobby/go/74cd80dd -d6f0-4609-8ed6-615cdf892847/downloads/02.12.20%20Trump %20Administration%20Zeroes%20Tribal%20Sc.pdf?ver=1584596710993

Diaz, N. (2020). *Postcolonial love poem*. Graywolf Press.

Dickason, O. P. (1984). *The myth of savage: And the beginnings of French Colonialism in the Americas*. University of Alberta Press.

Diné Policy Institute. (2018). *Land reform in the Navajo nation*. Diné College. http://hooghan.dinecollege.edu/institutes/DPI/docs/Land%20Reform%20 in%20the%20Navajo%20Nation.pdf

Division of Economic Development. (2010). *2009–2010 Comprehensive economic development strategy the Navajo nation*. http://www.navajobusiness.com/pdf /CEDS/CED_NN_Final_09_10.pdf

Donovan, B. (2015, February 19). Gallup candidates talk about racism and alcohol. *Navajo Times*. http://navajotimes.com/rezpolitics/gallup-candidates-talk -about-racism-and-alcohol/#.VRioi1xivjJ

Driskill, Q. (2010). Doubleweaving two-spirit critiques: Building alliances between Native and Queer studies. *A Journal of Lesbian and Gay Studies, 16*(1–2), 69–92.

Elliott-Groves, E. (2017). Insights from Cowichan: A hybrid approach to understanding suicide in one First Nations' Collective. *Suicide and Life-Threatening Behavior, 48*(3), 328–339.

Enos, A. D. (2017). With respect . . . In E. S. Hauman & B. M. J. Brayboy (Eds.), *Indigenous innovations in higher education: Local knowledge and critical research* (pp. 41–57). Sense Publishers.

Espinosa, L. J., Turk, J. M., Tayor, M., & Chessman, H. M. (2019). *Race and ethnicity in higher education: A status report*. American Council on Education (www. equityinhighered.org)

Estes, N. (2014, August 29). Welcome to Gallup, NM, where "They just want another person dead." *Indian Country Today*. https://indiancountrytoday.com /archive/welcome-to-gallup-nm-where-they-just-want-another-person-dead

Estes, N. (2015, January 14). "Blood money": Life and death in Gallup, NM. *Indian Country Today*. http://indiancountrytodaymedianetwork.com/2015/01/14 /blood-money-life-and-death-gallup-nm-158688

Estes, N., Yazzie, M. K., Denetdale, J. N., & Correia, D. (2021). *Red nation rising: From bordertown violence to Native liberation*. PM Press.

Faircloth, S. C., & Tippeconnic, III, J. W. (2010). *The dropout/graduation rate crisis among American Indian and Alaska Native students: Failure to respond places the future of Native peoples at risk*. The Civil Rights Project/Proyecto Derechos Civiles at UCLA (www.civilrightsproject.ucla.edu).

Farmer, P. (2005). *Pathologies of power: Health, human rights, and the new war on the poor*. University of California Press.

Feagin, J., & O'Brien, E. (2003). *White men on race*. Beacon Press.

First Nations Development Institute & Echo Hawk Consulting. (2018). *Reclaiming Native truth: A project to dispel America's myths and misconceptions*.

First Nations Development Institute & Echo Hawk Consulting. https://rnt .firstnations.org/

Fonseca, F., (2019). *Correction: Navajo Nation-electricity story*. Associated Press. https://apnews.com/article/north-america-us-news-ap-top-news-ut-state-wire -az-state-wire-c43c309a21e0486d942a98a5a41b726c

Freeman, C., & Fox, M. A. (2005). *Status and trends in the education of American Indians and Alaska Natives*. NCES 2005-108. National Center for Education Statistics, U.S. Department of Education, Institute of Education Sciences.

Freire, P. (1970). *Pedagogy of the oppressed*. Continuum International Publishing Group.

Fryberg, S. A., & Markus, H. R. (2003). On being American Indian: Current and possible selves. *Self and Identity, 2*(4), 325–344.

Fryberg, S. A., Markus, H. R., Oyserman, D., & Stone, J. M. (2008). Of warrior chiefs and Indian princesses: The psychological consequences of American Indian mascots. *Basic and Applied Social Psychology*, (30), 208–218.

Fryberg, S. A., & Townsend, S. S. M. (2008). The psychology of invisibility. In G. Adams, M. Biernat, N. R. Branscombe, C. S. Crandall, & L. S. Wrightsman (Eds.), *Commemorating Brown: The social psychology of racism and discrimination* (pp. 173–193). American Psychological Association.

Geiger, R. L. (2013). Postmortem for the current era: Change in American higher education, 1980–2010. *Higher Education Forum, 10*(1), 1–21.

Goodkind, J., Hess, J., Gorman, B., & Parker, D. (2012). "We're still in a struggle": Diné resilience, survival, historical trauma, and healing. *Qualitative Health Research, 22*(8), 1019–1036. https://doi.org/10.1177/1049732312450324

Gordon, A. F. (1997). *Ghostly matters: Haunting and the sociological imagination*. University of Minnesota Press.

Grande, S. (2003). Whitestream feminism and the colonialist project: A review of contemporary feminist pedagogy and praxis. *Educational Theory, 53*(3), 329–346.

Grande, S. (2004). *Red pedagogy: Native American social and political thought*. Rowman & Littlefield Publishers.

Grande, S. (2020). *The endemics of pandemics at the settler university* [webinar video]. https://arts.unimelb.edu.au/indigenous-settler-relations-collaboration/projects -publications-and-resources/resources/videos/the-endemics-of-pandemics -at-the-settler-university

Greenfield-Sanders, T. (Director). (2019). *Toni Morrison: The pieces I am* [Film; online video]. Hulu Originals.

Haederle, M. (1990, May 14). "Drunk City" faces up to its sobering problems: In Gallup, N. M., people are trying to reform their liquor laws and their community's image. *LA Times*. http://articles.latimes.com/1990-05-14/news/mn-135 _1_drunk-city

hooks, b. (1989). *Talking back: Thinking feminist, thinking black*. South End Press.

hooks, b. (2009). *Belonging: A culture of place*. Routledge.

Hope Center. (2020). *Tribal Colleges and Universities #RealCollege Survey*. Hope Center. https://collegefund.org/wp-content/uploads/2020/03/2019
_TribalCollegesUniversities_Report_Final.pdf

Huffman, T. E. (2013). *American Indian educators in reservation schools*. University of Nevada Press.

Iverson, P. (2002). *Diné: A history of the Navajos*. University of New Mexico Press.

Jaimes, A. M. (1992). *The state of Native America: Genocide, colonization, and resistance*. Boston South End Press.

Jim, R. L. (2000). A moment in life. In A. Krupat & B. Swann (Eds.), *Here first: Autobiographical essays by Native American writers* (pp. 229–246). Modern Library.

Johnson, D. R., Soldner, M., Leonard, J. B., Alvarez, P., Inkelas, K. K., Rowan-Kenyon, H., & Longbeam, S. D. (2007). Examining sense of belonging among first-year undergraduates from different racial/ethnic groups. *Journal of College Student Development*, 48(5), 525–542.

Keene, A., & Tachine, A. (2018, May 7). Colorado State University tour incident is nothing new for Native students. *Teen Vogue*. https://www.teenvogue.com/story/csu-incident-native-students-nothing-new-native-americans-in-united-states

Kickingbird, K. (1977). *Indian sovereignty*. Institute for the Development of Indian Law.

King, F. (2018). *The earth memory compass: Diné landscapes and education in the twentieth century*. University Press of Kansas.

Kirmayer, L. J., Gone, J. P., & Moses, J. (2014). Rethinking historical trauma. *Transcultural Psychiatry*, 51(3), 299–319. https://doi.org/10.1177/1363461514536358

Klein, R. (2015, March 3). The federal government has a lot of work fixing up Native American schools. *Huffington Post*. http://www.huffingtonpost.com/2015/03/03/bureau-of-indian-education-gao_n_6795568.html

Kluckhohn, C., & Leighton, D. (1962). *The Navaho*. Anchor Books.

Krol, D. (2019, January 8). Government shutdown hits tribes: Job losses, bad roads, no health-care. *Indian Country Today*. https://www.azcentral.com/story/news/local/arizona/2019/01/08/government-shutdown-effects-navajo-nation-yomba-shoshone-tribes/2516083002/

Kulago, H. (2016). Activating Indigenous knowledges to create supportive educational environments by rethinking family, community, and school partnerships. *Journal of Family Diversity in Education*, 2(1), 1–19.

Ladson-Billings, G. (2006). From the achievement gap to the education debt: Understanding achievement in U.S. schools. *Educational Researcher*, 35(7), 3–12. https://doi.org/10.3102/0013189X035007003

Lee, L. (2013). *Diné masculinities: Conceptualizations and reflections*. Createspace Independent Publishing Platforms.

Lee, L. (2017). *Navajo sovereignty: Understandings and visions of the Diné people*. University of Arizona Press.

Lee, L. (2020). *Diné identity in a 21st-century world*. University of Arizona Press.

Lee, R., & Ahtone, T. (2020, March 30). Land-grab universities: Expropriated Indigenous land is the foundation of the university system. *High Country News*. https://www.hcn.org/issues/52.4/indigenous-affairs-education-land-grab-universities

Lee, T. S. (2006). "I came here to learn how to be a leader": An intersection of critical pedagogy and Indigenous education. *InterActions: UCLA Journal of Education and Information Studies, 2*(1), 1–25. 10.5070/D421000557.

Leo, M. (2015, February 5). Feds fund Navajo schools 11 years after replacement was deemed a priority. *Cronkite News Online.* http://cronkitenewsonline.com /2015/02/feds-fund-navajo-schools-11-years-after-replacement-was-deemed-a -priority/

Leonard, Z. (2004). The color of supremacy: Beyond discourse of "white privilege." *Educational Philosophy and Theory, 36*(2), 137–152.

Litvin, Y. (2020, May 5). Indigenous leadership points the way out of the Covid crisis. *Truthout.* https://truthout.org/articles/indigenous-leadership-points-the-way -out-of-the-covid-crisis/

Locke, R. F. (1992). *The book of the Navajo.* Mankind Press.

Lomawaima, K. T., & McCarty, T. L. (2006). *To remain an Indian: Lessons in democracy from a century of Native American education.* Teachers College Press.

Lopez, J. D. (2021). Giving back as an educational outcome for postsecondary Indigenous students. In J W. Tippeconnic III & M. J. Tippeconnic Fox (Eds.), *On Indian ground: The southwest* (pp. 177–190). Information Age Publishing.

Lorde, A. (2020). *The selected works of Audre Lorde.* W. W. North & Company.

Lynch, S. N. (2015, April 14). *U.S. Consumer Bureau charges firms in tax refund scheme targeting Navajos.* Reuters. https://www.reuters.com/article/us-cfpb-taxes -fraud/u-s-consumer-bureau-charges-firms-in-tax-refund-scheme-targeting-navajos -idUSKBN0N51JQ20150414

Mabery, M. V. (1991). *Right after sundown: Teaching stories of the Navajos.* Navajo Community College Press.

Macarney, S., Bishaw, A., & Fotenot, K. (2013). *Poverty rates for selected detailed race and Hispanic groups by state and place: 2007–2011.* U.S. Department of Commerce Economics and Statistics Administration. http://www.census.gov /prod/2013pubs/acsbr11-17.pdf

Mankiller, W. (2004). *Everyday is a good day: Reflections by contemporary Indigenous women.* Fulcrum Publishing.

McCarty, T. (2002). *A place to be Navajo: Rough Rock and the struggle for self-determination in Indigenous schooling.* Taylor and Francis. https://doi .org/10.4324/9781410602503

Merskin, D. (2001). Winnebagos, Cherokees, Apaches, and Dakotas: The persistence of stereotyping of American Indians in American advertising brands. *Howard Journal of Communications, 12,* 159–169.

Milem, J., Bryan, P., Sesate, D., & Montano, S. (2013). *Arizona minority student progress report.* Arizona Minority Education Policy Analysis Center. https://highered.az.gov/sites/default/files/Executive%20Summary%20for%20 2013%20MSPR.pdf

Minthorn, R. S., & Nelson, C. A. (2018). Colonized and racist Indigenous campus tours. *Journal of Critical Scholarship on Higher Education and Student Affairs, 4*(1), 73–88.

Minthorn, R. S., & Shotton, H. J. (2018). *Reclaiming Indigenous research in higher education.* Rutgers University Press.

Morales, L. (2013, May 28). *Navajo schools lose funding due to sequestration cuts*. National Public Radio. https://www.npr.org/2013/05/28/186253246/navajo-schools-lose-funding-due-to-sequestration-cuts

Morales, L. (2015, January 6). *For many Navajo, a visit from the "water lady" is a refreshing sight*. NPR Code Switch. https://www.npr.org/sections/codeswitch/2015/01/06/374584452/for-many-of-navajo-nation-water-delivery-comes-monthly?utm_campaign=storyshare&utm_source=twitter.com&utm_medium=social

Morales, L. (2015, April 8). *The Navajo nation's tax on junk food splits reservation*. NPR Code Switch. https://www.npr.org/sections/codeswitch/2015/04/08/398310036/the-navajo-nations-tax-on-junk-food-splits-reservation

Moreton-Robinson, A. (2015). *The white possessive: Property, power, and Indigenous sovereignty*. University of Minnesota Press.

Morrison, T. (1975). Portland State, "Black Studies Center public dialogue. Pt. 2" [audio clip]. https://soundcloud.com/portland-state-library/portland-state-black-studies-1

Moya-Smith, S. (2018, September 13). Navajo kindergartner sent home from school ordered to cut his hair. *Indian Country Today*. https://indiancountrytoday.com/archive/navajo-kindergartner-sent-home-from-school-ordered-to-cut-his-hair

Musu-Gillette, L., de Brey, C., McFarland, J., Hussar, W., Sonnenberg, W., & Wilkinson-Flicker, S. (2017). *Status and trends in the education of racial and ethnic groups 2017* (NCES 2017–051). U.S. Department of Education, National Center for Education Statistics. http://nces.ed.gov/pubsearch

Nagle, R. (2018). Invisibility is the modern form of racism against Native Americans. *Teen Vogue*. https://www.teenvogue.com/story/racism-against-native-americans

Nash, M. A. (2019). Entangled pasts: Land-grant colleges and American Indian dispossession. *History of Educational Quarterly, 59*(4), 437–467.

National Education Association. (2014). *Rankings & estimates: Rankings of the states 2013 and estimates of school statistics 2014*. http://www.nea.org/assets/docs/NEA-Rankings-and-Estimates-2013-2014.pdf

Navajo Nation Division of Economic Development. (2010). *2009–2010 Comprehensive economic development strategy: The Navajo nation*. Navajo Nation Division of Economic Development. http://www.navajobusiness.com/pdf/CEDS/CED_NN_Final_09_10.pdf

Navajo Nation Office of Educational Research and Statistics Report. (2014). *Testimony of Timothy Benally, acting superintendent of schools, Navajo Nation Department of Diné Education*. Navajo Nation Office of Educational Research and Statistics. https://www.indian.senate.gov/sites/default/files/upload/images/5.21.14%20Testimony%20-%20Timothy%20Benally%20-%20Navajo%20Nation%20Department%20of%20Dine%27.pdf

Navajo Nation Roundtable on Remedial Education Summary Report. (2012). *Diné College, Navajo Technical College, Office of Navajo Nation Scholarship and Financial Assistance, and Department of Diné Education*. Navajo Nation Roundtable on Remedial Education. https://studylib.net/doc/12523801/navajo-nation-roundtable-on-remedial-education-summary-re

Nelson, C., & Tachine A. R. (2018). Native student financial aid as Native nation building. In S. J. Waterman, S. C. Lowe, & H. J. Shotton. (Eds.), *Beyond access: Indigenizing programs for Native American student success* (pp. 65–82). Stylus Publishing, LLC.

Nez, J. (2020, October 13–16). *Opening plenary session: Welcome to the 2020 National Tribal Health Conference* [Keynote address]. National Indian Health Board 2020 Conference, Virtual. https://www.youtube.com/watch?v=Z1b9mj5lJz8&t=62s

Norris, T., Vines, P., & Hoeffel, E. (2012). *The American Indian and Alaska Native population: 2010*. U.S. Census Bureau. https://www.census.gov/history/pdf/c2010br-10.pdf

Official Report of the Nineteenth Annual Conference of Charities and Correction (1892), 46–59. Reprinted in Pratt, R. H. (1892). *"The advantages of mingling Indians with Whites." Americanizing the American Indians: Writings by the "friends of the Indian" 1880–1900*. Harvard University Press, 260–271.

Orange, T. (2018). *There there*. Alfred A. Knopf.

paperson, la. (2017). *A third university is possible*. University of Minnesota Press.

Paris, D. (2019). Naming beyond the white settler colonial gaze in educational research. *International Journal of Qualitative Studies in Education, 32*(3), 217–224.

Paris, D., & Alim, H. S. (2017). *Culturally sustaining pedagogies: Teaching and learning for justice in a changing world*. Teachers College Press.

Patel, L. (2016). *Decolonizing educational research: From ownership to answerability*. Routledge.

Pete, L. T., & Ornelas, B. T. (2018). *Spider Woman's children: Navajo weavers today*. Thurms Books.

Quaye, S. J., Aho, R. E., Jacob, M. B., Dominique, A. D., Guido, F. M., Lange, A. C., Squire, D., & Stewart, D-L. (2018). *A bold vision forward: A framework for strategic imperative for racial justice and decolonization*. ACPA—College Student Educators International. https://www.aacu.org/sites/default/files/files/dlss19/CS%202%20Handout.pdf

Regan, S. (2014, February 18). *Unlocking the Wealth of Indian nations: Overcoming obstacles to tribal energy development*. PERC Policy Perspective No. 1. http://perc.org/sites/default/files/pdfs/IndianPolicySeries%20HIGH.pdf

Roessel, R. A. (1979). *Navajo education, 1948–1978: Its progress and its problems*. Navajo Curriculum Center, Rough Rock Demonstration School.

Rosay, A. B. (2016). *Violence against American Indian and Alaska Native women and men: 2010 findings from the National Intimate Partner and Sexual Violence Survey*. NIJ Research Report. http://doi.org/10.3886/ICPSR36140.v1

Sabzalian, L. (2019). *Indigenous children's survivance in public schools*. Routledge.

Schilling, V. (2018, May 10). Mohawk brothers detained by police on Colorado campus tour gain national attention. *Indian Country Today*. https://indiancountrytoday.com/archive/mohawk-brothers-detained-police-colorado-campus-tour-gain-national-attention

Senate Special Subcommittee on Indian Education. (1969). *Indian education: A national tragedy—a national challenge, 91st Cong., 1st sess., S. Rept. 91–501,*

1969. (Also known as the Kennedy Report.) Senate Special Subcommittee on Indian Education.

Sharpe, C. (2010). *Monstrous intimacies: Making post-slavery subjects.* Duke University Press.

Shirley, V. J. (2017). Indigenous social justice pedagogy: Teaching the risks and cultivating the heart. *Critical Questions in Education, 8*(2), 163–177.

Shone, C. (2010, October 22). For many on the Navajo Nation, it's been a long wait for power. *Cronkite News.* http://cronkitenewsonline.com/2010/10/for-many-navajos-its-been-a-long-wait-for-power/

Shotton, H. J., Lowe, S. C., & Waterman, S. J. (2013). *Beyond the asterisk: Understanding Native students in higher education.* Stylus Publishing, LLC.

Simpson, A. (2007). On ethnographic refusal: Indigeneity, "Voice" and colonial citizenship. *Junctures,* (9), 67–80.

Simpson, A. (2014). *Mohawk interruptus: Political life across the borders of settler states.* Duke University Press.

Simpson, L. B. (2013). *Islands of decolonial love: Stories and songs.* ARP Books.

Simpson, L. B. (2016). Indigenous resurgence and co-resistance. *Journal of the Critical Ethnic Studies Associations,* 2(2), 19–34. https://doi.org/10.5749/jcritethnstud.2.2.0019

Simpson, L. B. (2017). *As we have always done: Indigenous freedom through radical resistance.* University of Minnesota Press.

Soss, J., Fording, R. C., & Schram, S. F. (2011). *Discipling the poor: Neoliberal paternalism and the persistent power of race.* University of College Press.

Stanton, Z. (2020, July 16). How Native American team names distort your psychology. *Politico.* https://www.politico.com/news/magazine/2020/07/16/native-american-team-names-psychology-effect-redskins-indians-sports-logos-366409

Steele, C. M. (1997). A threat in the air: How stereotypes shape intellectual identity and performance. *American Psychologist, 52*(6), 613–629.

Stein, S. (2020). A colonial history of the higher education present: Rethinking land-grant institutions through processes of accumulation and relations of conquest. *Critical Studies in Education,* 61(2), 212–228.

Stetser, M., & Stillwell, R. (2014). *Public high school four-year on-time graduation rates and event dropout rates: School years 2010–11 and 2011–12. First look (NCES 2014-391). U.S. Department of Education.* National Center for Education Statistics. https://nces.ed.gov/pubs2014/2014391.pdf

Tachine, A. R., & Cabrera, N. L. (2021). "I'll be right behind you": Native American families, land debt, and college affordability. *AERA OPEN,* 7(1), 1–13. https://doi.org/10.1177/23328584211025522

Tachine, A. R., Cabrera, N. L., & Bird, E. Y. (2017). Home away from home: Native American students' sense of belonging during their first year in college. *Journal of Higher Education,* 88(5), 785–807. http://dx.doi.org/10.1080/00221546.2016.1257322

Tachine, A. R., Patel, P. R., & Daché, A. Z. (2021). Time-traveling through land and sea: Unearthing the past to cultivate seeds of present and future solidarity. *International Journal of Qualitative Studies in Education.* DOI: 10.1080/09518398.2021.1983663.

Tapahonso, L. (2008). *A radiant curve: Poems and stories.* University of Arizona Press.

Tinto, V. (1987). *Leaving college: Rethinking the causes and cures of student attrition.* University of Chicago Press.

Tippeconnic, III, J. (1999). Tribal control of American Indian education: observations since the 1960s with implications for the future. In K. G. Swisher and J. W. Tippeconnic, III (Eds.), *Next steps: Research and practice to advance Indian education* (pp. 33–52). ERIC Clearinghouse.

Tohe, L. (2012). *Code talker stories.* Rio Nuevo Publishers.

Trask, H. (1993). *From a Native daughter: Colonialism and sovereignty in Hawai'i.* University of Hawai'i Press.

Tuck, E. (2009). Suspending damage: A letter to communities. *Harvard Educational Review, 79*(3), 409–427.

Tuck, E., & Ree, C. (2013). A glossary of haunting. In S. Holman Jones, T. E. Adams, & C. Ellis (Eds.), *Handbook of autoethnography* (pp. 639–658). Left Coast Press.

United States–Navajo Tribe. (1868, June 1). *Treaty between the United States of America and the Navajo Tribe of Indians.* https://americanindian.si.edu/static/nationtonation/pdf/Navajo-Treaty-1868.pdf

U.S. Census Bureau. (2011). *Profile American facts for features: American Indian and Alaskan Native heritage month: November 2011.* http://www.census.gov/newsroom/releases/archives/facts_for_features_special_editions/cb11-ff22.html

U.S. Census Bureau. (2017). *American Indian and Alaska Native heritage month: November 2017.* https://www.census.gov/newsroom/facts-for-features/2017/aian-month.html

U.S. Department of Education Office of Civil Rights. (2014, March 21). *Civil rights data collection: Data snapshot: School discipline. Issue Brief No. 1.* National Indian Education Association. https://static1.squarespace.com/static/5cffbf319973d7000185377f/t/5db308fdfb61014c1859a24c/1572014336338/2-CRDC-School-Discipline-Snapshot.pdf

U.S. Executive Office of the President. (2014). *2014 Native Youth Report.* U.S. Executive Office of the President. https://obamawhitehouse.archives.gov/sites/default/files/docs/20141129nativeyouthreport_final.pdf

Vizenor, G. (1994). *Manifest manners: Post-Indian warriors of survivance.* Wesleyan University Press.

Waterman, S. J. (2012). Home-going as a strategy for success among Haudenosaunee college and university students. *Journal of Student Affairs Research and Practices, 49*(2), 193–209.

Wessler, S. F. (2014). Endless debt: Native Americans plagued by high-interest loans. *NBC News.* https://www.nbcnews.com/feature/in-plain-sight/endless-debt-native-americans-plagued-high-interest-loans-n236706

Wilder, C. (2013). *Ebony & ivy: Race, slavery, and the troubled history of America's universities.* Bloomsbury Press.

Wolfe, P. (1999). *Settler colonialism and the transformation of anthropology: The politics and poetics of an ethnographic event.* Cassell.

Wolfe, P. (2006). Settler colonialism and the elimination of the native. *Journal of Genocide Research, 8*(4), 387–409.

Williams, R. (1999). *Linking arms together: American Indian treaty visions of law and peace, 1600–1800*. Routledge.

Wright, B., & Tierney, W. (1991). American Indians in higher education: A history of culture conflict. *Change, 23*(2), 11–18.

Yazzie, E. P., & Speas, M. (2007). *Diné Bizaad Bináhoo'aah: Rediscovering the Navajo language*. Salina Bookshelf.

Yazzie, M. (2014, August 22). Brutal violence in border towns linked to colonization. *Indian Country Today*. https://indiancountrytoday.com/archive/brutal-violence-in-border-towns-linked-to-colonization

Youngbull, N. (2017). *The (un)success of American Indian Gates Millennium Scholars within institutions of higher education* (Publication No. 10252462) [Doctoral Dissertation, University of Arizona]. Proquest Dissertation Publishing.

Yurth, C. (2010, August 19). For 40 years, an Indian University program has provided dedicated teachers to Navajo. *Navajo Times*. http://navajotimes.com/education/2010/0810/081910teach.php#.VTxFHlwbvjI

Index

Note: Page numbers followed by n and number represent endnotes and note number respectively.

About the Author

Dr. Amanda R. Tachine is Diné (Navajo) from Ganado, Arizona. She is Náneesht'ézhí Táchii'nii (Zuni Red Running Into Water), born for Tł'ízí łání (Many Goats). She is an assistant professor in Educational Leadership and Innovation at Arizona State University, which resides on the home(lands) of the Akimel O'otham/Onk Akimel O'odham and Pee Posh/Piipaash peoples. Her dissertation, titled *Monsters and Weapons: Navajo Students' Stories on Their Journeys to College*, received the 2016 American Educational Research Association Division J Outstanding Dissertation Award. She has published works in the *Journal of Higher Education, Qualitative Inquiry, International Review of Qualitative Research, International Journal of Qualitative Studies in Education,* and other scholarly outlets. She also has published opinion pieces in the *Huffington Post, Al Jazeera, The Hill, Teen Vogue, Indian Country Today, Inside Higher Ed,* and *Navajo Times,* in which she advances ideas regarding discriminatory actions, educational policies, and inspirational movements.